SCHAUM'S OUTLINE OF

HTML

DAVE MERCER

CTO, Servata Online Applications

Schaum's Outline Series

McGRAW-HILL

New York   Chicago   San Francisco   Lisbon   London   Madrid   Mexico City
Milan   New Delhi   San Juan   Seoul   Singapore   Sydney   Toronto

Schaum's Outline of
HTML

Copyright © 2002 by The McGraw-Hill Companies, Inc. All rights reserved.
Printed in the United States of America. Except as permitted under the Copyright Act of 1976,
no part of this publication may be reproduced or distributed in any form or by any means, or
stored in a data base or retrieval system, without the prior written permission of the publisher.

1 2 3 4 5 6 7 8 9 10 11 12 13 14 15 16 17 18 19 20 PRS PRS 0 9 8 7 6 5 4 3 2 1

ISBN 0-07-137365-9

Sponsoring Editor: Barbara Gilson
Production Supervisors: Tina Cameron and Maureen Harper
Editing Liaison: Maureen B. Walker
Project Supervision: Keyword Publishing Services Ltd

Library of Congress Cataloging-in-Publication Data applied for.

McGraw-Hill

A Division of The McGraw·Hill Companies

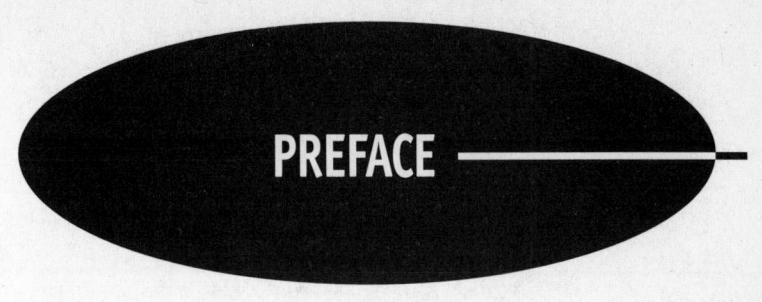

PREFACE

This book covers basic Web design and layout, graphics, scripting, CSS and DHTML, XHTML, XML, and of course all HTML commands, attributes, values, and usage parameters. The Outline complements any Web page design course focusing on HTML. Many code examples and illustrations of the resulting Web pages are provided. All code examples may be downloaded from the author's Website at www.e4free.com/Schaums.

Chapter 1 is an introduction to HTML. Chapter 2 covers basic page and text formatting commands. Chapter 3 discusses more advanced page and text formatting, as well as the construction of hyperlinks.

Chapter 4 is an introduction to graphics, with a discussion of the IMG element, and Chapter 5 continues the coverage of graphics with important IMG element attributes and a review of image maps.

Chapter 6 provides a thorough foundation for tables and frames, two important structures in Web page design. Chapter 7 examines HTML form building, with a review of how forms are connected to back-end processing scripts, and a short introduction to scripting with Javascript.

Chapter 8 provides a concise description of Dynamic HTML and the Cascading Style Sheets 2.0 language and the several ways to use style sheets and style elements in Web pages.

Chapter 9 gives a very complete introduction to XHTML and the primary differences between HTML and XHTML. Chapter 10 is an in-depth look at XML, and makes an excellent segue into advanced classes about XML.

Altogether, the book is a comprehensive companion to creating Web pages with HTML.

HTML 4.01 DTD Copyright Info

The HTML 4.01 Strict DTD can be found at http://www.w3.org/TR/html4/sgml/dtd.html.

The HTML 4.01 DTD is governed by the Software Notice, as follows:

W3C® SOFTWARE NOTICE AND LICENSE

The HTML 4.01 Specification is a Recommendation, as of 24 December, 1999.

All DTD code examples from the HTML 4.01 DTDs are subject to the following notice:

CONTENTS

Contents

Contents

CHAPTER 1

Introduction to HTML

1.1 Origins of HyperText Markup Language (HTML)

HTML was created by Tim Berners-Lee in collaboration with Robert Caillau while they worked at CERN in 1989 (CERN is a high-energy physics research institute in Geneva). It is a subset of Standard Generalized Markup Language (SGML). SGML was defined by International Standards in 1986 as ISO 8879:1986. The purpose of SGML is to provide a common convention for creating languages for communicating information in documents. People (or automated software tools) creating documents with SGML languages *markup* their documents by inserting commands (called *tags* in HTML). These tags define the appearance and workings of the document when it is viewed in an appropriate manner.

There are a number of markup languages (such as HTML) defined from SGML, and they are called SGML applications. Most SGML applications include the following components:

- An SGML Declaration specifying the characters and delimiters that are allowed in the application.

- A Document Type Definition (DTD) that specifies the syntax of markup elements. Chapter 2 covers the HTML DTD in more detail.

- A specification detailing the semantics of the application, and any constraints not defined within the DTD.

The vision for HTML was to create a platform-independent language for constructing hypertext documents to communicate multimedia information easily over the Internet. Using an Internet protocol called HyperText Transport Protocol (HTTP), HTML documents could be transmitted to any user on the Internet, and displayed by software called a browser. Even the first versions of HTML,

HTTP, and browsers were very powerful tools for conveying and displaying information, especially rich media information.

1.2 The HTML Specification

There is an organization called the World Wide Web Consortium (W3C), located at www.w3.org. It is the responsibility of this organization to maintain and update the formal specification for the HTML language. Because this organization recognizes that not every use of HTML will conform exactly to the specification, it calls the HTML specification a recommendation. HTML 4.0 became a recommendation in December 1997.

Rather than continuing to develop HTML, the W3C has begun recasting HTML into XHTML, a more formal version of HTML that follows the design principles of eXtensible Markup Language (XML). XHTML is covered in Chapter 9, and XML is covered in Chapter 10.

1.3 The Structure and Functions of HTML

HTML stands for HyperText Markup Language. It is considered to be a markup language as opposed to a programming language because it has very limited programmatic functionality. In fact, the primary purpose of HTML is to display data or content in a pleasing way. The majority of the commands in HTML assist the developer in arranging and modifying the display of text, graphics, and multimedia, and the only elements that approach traditional programmatic functionality are those that create links, tables, frames, and forms.

HTML is written in plain text commands (source code) that are conveyed to the end user as is, without being compiled (turned into machine language). The individual commands are called tags. Ordinary programming languages, on the other hand, must be compiled into machine language specific to the operating system (platform) they are intended to run on. The following code shows a minimal HTML document that will be displayed in Internet Explorer or Netscape Navigator:

```
<HTML>
<HEAD>
<TITLE>The Title</TITLE>
</HEAD>
</HTML>
```

Most HTML tags have both a beginning and ending (or closing) tag. The beginning tag is enclosed in angle brackets (less-than and greater-than signs < >). For example, the first tag you will ordinarily see in an HTML document is <HTML>. At the end of an HTML document, you will see the ending HTML tag (</HTML>). The difference is the forward slash (/). There are some HTML elements that have no ending tag, such as the IMG element

(< IMG SRC = "filename" >), and there are others for which an ending tag is not required, such as the P (paragraph) element. Chapter 2 will expand upon this theme, and discuss elements, tags, and attributes in greater detail.

In general, HTML tags have the following functions:

- Structure – HTML tags define the beginning and ending of major structures in the document, such as the head, body, forms, tables, frames, and so forth.
- Text formatting – There are quite a variety of tags that format text in a pleasing way, such as bold, italics, line breaks, paragraphs, lists, lines, and so forth.
- Object inclusion – There are tags for including images, objects, and hypertext links within an HTML document.
- Programmatic functionality – The INPUT element, when its *type* attribute is set to "submit", creates a button within a form that triggers the sending of filled-in information to a specified location when the button is clicked.

1.4 Browsers and Servers

You may be familiar with the term client-server. It refers to the traditional model of interaction between a host computer (or server) that provides files or services to client computers. Although the terms are sometimes used to refer to hardware, in fact they actually refer to the software running on these computers. The definitions are blurring because sometimes a client can act as a server, and vice versa, and there may be several tiers of functionality in modern distributed applications (n-tier or multi-tier applications). Still, on the Internet most relationships between one computer and another can be thought of as following the client-server model.

When you open your browser and connect to a Website, your browser sends a request to the Web server software on which the Website you wish to view resides. The request contains a surprising amount of information about your location on the Internet, the type of browser you are running, and what you are requesting. The Web server software on the other end interprets the request and, if everything is in order, it sends you a copy of the appropriate Web page. Your browser, in turn, interprets the Web page received by reading the HTML tags, and then displays the result on your screen. The format or protocol used for communicating these requests and responses between browser and server is called HyperText Transfer Protocol (HTTP).

1.5 The Role of HTTP

HTTP stands for HyperText Transfer Protocol. As the name suggests, it is a protocol used for transferring hypertext documents across the Web. A *protocol* is a specification for communicating information, and there are many protocols in use on the Internet. For example, File Transfer Protocol (FTP) is used for transferring files across the Internet. Protocols exist at many levels on the Internet and on networks in general, from very basic protocols defining how data packets are transmitted to very high-level protocols defining how applications construct and interpret data packets.

The current specification for HTTP is HTTP 1.1 as defined in Request For Comments (RFC) 2616. RFC is the name given to adopted changes to Internet standards, and many RFCs make up the standards for Internet communications. RFCs on various standards are maintained at the Internet Engineering Task Force (IEFT), located at www.ietf.org.

HTTP 1.1 defines the format of the messages Web servers and browsers use to communicate. It is considered an application-level, generic, stateless, protocol for distributed, collaborative, hypermedia systems, according to the abstract in RFC 2616. *Application-level* means that it works at the level of the end programs doing the processing, in this case the browser and the Web server. *Generic* means that it applies equally to many programs, and any program using it can communicate with other programs that understand the protocol. *Stateless* means that each request is treated as an individual, and that no identifying data or values are kept from one request to the other. *Distributed* means that the resources (files) included in a Web page may reside at multiple locations distributed anywhere on the Internet. *Collaborative* means that content producers and programmers can provide data and functions to the overall document or application while working together. Finally, *hypermedia* means that rather than just hypertext, HTTP can work with many media formats within a Web page.

1.5.1 HOW HTTP WORKS

In operation, HTTP is a request/response protocol. When you make a request, the request contains a request method, a Uniform Resource Identifier (URI), and protocol version. It may also contain request modifiers, client information, and perhaps the names and values of a form on the page from which the request originated. The server responds by sending back a status line that contains the protocol version, success or error codes, server information, and perhaps content such as a Web page.

While many requests and responses take place between your browser and a web server directly, sometimes there are intermediate steps. For example, suppose there is a proxy or gateway between your browser and the Web server. Requests and responses will be interpreted and passed along by each intermediate application.

1.5.2 URIs AND URLs

URI stands for Uniform Resource Identifier. The word *Uniform* in this case means that the syntax follows a standard convention, even when extended into new addresses. *Resource* means anything that has an identity, such as a file, a program, an image, and so forth. The *Identifier* portion is the reference to the resource. URIs include URLs (Uniform Resource Locator) and URNs (Uniform Resource Name).

The term URI is functionally equivalent to the URL that we are familiar with as a domain name, path, and filename. A URL includes the following components:

- http:// – The http refers to the overall *protocol* being used (but not the version number) and following that must be the colon and two forward slashes.

- The name of the *host computer* on which the resource resides – Typically this is the domain name (for example, www.e4free.com). Note that there is no requirement to include "www" as the first part of the host name, and that the IP address works just as well in place of the domain name, but according to the specification should be avoided whenever possible.

- The *port* on which the Web server is listening – This is typically 80, and must be preceded by a colon (:). If it is not explicitly stated it is assumed to be :80. Ports are logical addresses to which messages may be sent in an operating system, and networked operating systems have many ports, because they typically have many servers running, all listening to various ports in the operating system.

- The *absolute path*, preceded by a forward slash (/), to the folder where the file is located, including the filename – For example, a typical URL might be www.e4free.com/asubfolder/afile.htm. Notice the slashes separating folders and files in the path are forward, not backward.

- If there is a *query* attached to the URL, it begins with a question mark, and the name/value pairs in the query are separated by ampersands.

Although a fully qualified (complete) URL is required in order to make a request directly from a browser via the address entry area (typing the URL into the browser manually), subsequent requests made via links do not require complete URLs to function correctly. Fully qualified URLs are referred to as *absolute* URLs, and incomplete URLs are referred to as *relative* URLs. For example, it is common practice to code hypertext links and image source references with simply the filename of the resource, rather than the complete URL, when the file resides in the same folder on the same host computer as the file currently displayed in the browser (the file in which the link is being clicked or the image is being displayed). This subject is discussed in more detail in Chapter 3.

As you have certainly noticed, leaving off the path and filename when making a request to see a particular Website will cause the Web server to search for the beginning page of the Website on its own. Web servers can be programmed to search for any filename in the absence of a path and filename in the URL, but are typically programmed to search for index.html. Other commonly used names for the first page of a Website are index.htm, default.html, and default.htm.

1.5.3 HTTP MESSAGES

Communication between browser and Web server consists of requests from the browser to the server and responses from the server back to the browser. These are called HTTP messages, and they have a start line, header fields, an empty line, and then the message body (if one is included). There are a number of categories of header fields, including:

- General Header Fields – Contain information that may apply to both requests and response messages, but not the document being transferred.

- Request Header Fields – Allow the sender to include information about itself (the browser type, for example), and to modify the request (the type of language or character set to be used, for example).

- Response Header Fields – Let the server pass along information about the response, such as the server software used to create the response.

- Entity Header Fields – Provide information about the document being transmitted (if there is one) or about the resource being requested. For example, the natural language the document uses can be specified with the Content_Language field.

The order in which header fields are sent or received does not matter. Header fields are constructed starting with the name of the field followed by a colon, and then the value for the field. For example, the following listing shows the name and value of a request header field; in this case, the browser type making a request:

```
HTTP_USER_AGENT: Mozilla/4.0
(compatible; MSIE 5.0; Windows 98)
```

1.5.4 REQUESTS AND RESPONSES

In a request from a browser to a Web server, the first line is called the Request Line. The Request Line includes the Method, the Identifier (meaning the URL), and the protocol version (meaning what version of HTTP is being used). Methods include the commonly used "GET" and "POST", among others. The "GET" method is designed to retrieve whatever output is associated with the request, and the "POST" method is designed to insert the contents of submitted forms. Both methods have other applications as well, although their usage is not so significant, and there are quite a few other methods in the current HTTP RFC.

In a response from a server to a browser, the first line is called the Status Line. The Status Line includes the protocol version and a numerical status indicator code followed by a short reason phrase. For example, 404 Not Found is a common status code and reason. Status codes beginning with a 1 are informational, with a 2 are successful, with a 3 redirect the browser to another location, with a 4 indicate a client error, and with a 5 indicate a server error.

1.6 The Document Object Model (DOM)

HTML 4.0 is associated with a Document Object Model (DOM). An object model is a representation of the relationships of various functions, objects, collections, properties, methods, and so forth within a particular language, technology, or application. The purpose of the model is to allow people to review and analyze those relationships, so that they may more easily understand how to work with them.

The DOM for HTML is considered an application-programming interface (API) for HTML documents (and XML documents as well). The current DOM is called the DOM Level 1 Specification (approved on October 1, 1998). It uses traditional object-oriented programming techniques to define the objects that make up an HTML document. The DOM allows developers to build documents in which the objects contained in it can be navigated and modified in real time. For example, the BODY element has an attribute for background color. In the DOM, the BODY element can be thought of as an object with a collection of attributes. Programmatically, these attribute values can be read and written to, changing the existing background color from one to another, in response to events affecting the BODY element. Therefore, the background color of the body of an HTML document can be programmatically manipulated (changed from one color to another) while the user works with the page. Javascript is capable of reading and changing background colors in a Web page.

A typical representation of objects within the DOM is the parent-child relationship. For example, the FORM element can be considered a parent object to text boxes within it. Since you can name most HTML elements, the name of a form provides a means of accessing a particular form on a document (as with many object-oriented programming languages you can also access a particular object using an index number). By naming the form and the text boxes within it, you can then access a particular text box, and from there you can access the properties and methods associated with that object. The text boxes and other elements residing in a form are considered as child objects of the parent form object.

1.7 Coding HTML Documents

In the classes I teach, older students familiar with the early word-processing programs such as WordPerfect tell me that HTML reminds them of the way WordPerfect used to work. In order to make an old WordPerfect document format characters, they had to insert tags to give the printer formatting commands. Knowing the commands was a prerequisite to efficient use of the program.

Today, few people would attempt to rewrite the codes inside a typical word-processing document in order to modify its formatting. If you use Notepad to open a small document created in Word, however, you can see the many lines of special characters Word uses to format documents.

As Web page creation tools such as Microsoft FrontPage and Macromedia Dreamweaver become better at writing the HTML code behind the scenes, it becomes less and less necessary to know how to write each HTML command by hand. But there are several crucial differences between the code required for Web pages and the characters defining the look of a document in Microsoft Word. First, HTML is a standard, whereas word-processing formats are unique, even from version to version of the same program. Second, Web pages are built to contain many languages, often within the same document. There are few tools accessible to the average person that can write most of the HTML, Javascript, ASP, VBScript, SQL, Perl, Php, and so forth that goes into modern Web pages. Therefore, I believe the requirement to understand HTML will exist into the foreseeable future.

At the same time, I also believe that using a good HTML editor such as FrontPage or Dreamweaver can dramatically speed up the process of creating Web pages. Purists will tell you that the only effective way to code is by hand, but I find developing with a modern HTML editor easier, quicker, and effective for producing readable code.

1.8　Other Web Page Languages and Scripting

One of the most common languages included in Web pages is Javascript. It finds its way into so many Web pages because it offers rudimentary programmatic functionality that HTML doesn't possess, and because most browsers can process Javascript commands without special help. Javascript is called a scripting language because it doesn't need to be compiled. Instead, it is interpreted at run-time within the browser. This means it runs slower than a compiled program, but since Javascripts are usually very short anyway, the difference in speed is most often not noticeable.

VBScript (Visual Basic Scripting Edition) is the Microsoft answer to Javascript. It is a scripting language very similar to Visual Basic, so it is quite familiar to many programmers without a large learning curve, yet at the same time many of the functions Javascript can perform are also found in VBScript, meaning that it can easily substitute for Javascript in many situations. However, support for VBScript in browsers is not widespread enough to make it a reasonable alternative to Javascript; notably, Netscape's browser does not support it.

To insert functions created with Javascript or VBScript in a Web page, the SCRIPT element is used, as shown here with a simple Javascript:

```
<SCRIPT LANGUAGE="Javascript">
function pushbutton() {
        alert("Hello!");
}
</script>
```

The function defined can then be called from within the body of the page using a variety of methods based on object events, as in the following example using the OnClick event of a FORM element (a button named Button1):

```
<form>
  <p><input TYPE="button" NAME="Button1" VALUE="Press Here"
ONCLICK="pushbutton()"></p>
</form>
```

Practical Extraction and Reporting Language (Perl) has been used as the language of choice for scripting server-side programs for many years, and is still in use and being updated often on the bulk of the Websites in operation (at least, those having back-end programming). Perl scripts can be written with Notepad or any plain text editor in the Windows environment, but when used on Unix machines they sometimes require further processing to eliminate special characters and set the file permissions for execution. An extremely simple Perl script is shown in the following example:

```
#!/usr/local/bin/perl
# prints Hello World back to the user
print 'Hello world.';
```

Programmed Hypertext Preprocessor (Php) is a server-side scripting language that has many of the same features and capabilities as ASP, and it is growing rapidly in popularity on Unix-hosted Web servers. It allows rapid development of Web applications that can perform functions ranging from simply feeding data back to the user to full database search, retrieval, and data processing. The source code for Php is embedded within HTML, making it easy to format responses to the user as Web pages. Again we provide a simple example showing common Php syntax:

```
<?php echo "Hello World<p>"; ?>
```

Microsoft's Active Server Pages (ASP) technology is not a programming language per se, it is a set of objects (accessible to a scripting engine, with the default scripting language being VBScript). Like Php, it allows developers to incorporate processed data into Web pages, and it can perform many application-like functions, including database operations. Here is an example of a simple ASP script that feeds back a statement to the user:

```
<% Response.Write "Hello, world" %>
```

Structured Query Language (SQL) is used to perform queries and execute operations on databases, and the majority of Database Management Systems (DBMSs) understand SQL commands. Php and ASP both allow the inclusion of SQL commands within their statements, and allow the data returned to be held in table-like structures for further processing. To select records from a table with SQL, the following commands can be used (the asterisk is shorthand for all records, and to embed the statement in Php or ASP it would be formatted as a string):

```
SELECT * FROM myTable
```

1.9　Web Page Design

It's easy to start building a Web page. Just open Notepad (if you intend to write the page by hand) or a good HTML editor such as FrontPage or Dreamweaver. You will have a blank page on the screen, ready to become the next billion-dollar Website. Unfortunately, the very ease with which new Web pages can be created undermines the success of many Websites. Inexperienced developers begin to create pages before they've really thought through the purpose of the Website, and lose their audience in a maze of disjointed, seemingly unconnected pages.

One of the first considerations when creating a Website must be the type of functions it is required to perform. For example, some Websites are meant to convey large amounts of technical information, while other Websites are specifically for searching, and still others are mainly for entertainment.

Although it is possible that a Website could perform many of these functions, the user interface for each function will be somewhat different. To determine the functions a Website should perform, it is important to establish objectives. Objectives help to focus the Website to one or more specific tasks, such as sales, customer assistance, the distribution of information, and so forth. As the user performs these tasks or processes with the assistance of the Website, the results can be measured. Measuring results helps you determine whether or not the objectives of the Website are being met.

Once objectives are established and functions are defined, it is easier to proceed to the physical design of the Website. Ease of use (usability) is always an important factor in Website design, but usability must often be balanced with capability and flexibility. Unfortunately, the more capable and flexible a Website is, the less easy to use it tends to be. Building flexibility and capability into a Website while retaining ease of use is a constant challenge to professional Website designers.

Bandwidth is also an important consideration in the development of Web pages and Websites. There are two kinds of bandwidth that should be taken into account: the bandwidth required to download your pages at a reasonable speed (user's bandwidth available) and the amount of bandwidth allocated by your hosting company for your site over a given time period. As a general rule, the size of Web page files should be kept to a minimum, to make downloads faster and cheaper for users, and to reduce the Website owner's transmission costs. Although they are appropriate in some circumstances, in most cases large Web pages will be avoided by users. In addition, Website owners often pay extra when their allocation of data to be transmitted within a given period is exceeded. For example, if your Web hosting account allows 1 GB of data to be transmitted by the web server in a month, transmitting more than that may incur a fee of $10 for every extra gigabyte sent out. A very popular site could end up costing the owner quite a bit more in extra transmission charges.

1.9.1 USABILITY AND PAGE LAYOUT

Usability engineering and marketing go hand-in-hand when designing the page layout and structure of a Website. Usability engineering is the practice of testing the usability of a particular product or service, and in the context of Website design refers to examining the user interface (the part of the Website seen by users in their browser) for ease of use. Focus groups are often used in larger Website design projects, and thus it is natural to gather marketing information at the same time.

Fig. 1-1. A typical Web page layout.

The idea is to combine usability data with marketing data to form a page layout and Website design that is easy to use and at the same time communicates well. For example, Fig. 1-1 shows a typical Web page design. Across the top there is a banner, down the left-hand side there is a menu of links or buttons, and in the larger right-hand side of the page the content of each page appears. This layout is certainly not considered innovative, but has the advantage of being well-known and easy to use.

1.9.2 PLATFORM OR BROWSER DEPENDENCE

Another major consideration in Website design is the platform on which it will run. HTML is said to be platform-independent, but this term actually refers to independence from the operating system. The look, feel, and workings of a Website still depend rather heavily on the browser software used, and the browser can be thought of as a platform of another kind.

Although the World Wide Web Consortium (W3C) maintains the specification for HTML, browser manufacturers compete for market share by making their browsers understand nonstandard HTML tags and other specialized or proprietary Website components. The result is each browser understands common HTML tags, but usually not competitors' tags. In addition, newer versions of a browser may recognize more recent tags than older versions, even within the same brand of browser.

For designers, this means using only the common denominator HTML tags, or coding several versions of a Website so all the major browsers and versions are covered. Fortunately, there are ways to discover in real-time what browser a given user is running, and feed them back the version of the Website that looks best on that browser.

As discussed in section 1.5 (The Role of HTTP), one of the details passed by the browser to the server during a request for a page is the type of browser. Scripting technologies such as ASP provide a Request object that assembles, within a collection, all the values passed to the server when a request is made. The value for the browser type can be programmatically extracted, and used to conditionally send Web pages back to the browser. By checking the browser type, your Website can automatically send back Web pages appropriate for the browser type and version.

Internet Explorer and Netscape Navigator (or Communicator) are the most popular Web browser clients in the market today. Naturally, no one source has perfect statistics, but the consensus seems to be that Internet Explorer has over 50% of the market and Netscape Navigator has close to 30%. Other browsers of note are the AOL browser, the Web TV browser, and Opera, although these have small percentages of the overall market. And with the coming of ubiquitous wireless devices and other devices without a user interface at all, Web designers will be facing hundreds of platforms that could potentially require a special version of your Web pages.

1.9.3 STORYBOARDING THE WEBSITE

The primary focus of Website design with HTML is the front end, or user interface. These are the pages and functions people see directly on their screens. Since a Website can be thought of as a series of screens people see, a storyboard can be used to rough out the content, look and feel, and navigation of each page. Usually a Website storyboard will also include lines showing the links connecting each page.

The storyboard can be done using plain paper and pencil, rapidly drawing and discarding ideas while the client offers input. Although the finished product may have a more polished look to it, the most productive aspect of the process of storyboarding is the brainstorming that occurs. A good technique for arriving at a useful design is to start with the premise that no idea is bad, and simply draw and include them all. Then, begin to weed out features that are unnecessary in terms of the objectives. For instance, if a feature will cost too much to include or maintain, throw it out. If a feature is of little use to the target audience (no matter how cool it looks), throw it out. The end result will be a storyboard that allows developers to make pages that are easy to understand and navigate, and fulfill the client's objectives.

1.9.4   CODING AND MANAGING WEBSITE DEVELOPMENT

Creating Web pages can be done with a plain text editor such as Notepad, or with a specialized programmer's text editor (such as Programmer's File Editor 1.01, found at www.download.com). Specialized text editors offer features, such as line numbering and the capability to store macros, that make coding easier. Line numbering comes in handy when you are debugging Javascript or ASP code.

More sophisticated HTML editors such as FrontPage and Dreamweaver can also be used, and they often provide Website management features. Website management features include the ability to display groups of Web pages depicting the links between them and their relationship to each other. FrontPage 2000, for example, can show Web pages connected to each other in a structure similar to a storyboard, and allows the developer to change the relationship of pages to one another using a visual interface (as shown in Fig. 1-2). Unfortunately, this feature requires the use of a proprietary system of navigation bars and buttons, and is not standard HTML.

Another helpful feature of high-end HTML editors is the ability to rename files and change links on each affected page automatically. The problem with larger Websites is that, once filenames are established and file references are coded into hypertext links, changing filenames and their associated links can be very time-consuming. Automatically making the changes saves time and reduces the possibility of human error.

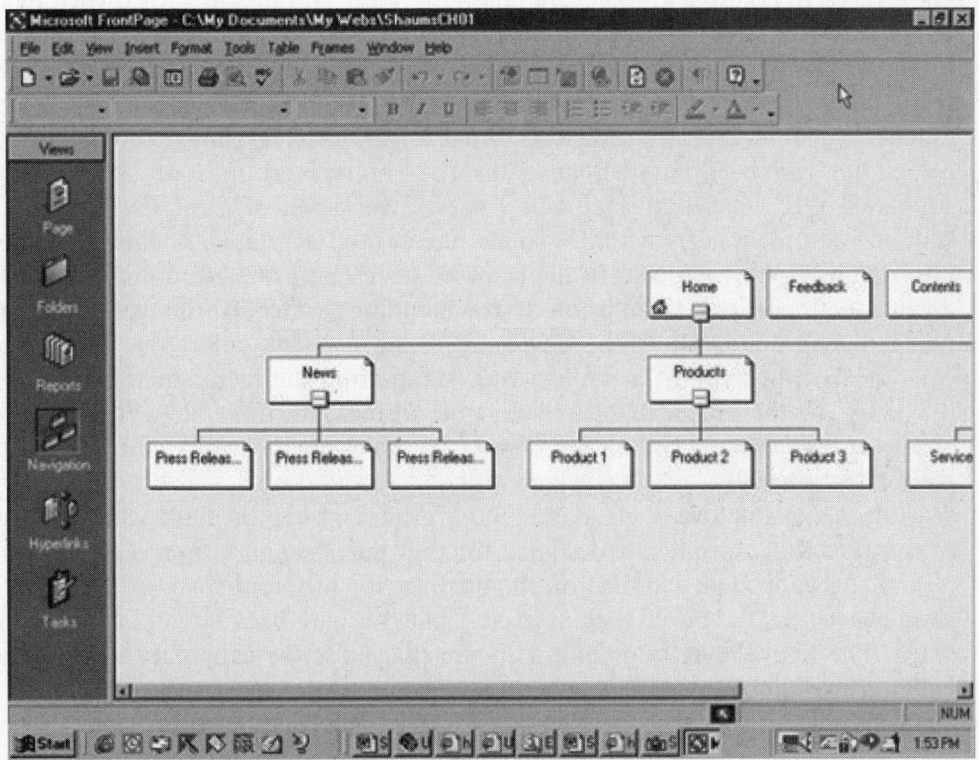

Fig. 1-2.   A FrontPage 2000 Website in navigation view.

Sophisticated HTML editors also offer a variety of visual tools that make the process of building common HTML structures considerably easier than doing the same work by hand, with less chance for error. For example, there are visual and menu-driven tools in FrontPage and Dreamweaver that make building and modifying complex table structures easier to perform and to comprehend. Building complex table structures by hand can be difficult simply because it is sometimes hard to find the beginning and ending table or row tags in larger Web pages.

1.9.5 WEBSITE CONTENT DEVELOPMENT

Content is the word used to describe all information communicated within a Website, meaning text, graphics, programmed functions, video, audio, 3D, multimedia, and so forth. Content development can be as simple as entering text into a page, or as complex as a complete video production formatted for delivery from a Website. Deciding what content to include in a Website depends upon the objectives of the Website and the tastes of the designer and client.

Text content can be gathered from existing hard copy material (which can be scanned and converted to machine-readable text using Optical Character Recognition (OCR) software, or entered manually), from existing electronic files (such as Word documents or other Web pages), or written from scratch.

Graphics can be produced from digital photographs, scans of hard copy photographs or artwork, free graphics found on the Web, graphics already owned by the Website owner, or newly created by a graphic artist. The Compuserve Graphics Interchange Format (GIF) and Joint Photographic Experts Group (JPG) image file formats are commonly supported by browsers. JPG images support a large number of colors and are therefore suited to photos. GIF images support fewer colors but can be animated, have transparent backgrounds or be interlaced. Animated GIF images are actually a special variation of the GIF format, and contain multiple images within a single file, as well as playback data. Interlaced GIF images begin to appear in the browser screen before the full image has been downloaded, and give the illusion of downloading faster. GIF images with transparent backgrounds allow the developer to set a single color (the background color) to be transparent in the browser, eliminating the rectangular structure of the image file on screen. Another image file format (Portable Network Graphics, or PNG) is beginning to gain acceptance on the major browsers, but only with a limited feature set.

Multimedia and audio, video, and 3D productions can be made using a variety of software tools specifically designed for that purpose, and often require special *plug-in* software to be installed on the browser for proper display or playback. A good example is the popular Real Player that can play back streaming audio and video. The Real Player is plug-in software that adds the capability to play back video and audio from within your browser. *Streaming* means that the video or audio files do not have to be completely downloaded before they begin to playback, a big advantage on the Internet, where download times for larger audio and video files can be excessively long.

Production of multimedia formats carries with it all the requirements of production of ordinary video/audio production. For example, to create a short video for display on a Website, it is necessary to first produce the video like any other video, with high production standards, scripts, storyboards, production crews, good lighting and direction; effectively everything that goes into the making of a commercial, including the expense. Then, to convert to a format suitable for broadcasting on the Internet, it must be processed and compressed. Finally, it must be loaded on a server and connections must be made in the Web page to activate the download or streaming process when a link is clicked.

1.9.6   INTELLECTUAL PROPERTY

The term *intellectual property* refers to property rights for ideas, concepts, processes, written and other types of works, and usually means patents, copyrights, trademarks, and so forth. On the Internet, because of the ease with which content can be obtained, copied, and misused, laws are changing rapidly. However some fundamentals seem to be holding (with a bit of modification).

First, copyright law protects text, graphics, and other works of this type from misuse, except in a very narrow set of circumstances labeled *fair use*. Fair use is when the work is excerpted in a small portion for the purpose of example or criticism, or when it is considered simply a fact or set of facts. Second, the nature of the Web is that any resource can be linked to by any other (meaning you can make links from your Web page to any other Web page on the Internet). However, restrictions on the type of link you can make are beginning to appear. For example, a recent court case ruled that links to certain sites, when there is an intent to facilitate an illegal act, may be illegal in themselves. This court case is certain to be reviewed, but should make all Web developers wary of indiscriminate linking.

It is important to monitor the production of content so that copyrights will not be violated. The ease with which material can be copied from the Web can make it difficult to verify the original author or creator of content. The fact that any work, as soon as it is produced, has copyright protection (whether or not the copyright symbol is attached to the work) means that every work is suspect unless originally created by the developer or the developer's team. If a third party creates or provides content, a contract assuring the Website owner of indemnification (by the third party) in the event of legal action over the content is a common approach.

1.9.7   HOSTING, LOADING, AND MANAGING WEBSITE CONTENT

A primary consideration in the production of a Website is the system for hosting the Website and delivering the content it contains. When the initial production of Web pages and content is finished, the next task is to load them on to a Web server. In this case the term Web server stands for both the hardware and software, as well as the Internet connection, that broadcast copies of the requested Web pages to users around the world. Typically, the hardware is a computer (or load-balanced, clustered network of computers) that are specially designed and optimized for delivering Web pages and content to users. Some of the features of Web servers are:

- Multiple Central Processing Units (CPUs) to speed processing of requests and back-end programming logic.
- Large amounts of RAM to accommodate many simultaneous requests.
- Redundant hard drives configured in a RAID (Redundant Array of Inexpensive Disks) array and hot-swappable power supplies, so that failing drives or power supplies may be removed and replaced without disrupting service.
- Uninterruptible Power Supplies (UPSs) or backup generators that allow operation for many minutes in the event of a power failure, so systems can be properly shut down or kept running until utility power is restored.
- Backup systems, such as optical or tape drives, so in the event of total failure files can be restored, and mirroring systems, so that in the event of failure of one site, an identical site can take over the load in a manner transparent to the user.
- High-speed, multi-homed connections to major Internet Service Providers, so that content can be delivered rapidly to the least congested connection.

The Operating System (OS) on which the Web server runs is also important, because it forms the basis for the decision of what Web server to use, and what back-end communication technology will be employed. For example, if a Microsoft OS such as Windows NT is used, the Web server software will likely be some version of Internet Information Server (IIS), and the back-end communication technology will probably be ASP. Although it is possible to use other Web servers and back-end technologies, IIS and ASP are most commonly used because they are offered with the OS at no additional charge, and because there is a perception that Microsoft servers and technologies will work best on Microsoft OSs, and will receive better continuing support from the company than third-party servers and technologies.

Loading Web pages or creating them online can be performed in several different ways, each with its own pros and cons. For example, standard Web pages are easily loaded to a Web server across the Internet (from wherever they are created) using utility FTP programs such as CuteFTP and WS_FTP. However, Web pages created with Microsoft FrontPage must sometimes (when the pages are dependent upon FrontPage Server Extensions) be loaded with the FrontPage Publish utility, or must be created online. In either of these cases, the FTP host address, username, and password for the Website must be known to make a connection. Common practice these days is to make the FTP host address equivalent to the domain name (for example, www.e4free.com).

Managing and maintaining Web content is the process of adding new pages, fixing errors, updating information, deleting information, and weeding out old pages. It is also frequently necessary to completely make over a site, both to upgrade the look and feel and to make the site more manageable. A good example of making a site more manageable is the case of a site that has undergone rapid growth in content and users. When this occurs the number of Web pages may skyrocket from tens to thousands. Periodically, the content and purpose of the growing number of pages should be reassessed, so that pages or content that are outside the general scope or objectives of the Website can be culled, and so that required pages in a static format can be changed to a dynamic format.

Static Web pages are pages in which the content is hard-coded, a direct part of the HTML file. In Dynamic Web pages the content is stored in separate files in a database or other data store, distinct from the HTML files. Dynamic Web pages can be built with Server-Side Includes (SSI), for example. A Web page built with SSI has references within it to other text files that contain content and tags. These other files are dynamically included within the Web page requested at the time of the request, by the Web server. The user sees only the finished product. Site management is enhanced because the content of an include file need only be changed once, but it can be included simultaneously in many pages. For example, a copyright statement can be updated once a year, but this statement can be included in every page on the site from the single include file.

Dynamic Web pages can also be produced using scripting technology. ASP scripts can perform database record retrievals to insert content in Web pages in real time, including product lists in drop-down menus, catalog listings, and so forth. When content is stored in a database it is much easier to modify efficiently, especially for large amounts of repetitive data. As an example, suppose you are in charge of maintaining prices for a large ecommerce retailer with thousands of products for sale. Would you rather change prices on thousands of individual HTML pages one at a time, or change them *en masse* using an update query in a database?

1.9.8 CHECKING AND PUBLICIZING A WEBSITE

Like most software development, the design and construction of a Website usually involves errors and bugs. With HTML, the bugs are often broken links and the errors are often misspellings. Utility programs and Websites are available to check for broken links, misspellings, and even grammar, as well as poorly constructed HTML. It's easy to find HTML validation Websites. Just go to your favorite search engine and enter the search term "Check HTML". You'll receive a list of sites that perform the service. For example, the top listing on a search done at the time of this writing produced the following link: http://www.unimelb.edu.au/html-check/validation-form.html. This is an online HTML validation service provided by the University of Melbourne.

Poorly constructed HTML can have hard-to-find consequences, depending upon the HTML editor and browser you are using during the construction process, and may react differently on your development computer than on the Web server computer. For example, accidentally leaving off an ending table tag causes no discernible effect if you are checking your work in Internet Explorer, but will cause the entire page to be blank when viewed in Netscape Navigator. And it is not uncommon to find that the structure of your folders is slightly different on the development computer than on the Web server computer. Therefore, it is important that you check your work with a utility program or validation service both before and after uploading.

Publicizing your Website is an important step in letting potential users know the service is there. There are many kinds of publicity, including traditional marketing and advertising (radio, print, TV, direct mail, and so forth), but one of the most important (and least costly) is to register your site with search engines. There are only about 20 major search engines, so registering with the thousands that offer themselves is really only a sure way to bring yourself a flood of spam. You can manually register with the top search engines, or you can make use of Websites that perform an automatic registration for you. Either way, the search engines will send requests to your site (using what's called *spider* or *crawler* software) and index the keywords on your site. Each search engine has different criteria by which they rate your site, and the criteria change over time. Your rating affects your place on the search engines for each keyword or search phrase used, and having a higher rating and placement can mean the difference between being found and being lost. The construction techniques you use on your pages should conform to what is known about search engine placement at the time you build the site, and you may want to revise the site periodically to keep the search engine rankings high.

Review Questions

1.1. What organization maintains the specification for the HTML language, what is the URL for the organization, and what is the most recent major version number for HTML?

1.2. What is the primary purpose of HTML, and what capabilities within HTML support this purpose?

1.3. What is SGML, and what are languages defined from it called?

1.4. HTML is a fairly mature markup language after the number of revisions it has seen. What does the W3C intend to do next with the HTML language?

1.5. What is HTTP, and what role does it play in Websites?

1.6. HTTP is stateless. What does this mean?

1.7. What are the parts of a URL?

1.8. Why is it not necessary to include the filename when entering the address for a Website, in many cases?

1.9. What is a Request For Comments (RFC), and what is the current RFC for HTTP 1.1?

1.10. In general, how do HTTP communications work?

1.11. What parts may be included in an HTTP request or response?

1.12. What types of header fields may be contained in the header fields section of an HTTP message?

1.13. What is the first line of an HTTP Request message called, and what does it include?

1.14. What is the first line of an HTTP Response message called, and what does it include?

1.15. What language is most commonly used with HTML to provide programmatic functionality within Web pages? What kinds of functions can be performed with this language that HTML alone cannot do?

1.16. Give some examples of languages and technologies that are used on the server to provide programmatic functionality, including database access.

1.17. At what point does content you create become protected by copyright law in the United States?

1.18. What image file formats are supported by the major browsers? What recently developed image file format is beginning to gain acceptance?

1.19. What is the simplest (but not necessarily the most efficient) way to provide access to multimedia content or other file formats within a Web page? What technology can make this access more efficient?

1.20. What are some of the attributes of a professional Website hosting server, and why are they important to Website developers?

1.21. What two operating systems host the majority of Websites today?

1.22. What are static Web pages. Why are they more difficult to maintain than dynamic Web pages?

1.23. Name two common mistakes that occur in the development of Websites.

1.24. How do search engines index Websites?

Solved Problems

1.1. What delimiters are used to denote HTML tags?

The less-than (<) and greater-than (>) signs, also called angle brackets. For example, here is a minimal HTML document:

```
<HTML>
<HEAD>
<TITLE>The Title</TITLE>
</HEAD>
</HTML>
```

1.2. What is the notation used to define the protocol for a Web page URL?

The notation is http://

1.3. How much bandwidth do you have available if you are running a 28.8 modem for your Internet connection?

A 28.8 modem transmits and receives data at 28,800 bits per second, so your bandwidth available is 28,800 bits per second.

1.4. If you have a 1 kilobyte (KB) file (meaning the file size is 1000 bytes) on your Website, and it is the only file there, and one person requests it once, how much bandwidth has been consumed?

1000 bytes.

1.5. If you have a single file on your Website that, when added together with its associated graphics files, totals 1 MB in size, and an average of 33 people request the file per day, how much bandwidth is your site consuming in a month, assuming there are 30 days in a month?

One MB times 33 people (or hits) equals 33 MB per day. Thirty-three times 30 equals 990 MB per month.

1.6. You have produced a Website on which each page contains, at the bottom, the following statement: "For further information contact webmaster@e4free.com". The Website has now grown to over 100 pages. Employing what technology would be useful to avoid labor each time the email address changes?

Creating a separate text file and using Server-Side Include (SSI) technology would allow you to include the statement on every page while only needing to maintain the statement in a single file.

1.7. You want to build a Javascript into a Web page. Give an example of the beginning and ending tags to use.

Javascript functions begin with the < SCRIPT LANGUAGE = "Javascript" > tag, and end with the < /SCRIPT > tag. Notice the language attribute setting.

1.8. Give an example of the delimiters used to embed Php scripting within a server-side script.

A Php server-side script begins and ends with question marks inside greater-than and less-than signs, like this: < ?php echo $name? > .

1.9. Give an example of the delimiters used with ASP server-side scripts.

An ASP script begins and ends with percent signs inside greater-than and less-than signs, like this: < % Response.Write "This text goes back to the user" % > .

Answers to Review Questions

1.1. The World Wide Web Consortium (W3C) maintains the specification for HTML and the URL is www.w3.org. The most recent major version of HTML (at the time of this writing, in summer 2000) is 4, with a minor version number of .01.

1.2. The primary purpose of HTML is to provide a means for formatting hypertext documents to display text, graphics, and other media in a pleasant manner, across disparate platforms. Text formatting commands, as well as commands that create and/or insert images, hypertext links, tables, frames, and forms support this purpose.

1.3. SGML stands for Standard Generalized Markup Language, and it is a framework for producing document languages. Languages produced within the framework of SGML are called SGML applications.

1.4. There are many aspects of HTML that are worth preserving, and there are many legacy documents written in HTML, so the W3C has created XHTML, an XML-compliant version of HTML, to be the next version of HTML.

1.5. HTTP is a protocol used on the Internet for communications between Web servers and browsers. It transmits hypertext documents, along with a significant amount of other information, such as browser type, status messages, and IP addresses.

1.6. Stateless means that each request from a browser is individual, carrying no information over from past requests that would create a "session" comprised of all requests and responses in a particular time frame.

1.7. The parts of a URL are the protocol, the domain name of the host computer, the port, the folder or folders in the path to the resource (if any), and the filename of the resource.

1.8. In many cases, it is not necessary to include the filename of the first file on a Website because the Web server has been programmed to automatically find the first file by looking for the filename index.html. Some Web servers will also look for other filenames (such as index.htm, default.htm, and default.html) if they do not find index.htm.

1.9. An RFC is the means by which standards are adopted and modified on the Internet. The current RFC for HTTP 1.1 is RFC 2616.

1.10. HTTP communications work using a request/response method. When a person enters a URL in their browser while on the Internet, the browser sends a request to the Web server specified by the URL. The Web server determines the location of the resource requested within the URL and copies it to the browser as a response.

1.11. Included in an HTTP message may be a start line, header fields, an empty line, and then a message body. Not all HTTP messages include message bodies.

1.12. Header fields may include general header fields, request header fields, response header fields, and entity header fields.

1.13. The first line of an HTTP Request message is called the Request line, and it includes the Method, the URL, and the protocol version.

1.14. The first line of an HTTP Response message is called the Status line, and it includes the protocol version and a numerical status indicator code followed by a short reason phrase.

1.15. The most commonly used language for adding programmatic functionality to Web pages is Javascript. Javascript can perform arithmetical operations, comparisons, and store values in variables, while HTML cannot perform these functions.

1.16. Active Server Pages (ASP) and Programmed HTML Preprocessor (Php).

1.17. As soon as it is created. Although you can apply formally for a copyright, doing so is not required for protection, and neither is displaying a copyright symbol with the published work.

1.18. The Joint Photographic Experts Group (JPEG or JPG) and Compuserve Graphics Interchange Format (GIF) image file formats are supported by the major browsers. The Portable Network Graphics (PNG) image file format is gaining support but only for a limited set of features at the time of this writing.

1.19. The easiest way to provide access to multimedia and other file formats within a Web page is to simply make a link directly to the file. If the file cannot be opened natively in the user's browser, the browser will offer the user the choice of downloading the file and saving it, or of specifying an application program with which to open the file. Streaming technology allows the user to begin playing back the multimedia file before the entire file is downloaded (if the appropriate plug-in software is installed) and thus makes the process of using the resource more efficient.

1.20. Professional Website hosting computers are optimized for delivering Web content, and often contain multiple CPUs, large amounts of RAM, redundant hard drives and power supplies, Uninterruptible Power Supplies (UPSs), backup generators, and data backup devices. These attributes are important to Website developers because they constrain Web content delivery.

1.21. Unix variations and Windows NT versions host the majority of Websites in operation today.

1.22. Static Web pages are pages in which the content is coded directly into the HTML. They can be changed fairly easily when only a few exist on the Website, but when the number of pages grows large, maintenance can become problematic. Dynamic Web pages relieve some of the maintenance burden by allowing Website developers to place repetitive content in separate text files or in databases. This makes the data or content easier to manage because it can be changed just once for many pages, or can be changed once for many records.

1.23. Misspellings and broken links are two common mistakes made in the development of Websites.

1.24. Search engines respond to Website submissions by making requests of Websites to retrieve the HTML code and content. The code and content are indexed by a variety of criteria that are different for each search engine and change over time.

CHAPTER 2

HTML Page Formatting Basics

2.1 The HTML Document Type Definition (DTD) and Elements

When writing an HTML document manually, it is easy to create a page rapidly simply by writing a few tags (< HTML > , < HEAD > , < TITLE > , and so forth). Major browsers will display a page properly with just these tags, but there are more tags that constitute a well-written (or well-formed) HTML document. For example, there is the DOCTYPE element, containing the Document Type Declaration (DTD).

A (DTD) declares element types. In HTML, there are several elements present in every finished document. An element is a part of the overall structure of a document, and may contain some functionality. For example, the HEAD section (constructed using the HEAD element) of a Web page must be present in every HTML document, and a FORM section (if a FORM element is present), has the capability to transmit information from the document to another location. Shown here is an example of the DTD for the line break element (BR):

```
<!ELEMENT BR -- O EMPTY    -- forced line break -->
<!ATTLIST BR
  %coreattrs;                -- id, class, style, title --
  >
```

Notice the BR is not contained inside angle brackets in the DTD, and it has a definition next to it. It is formally defined as an *element*, and it has a list of *attributes* (called %coreattrs;, for core attributes) below. The core attributes of the BR element are *id*, *classs*, *style*, and *title*. Elements often have additional attributes defined, as well as intrinsic events that can be manipulated within the Document Object Model (DOM). We will discuss the attributes for the BR element more comprehensively in the section on text formatting.

Within the DTD, element type declarations define the starting tag, attributes, events, permissible content, and the ending tag. Note that tags are not the same thing as elements. There is only one HEAD element, but there is a starting HEAD tag (< HEAD >) and an *ending* HEAD tag (< /HEAD >). Tags include the names of the tag (for example, the starting HTML tag is written < HTML >), and the ending tag has a slash (/) before the name and is written < /HTML >. Starting and ending tags delimit content (and other tags or elements) contained within them.

Not all elements are required to have ending tags. For example, the paragraph element (P) does have an ending tag (< /P >), but it is not required. Some elements not only are not required to have ending tags, but ending tags for them do not exist and are forbidden. The line break element (BR) has no ending tag; its function is to break a line at the point in which it is inserted. Another interesting feature of the BR element is that it contains no content.

2.2   Writing Well-formed HTML

A plain-text editor, such as Notepad, Wordpad, or Simple Text can be used to write HTML manually, or a sophisticated HTML-editor such as FrontPage or Dreamweaver can be used. There are many in-between tools as well, both for writing the HTML and for checking its accuracy. For example, there is a free utility program, linked to the W3C website, called HTML Tidy. HTML Tidy reads your HTML and cleans it up, making tags match, placing tags in the proper order, and so forth.

In the official HTML 4.01 recommendation, there is a conformance guide. Throughout the recommendation, within the descriptions of HTML tags are words such as MUST, MUST NOT, REQUIRED, and so forth. These words indicate whether or not a particular directive has to be followed to the letter to maintain conformance, or whether it can be followed partly or not at all. Directives that do not require strict conformance should probably still be followed just for good coding practice.

Also in the recommendation, you'll find tags defined as deprecated or obsolete. *Deprecated* means that the tag has become outdated, perhaps superseded by a newer element, but can still be used and should be managed properly by browsers. *Obsolete* means the tag is no longer supported and there is no guarantee that a browser will render it effectively. Deprecated and obsolete tags should be avoided, if possible, but are sometimes employed in versions of Web pages designed for a user base still relying on older browsers.

HTML can be written in a variety of formats, which has some interesting consequences. First, HTML tags are *case-insensitive*. You can write them uppercase, lowercase, or even a mixture of cases, and it won't affect their functions. Second, HTML can be written as one long string of characters, without carriage returns or line feeds (the invisible characters that tell your text editor to go to the next line). The reason most people (and HTML editors) don't do this is that it can be very hard to read and debug from the developer's standpoint. Third, because not all directives must be followed strictly, HTML code that still works properly in modern browsers may have missing tags, missing delimiters, and so on. We will always try to conform to good coding practice as well as the strictly interpreted directives in this book, because the next generation of HTML (XHTML, covered in Chapter 9) will be quite a bit stricter, and we want to be ready for it.

2.3   Attributes

An HTML element may have attributes or properties associated with it. These properties may be set to the default (without even being declared in the element, in some cases) or they may be given a value. For example, the background color of a Web page may be set by specifying a color code within the beginning BODY tag, using the bgcolor attribute. The syntax and attribute/value pair for setting the background color to white would be:

```
<BODY bgcolor="#FFFFFF">
```

Legal attributes are defined in the HTML specification, and any legal attributes are included before the ending angle bracket (>) within the starting tag of an element. They can be in any order. Generally, *attribute values are placed in quotes*, but in some cases this is not necessary. *Attribute names are case-insensitive*, but the values assigned to them are sometimes case-sensitive. For example, in the following code example, an image tag specifies the name of an image file to be inserted in an HTML document, and the filename is case-sensitive:

```
<IMG SRC="MyLogoFile.jpg">
```

2.4   Intrinsic Events

When a user requests a page the document must first be loaded, and then the user is free to roam the document, clicking and double-clicking buttons and links, scrolling up and down, placing the mouse over sections of text or images, or tabbing from field to field on a form. Loading, clicking, tabbing, and so forth can all be considered *events*, and the occurrence of these events can be detected and used to trigger script actions. Triggering script actions is accomplished through the use of intrinsic events coded into beginning HTML tags. Many HTML elements support a variety of intrinsic events, such as *onload, onmouseover, onclick*, and so forth. The DTDs throughout this book explain the events supported by each HTML element. Creating event-driven functions with scripting languages will be discussed in more detail in Chapter 7.

2.5   Character Entity References (Special Characters)

There are some characters that, if simply inserted into a plain text HTML file, would not display properly. The less-than sign (<), for example, would indicate to the browser the beginning of an HTML tag and would not be displayed (although browsers are notorious for "excusing" coding mistakes, and will sometimes display characters such as this anyway). In order to force the display of these characters, *character entity references* (often called special characters) are used.

The correct syntax for displaying special characters is to start them with an ampersand, end them with a semi-colon, and in between place either a pound sign (#) and a numeric value signifying the character to be displayed, or an abbreviation for the character to be displayed (without including the pound sign). Both methods of coding special characters are shown here, using the correct value to display a less-than sign:

```
&#60;
&lt;
```

The numeric values that may be used in an HTML document are listed in the Universal Character Set (UCS), defined by ISO10646. ISO stands for the International Standardization Organization. The UCS includes thousands of characters used in English as well as other languages and alphabets.

2.6   The Basic Structure of HTML Documents

HTML documents are made up of three parts: a line containing the *version information*, the *head* of the document, and the *body* of the document. Technically, HTML documents should start with a line indicating the DTD to be used (the version information). The DTD is contained within the < !DOCTYPE > element. In this tag it is called the Document Type Declaration, but it is not enforced by browsers and so therefore is left off many popular Website pages. An example of a common declaration line is:

```
<!DOCTYPE HTML PUBLIC "-//W3C//DTD HTML 4.01
Transitional//EN">
```

The HTML 4.01 recommendation lists three DTDs that can be used for HTML documents, and they each include a reference to an online DTD file. The files contain information browsers may need to understand the documents. This line becomes very important when dealing with XHTML and XML, but is not nearly so important in basic HTML documents. The three DTDs are:

```
<!DOCTYPE HTML PUBLIC "-//W3C//DTD HTML 4.01//EN"
"http://www.w3.org/TR/html4/strict.dtd">
<!DOCTYPE HTML PUBLIC "-//W3C//DTD HTML 4.01
Transitional//EN"
"http://www.w3.org/TR/html4/loose.dtd">
<!DOCTYPE HTML PUBLIC "-//W3C//DTD HTML 4.01
Frameset//EN"
"http://www.w3.org/TR/html4/frameset.dtd">
```

The *strict* DTD includes only elements and attributes that have not been deprecated and are not part of the *frameset* DTD. The *loose* DTD includes elements and attributes in the strict DTD as well as those that have been deprecated. The frameset DTD includes everything in the other two DTDs, as well as frames (frames are discussed in Chapter 6).

2.7   The HTML Element

The HTML element is considered the root element of an HTML document, according to the DOM, and strangely enough it is optional (both starting and ending), although it is rarely omitted. The syntax of an HTML tag is simply < HTML > for the starting tag and < /HTML > for the ending tag. An HTML tag begins and ends HTML documents (following the DOCTYPE tag, if included), and all document content is contained within these two tags.

The HTML tag can have two attributes: the *lang* attribute and the *dir* attribute. The *lang* attribute specifies the language of the document (using a two-character code for the country) and the *dir* attribute specifies the direction (left-to-right or right-to-left) in which text proceeds across the page. These attributes can be found in other tags as well. The DTD of the HTML element is:

```
<!ENTITY % html.content "HEAD, BODY">
<!ELEMENT HTML O O (%html.content;)    -- document root
                                          element -->
<!ATTLIST HTML
 %i18n;                                 -- lang, dir --
 >
```

2.8   The HEAD Element

The HEAD tag marks the beginning of the document head element. Typically, nothing contained in the HEAD element is displayed to the user, except the title (in the title bar of your browser). This element serves as a container for other elements (such as TITLE and META tags), and is optional (both starting and ending). Like the HTML tag, it contains the lang and dir attributes. It also contains the *profile* attribute. The profile attribute is used to specify the location of a meta (information *about* information) data profile, which is a file that helps define information *about* the document. As a matter of fact, there are META tags that can be included in the header of an HTML document. For example, the meaning of the word "author" (as in the author of the document) could be defined in the profile, and then a META tag could be used to specify the actual author of the document. The DTD of the HEAD element is:

```
<!-- %head.misc; defined earlier on as "SCRIPT|STYLE
  |META|LINK|OBJECT" -->
<!ENTITY % head.content "TITLE & BASE?">
<!ELEMENT HEAD O O (%head.content;) +(%head.misc;)
                                           -- document head -->
<!ATTLIST HEAD
  %i18n;                        -- lang, dir --
  profile   %URI;   #IMPLIED -- named dictionary of meta info --
  >
```

2.9   The TITLE Element

The TITLE element contains the title of an HTML document, and both the starting and ending tags are required. As mentioned, the title appears in the title bar of your browser. An HTML document must have exactly one title. The DTD for the TITLE element is:

```
<!ELEMENT TITLE -- (#PCDATA) -(%head.misc;)
                                           -- document title -->
<!ATTLIST TITLE %i18n>
```

2.10   The META Element

META tags are not required, but can be included in HTML document head elements to provide (as the name suggests) information about the information contained in the page. A common use of META tags is to provide keywords and descriptions pertaining to the page for search engine usage. For META elements, the starting tag is required but an ending tag is forbidden (not just optional). The element itself consists of the definition of a property (keywords, for example) and a value (the individual keywords, for example). Coding a META element for a gift shop Web page might be done as follows:

```
<META Name="keywords" Content="gifts, birthdays,
Christmas, presents">
```

The DTD for the META element is:

```
<!ELEMENT META -- O EMPTY      -- generic metainformation -->
<!ATTLIST META
  %i18n;                       -- lang, dir, for use with
                                  content --
  http-equiv  NAME  #IMPLIED  -- HTTP response header name --
  name        NAME  #IMPLIED  -- metainformation name --
  content     CDATA #REQUIRED -- associated information --
  scheme      CDATA #IMPLIED  -- select form of content --
  >
```

The attributes of the META element are:

- *Name* – The name of the property being established, such as keywords, description, and so forth.
- *Content* – The value that is assigned to the property, such as a set of keywords, a short description, and so forth.
- *Scheme* – The type of data contained in the value would be set (text is the default).
- *Http-equiv* – This attribute can be used rather than a name, and if so the Web server will use the META element to collect data for HTTP response headers. For example, the character set can be specified with this type of META element.
- *Lang* and *Dir* – These attributes can be used to define the language in which the document is constructed and the direction of text within the document.

Here is an example of a typical Web page with HTML, HEAD, TITLE, and META tags:

```
<!DOCTYPE HTML PUBLIC "-//W3C//DTD HTML 4.01//EN"
"http://www.w3.org/TR/html4/strict.dtd">
<HTML>
<HEAD>
<TITLE>Here is the title of your page</TITLE>
<META http-equiv="Content-Type" content="text/html;
charset=iso-8859-1">
<META name="keywords" content="first, second, third">
<META name="description" content="This is a description">
</HEAD>
</HTML>
```

2.11 The BODY Element

The BODY element contains the major portion of Web page content that is actually visible on the screen in your browser. Within the BODY element you may insert text, images, links, tables, and forms, but not frames. Interestingly, the starting and ending tags are optional, although in practice they are almost never left out. The DTD of the BODY element is:

```
<!ELEMENT BODY O O (%block;|SCRIPT)++(INS|DEL)
                              -- document body -->
<!ATTLIST BODY
  %attrs;                               -- %coreattrs, %i18n,
                                           %events --
  onload      %Script;   #IMPLIED -- the document has been
                                      loaded --
  onunload    %Script;   #IMPLIED -- the document has been
                                      removed --
  >
```

The starting BODY tag can include several attributes setting the background color of the screen, the foreground color of text, and so forth. Here are the attributes and events of the BODY element:

- *Background* – This attribute specifies the location of an image file, which is then tiled across the background of the browser display area, starting at the top left. It is typically used to provide smoothly textured backgrounds for Web pages.

- *Bgcolor* – This attribute specifies a color for the background (we will discuss this further in the next section).

- *Text*, *Link*, *Vlink*, and *Alink* – These attributes all set a color for either text, hypertext links, links that have been visited (*vlink*), or links that are active (*alink*). Active links show their color when the mouse is over them and the left mouse button is pressed down.

All of the attributes above have been deprecated, meaning they still work but are being phased out, in favor of style sheets. Style sheets should now be used for defining these attributes.

- *Id*, *Class* – These attributes apply to the BODY element (and also to other elements) and can be used to assign a unique name (*id*) to an element and to assign an element to a group (*class*). Once assigned a name or to a group, other tags can reference the element or group and apply styles or perform other selective functions.

- *Lang*, *Dir*, and *Title* – The *lang* and *dir* attributes perform the same functions here as before, while the *title* attribute (unlike the TITLE element) gives a title to the element it is coded into. Think of *title* attributes as popup labels (such as you might see if you put your mouse over a link or image).

- *Style* – This attribute specifies style information or an external style sheet for a page. Style sheets will be covered in more detail in Chapter 8.

- *Onload, onunload, onclick, ondblclick, onmousedown, onmouseup, onmouseover, onmousemove, onmouseout, onkeypress, onkeydown, onkeyup* – These are all *events* to which the BODY element may be programmed to respond, but the BODY element can only be programmatically affected when a scripting language such as Javascript is used.

2.11.1 BODY ELEMENT BACKGROUND COLOR

Those of you familiar with early Web pages will probably remember when backgrounds were gray. Adding color to the background of a Web page makes it much more visually appealing, and that is the function of the *bgcolor* attribute of the BODY element. The *bgcolor* attribute can also be used with tables, and setting the color values (discussed next) works the same for the *text*, *link*, *vlink*, and *alink* attributes of the BODY element.

Colors are specified in HTML using the Red, Green, Blue (RGB) color space. This means that colors are created using a combination of red, green, and blue color values from zero to 255 (a total of 256 values for each primary color, because zero is a value, giving 256^3 or 16.7 million colors in all).

Color value are coded in HTML by setting the attribute equal to the hexadecimal value for the appropriate color, preceded by a pound sign, like this:

```
<BODY BGCOLOR="#FF0000">
```

In this example, the background color of the page would be pure red, because the hexadecimal value for 255 (FF) has been inserted into the first two characters of the color code, while the other values are set at zero.

Most image-editing software programs provide decimal values for the colors red, green, and blue when you use their color picker functions, and these decimal values can be converted to hexadecimal values with any decent calculator, including the calculator provided as an accessory program with the Windows operating system.

2.11.2 CONTENT WITHIN THE BODY ELEMENT

Inside the BODY element of your HTML document all the content you wish to display to the user appears. In standard HTML text, images, forms, tables, and so forth appear on screen in the order you write them, so it is common practice to write HTML documents from top to bottom, with the elements and objects in roughly the same location as you would find them on the finished page in your browser. This makes it easier to read the HTML and find errors or problems in the code reflected in the finished page. For example, if you have several images on a Web page, and one is missing in the browser, you can read down through the HTML to approximately the same location and quickly find the broken image file reference (assuming that is the problem).

Unless you are using absolute positioning, elements in an HTML document cannot appear to overlay each other, and they will start at the top left of the finished page, proceed from left to right across the screen until they run out of room, and then drop down to the next line. If there is enough content a vertical scrollbar will appear allowing the user to scroll down the page, but a horizontal scrollbar won't appear unless you use tags to prevent line breaks or images or other objects wider than the screen width. As you are designing your pages, keep in mind that people hate to scroll horizontally.

Although you may make Web pages as long as you like, as a practical matter some pages work better with about enough content to fill only one screen (such as the first page of a Website), others may contain 3 or 4 screens of content (most pages), and some may contain 10 or 20 screens of content (catalog pages, for example) although from a design standpoint there should be relatively few of these. If you do build pages with more than 3 or 4 screens of content, make sure to provide some navigation mechanism that relieves the user of the burden of finding where they are within the page, because it's easy to lose your way, and a frustrated user will be more likely to leave your site.

Although browsers will handily display plain text, many of the elements explained in this chapter serve to liven up Web pages by making text more readable. For example, the P element breaks text into paragraphs. Text that runs together in one large block is going to be harder to read than nicely separated paragraphs, obviously. Note that the P element, although it breaks up blocks of text, doesn't indent text at the beginning of a paragraph, as most people are used to. Indentation must be specifically applied.

There are also elements for applying bold, italics, and underlining to text, creating headings of various sizes, adding visible lines to break sections of text, and so forth. Many of these elements have been deprecated in favor of style sheets, but you'll still find them widely used because of their simplicity and because of the habits of Web page designers.

Also, some of the HTML elements are used because they produce graphical effects without the need for graphics. In the early days of Website design, any time you could produce an effect with code rather than graphics you did it because you knew you were saving the user download time. For example, inserting a horizontal rule (a visible line across the screen) was preferred to using an image file of a bar, because the horizontal rule was only four characters to download.

In the HTML recommendation browsers are referred to as user-agents, and user-agents as a class includes a broad spectrum of software that is capable of rendering HTML documents in one format or another. We are probably most familiar with the typical visual browsers such as Netscape Navigator and Internet Explorer, but there are user-agents that display only plain text, synthesize speech, or in some way or another radically change the output from what we might have in mind. HTML has mechanisms built in to accommodate some of this modification, and we should be aware of users who may not use a standard visual browser.

Interestingly, even visual browsers have a great deal of control over the display of content on Web pages. For example, browsers decide where to break lines and how to wrap words on a Web page. If you, as the user, change the size of the display screen window with your mouse, the browser will automatically try to re-wrap lines of text to fit the new screen size. This can completely change the look and feel of the Web page, although there are HTML elements offering the developer some control over these text layout functions.

In the final analysis it is up to you as the Web page designer to ensure a pleasant, appealing, easy-to-navigate, and easy-to-download Website, through judicious use of the appropriate HTML elements and attributes. Keep in mind that user-agents come in a variety of types and versions of each type, and that users sometimes set their browser settings somewhat differently than you yourself might, and you'll design pages that the vast majority of users can use profitably.

2.12   Block-level/Inline-level and Grouping Elements

Elements within the BODY element can be defined as block-level or inline-level elements. Think of *block-level elements* as larger structures such as a whole section of a document, while *inline elements* may be a single image or paragraph. For example, the DIV element is a block-level element that serves to provide an identity for a section of a page.

In general, block-level elements may contain other block-level elements and inline elements, while inline elements may contain other inline elements and data such as text. Block-level elements typically begin on a new line, while inline elements remain on whatever line they happen to be placed on, unless there is not enough room on the screen for them, in which case they would flow down to the next line. For example, if a picture (an inline element) is placed next to some text, and the text extends to the right far enough, the picture will flow down to the next line.

2.13   The DIV Element

The DIV element creates a generic block-level element within an HTML document, meaning the author of the document can use the *id*, *class*, *lang*, and *style* attributes to set an effect for the block defined by the DIV element as a whole. The start and end tags are required. Here is the DTD for the DIV element:

```
<!ELEMENT DIV -- - (%flow;)*      -- generic language/style
                                     container --
>
<!ATTLIST DIV
  %attrs;                          -- %coreattrs, %i18n,
                                     %events --
  >
```

In addition to the id, class, lang, and style attributes, the DIV element includes the id, title, and align attributes. The align attribute can take on the values of *left*, *right*, *center*, and *justify*. The meaning of the first three values is fairly obvious (they affect the horizontal placement of the element) and the last, justify, means that both ends of a block of text will have even margins (like in a newspaper column).

The DIV element can be programmatically affected by the onclick, ondblclick, onmousedown, onmouseup, onmouseover, onmousemove, onmouseout, onkeypress, onkeydown, and onkeyup events.

The DIV element affects whatever block and inline elements are contained inside it, as the following example illustrates:

```
<DIV align="right">
<P>Here is my first paragraph. This one will be aligned to the
right.
<P>Here is my second paragraph. This one will also be aligned to
the right
<P>Here is my third paragraph. This one will be right-aligned
as well.
</DIV>
```

If you are using an HTML-editor such as FrontPage, it may use the DIV element to align blocks of text or other elements, rather than the align attribute of the paragraph element. Use of the alignment attribute works, but has been deprecated in favor of style sheets.

2.14 The SPAN Element

The SPAN element is similar to the DIV element in that it allows the use of the same attributes, and has a similar DTD:

```
<!ELEMENT SPAN -- (%inline;)*   -- generic language/style
                                   container --
>
<!ATTLIST SPAN
  %attrs;                        -- %coreattrs, %i18n, %events --
>
```

Like the DIV element, the SPAN element starting and ending tags are required, and the same events affect it. The primary difference between the DIV and SPAN elements is that the DIV element defines a section of content as block-level, while the SPAN element defines a section of content as inline.

2.15 The H Element (Headings 1–6)

The H element comes in a variety of sizes, starting with the largest (H1) and ending with the smallest (H6). Headings are not measured in point sizes like ordinary text. When displayed in a browser H1 is very large, H2 is large, H3 and H4 are close to the size of standard text, H5 is small, and H6 is very small. A heading begins with a blank line, then comes the heading text, then another blank line. The H element also sets the text in the heading to Boldfaced.

The starting and ending tags are required for a heading, and the same attributes and events as DIV and SPAN are allowed. For example, the following heading is large and aligned to the center of the page:

```
<H2 align=center>Welcome to My Page</H2>
```

Typically, headings are used the same way they are in a book, meaning you would use them to separate sections within a page of text, with larger headings identifying broad subjects, while smaller headings identify subsections within the broad subject.

2.16   The ADDRESS Element

The ADDRESS element is sometimes used to supply contact information such as addresses, but is not seen that frequently. The starting and ending tags are required, and the same attributes and events are allowed as for the DIV, SPAN, and heading elements. For example, the following is a typical usage of the ADDRESS element:

```
<ADDRESS>
John Doe
11223 Spring Street
San Diego, CA 92108
</ADDRESS>
```

Using this element causes the address to be displayed in italics in Internet Explorer. Although the ADDRESS element does not provide conspicuous formatting for typical browsers, it might be helpful for users using speech-synthesis browsers, because those browsers could then identify to the user the specific type of information being rendered.

2.17   Text Formatting in Web Pages

In HTML, text formatting is performed by a combination of the tags used by the document author and settings or preferences within the user's browser. It takes a little getting used to, and the sharing of control can be disconcerting. For example, word wrapping is by default controlled by the browser, so that when the user resizes the browser window the text automatically rewraps, rather than going off the side of the screen. Unless line breaks are inserted by the author to force breaks at specific points, the author will not know where line breaks are going to occur for any given combination of browser, screen size, and screen resolution.

Browsers also allow only one white space between words. If more white spaces are inserted within the HTML (in plain text) they are completely ignored, as are tabs, carriage returns, and line feeds. Additional white spaces can be inserted using the character reference * * (and HTML-editors like FrontPage write these into the HTML when the space bar is pressed).

2.18 Structured Text Elements

The EM, STRONG, DFN, CODE, SAMP, KBD, VAR, CITE, ABBR, and ACRONYM elements are all referred to as Phrase elements. They denote document structure, meaning they assign specific identities to sections of text. For example, the CODE element refers to a segment of code (such as programming language code), and may be rendered in a font that might be expected by most users. The DTD for Phrase elements is:

```
<!ENTITY % phrase "EM | STRONG | DFN | CODE |
                   SAMP | KBD | VAR | CITE | ABBR | ACRONYM" >
<!ELEMENT (%fontstyle;|%phrase;) -- (%inline;)*>
<!ATTLIST (%fontstyle;|%phrase;)
  %attrs;                      -- %coreattrs, %i18n, %events --
>
```

The Phrase element starting and ending tags are required, and they offer all the same attributes and events as the block-level elements, with the exception of the *align* attribute. Often they are rendered in a manner similar to other text formatting tags, such as boldfaced for the STRONG element and italics for the EM element. In general, these elements are more useful when it is necessary to define a particular kind of data within a document, rather than for display purposes.

2.19 The BLOCKQUOTE and Q Elements

The BLOCKQUOTE and Q elements are for defining a phrase or section of text as a quotation, with the BLOCKQUOTE element referring to a whole block of text or paragraph and the Q element indicating the placement of quote marks. The DTD for these elements is:

```
<!ELEMENT BLOCKQUOTE -- (%block;|SCRIPT)+
                              -- long quotation -->
<!ATTLIST BLOCKQUOTE
  %attrs;                      -- %coreattrs, %i18n, %events --
  cite      %URI;     #IMPLIED -- URI for source document or
                                  msg --
  >
<!ELEMENT Q -- (%inline;)*    -- short inline quotation -->
<!ATTLIST Q
  %attrs;                      -- %coreattrs, %i18n, %events --
  cite      %URI;     #IMPLIED -- URI for source document or
                                  msg --
  >
```

Both starting and ending tags are required for these elements, and they allow the same attributes and elements as the Phrase elements. Each of these elements also permits the use of the *cite* attribute (not to be confused with the CITE element). The *cite* attribute allows the document author to place a citation URL value within the starting tag, and BLOCKQUOTE elements are rendered as an indented block of text. For example, the following code will display as an indented block, with a reference or citation URL of www.mcgraw-hill.com:

```
<blockquote cite="www.mcgraw-hill.com">The McGraw-Hill
Companies <font face="Arial, Helvetica, sans-serif"
size="1">(NYSE:MHP)</font> is a global publishing, financial,
information and media services company with 16,500 employees
located in 400 offices in more than 32 countries. It includes
such renowned brands as Standard &amp; Poor's, Business Week,
and McGraw-Hill educational and professional materials.
</blockquote>
```

Although the Q element has a place in the specification, it does not appear to be well supported by HTML-editors or browsers, and the HTML 4.01 recommendation itself recommends that style sheets be used to provide quotation marks, rather then the Q element.

2.20   The SUP and SUB Elements

The SUP and SUB elements provide superscript and subscript formatting. Their starting and ending tags are required, and they support the same attributes and events as the Phrase elements. Their DTD is:

```
<!ELEMENT (SUB|SUP) -- (%inline;)*
                         -- subscript, superscript -->
<!ATTLIST (SUB|SUP)
  %attrs;                -- %coreattrs, %i18n, %events --
  >
```

These elements are useful for ordinary super- and sub-scripting, as in the following example of the presentation of written dates like July 1st, 2000:

```
July 1<sup>st</sup>, 2000
```

2.21   Paragraphs and the P Element

Paragraphs are formatted in HTML using the P element. Interestingly, though the content (such as text) of a paragraph may be contained within beginning and ending paragraph tags, the ending tag is optional. However, there must be a starting paragraph tag at the beginning of the next paragraph, or the two blocks of text will run together (in the absence of any other tags) even if there is white space separating them. The DTD for the P element is:

```
<!ELEMENT P -- O (%inline;)*       -- paragraph -->
<!ATTLIST P
  %attrs;                          -- %coreattrs, %i18n,
                                      %events --
  >
```

When a P tag is placed on a line of text, it forces the browser to display a single blank line. The P element has the same attributes and events as the DIV and SPAN elements, and can use the *align* attribute to align text (left, right, center, or justify). It cannot contain other block-level elements, including other P tags. Some versions of browsers will display multiple blank lines in a document if multiple P tags are present, but this is discouraged in the HTML 4.01 recommendation.

2.22   Line Breaks and the BR Element

Since browsers control word-wrapping, the BR element should be used in places when the author wants to force a line break. The <BR> tag produces a BR

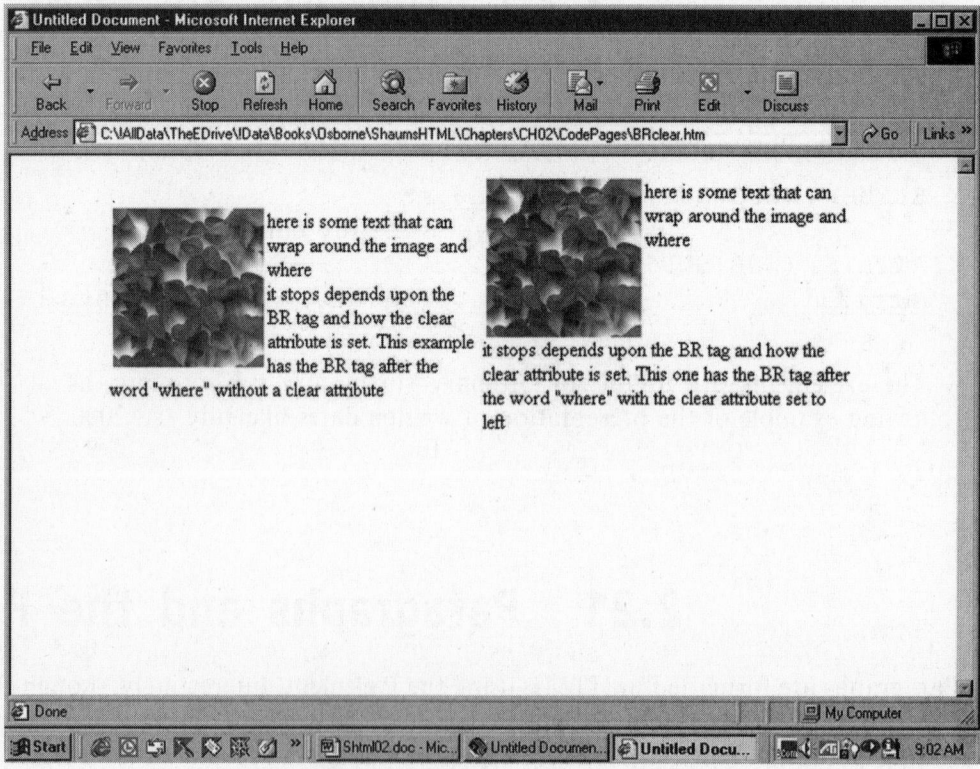

Fig. 2-1.   Setting the clear attribute of the BR element.

element, and only the starting tag is allowed (an ending tag is forbidden for the BR element). Other than the *id*, *class*, *title*, and *style* attributes, its only notable attribute is the *clear* attribute. This attribute indicates where text will continue if the text is next to a floating element such as an image (the default value is *none*, but the *clear* attribute can also assume the values *left*, *right*, and *all*). For example, if text is wrapping next to an image and the BR element is put in place in the middle of one of the lines, setting the *clear* attribute to *none* will make the text continue on the next line down, while setting the clear attribute to *left* will make the text continue below the bottom of the image. Figure 2-1 shows an example.

2.23   Alignment and the *align* Attribute

The *align* attribute can be set for a variety of elements, such as the IMG (image), the H (heading), and the P (paragraph) elements, and of course the effect it produces is the horizontal alignment of the element it is attached to. For example, to align a heading to the center of a page, the following code could be used:

```
<H2 align="center">This is the Heading</H2>
```

The values the align attribute can take are *left*, *center*, and *right*. By default, elements are aligned to the left, but for some elements, such as IMG, forcing left alignment causes a change in word-wrapping, as we shall see in Chapter 5.

2.24   Text Style Elements

Visually appealing text is enhanced by the use of bold, italics, underlining, teletype, and so forth. The HTML elements producing stylistic effects (B, I, U, BIG, STRIKE, TT, SMALL, and S) are not all deprecated, but the recommendation expresses preference for using style sheets to accomplish these effects.

These text style elements can be combined or nested, meaning, for example, that an author can place <I> tags inside <B> tags, like this:

```
<B><I>This text will be bold and italicized</I></B>
```

Both the starting and ending tags are required, and the DTD for these elements is:

```
<!ENTITY % fontstyle
  "TT | I | B | BIG | SMALL">
<!ELEMENT (%fontstyle;|%phrase;) -- (%inline;)*>
<!ATTLIST (%fontstyle;|%phrase;)
  %attrs;                   -- %coreattrs, %i18n, %events --
  >
```

These elements can be modified using the standard id, class, lang, dir, style, and title attributes, and the standard events.

2.25   Lines and the HR Element

The use of a line across the page makes text more readable by breaking it up into easily discerned blocks. The Horizontal Rule (HR) element creates a line across the page, and essentially acts as a paragraph break, because even if it is set to extend only partially across the page (50% width, for example) it still pushes other elements off the line on which it resides.

The DTD for the HR element is:

```
<!ELEMENT HR -- O EMPTY -- horizontal rule -->
<!ATTLIST HR
  %attrs;                    -- %coreattrs, %i18n, %events --
  >
```

The HR element is one of those few that has a required starting tag but a forbidden ending tag. It allows the standard *id*, *class*, *lang*, *dir*, *title*, and *style* attributes, and the standard events. It also allows the attributes *align* (the default is center for this element), *noshade* (renders the line as solid instead of etched into the page), *size* (height in pixels), and *width* (length as a percentage). However, all these additional attributes are deprecated for the HR element. Figure 2-2 shows some examples of the HR element with various attribute settings.

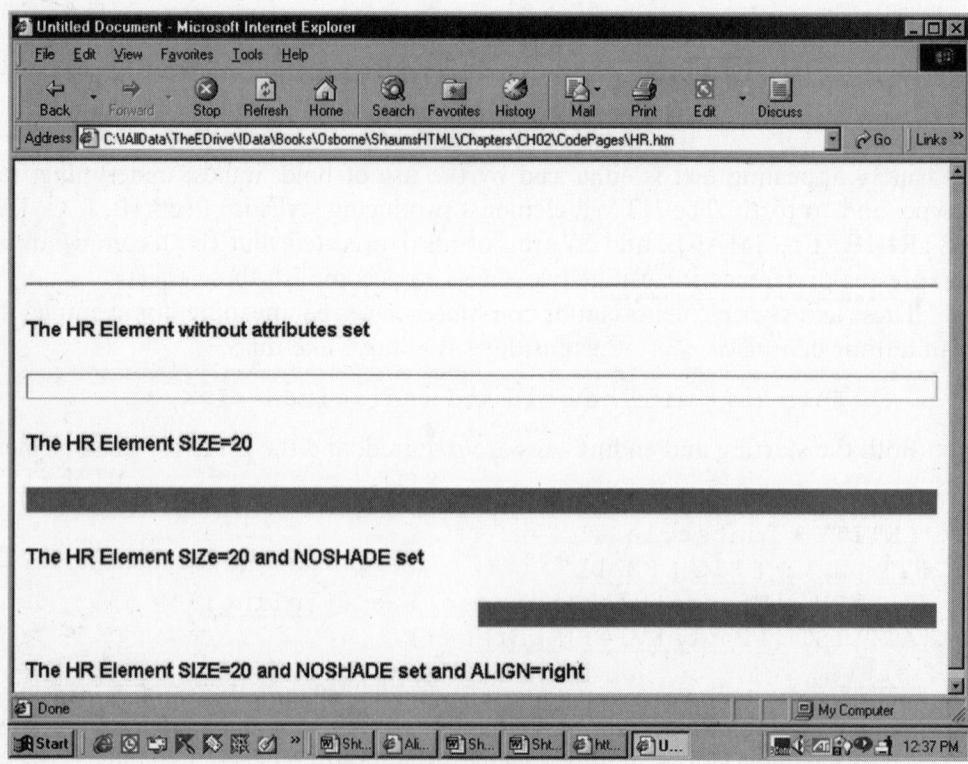

Fig. 2-2.   The HR element.

2.26   A Formatted HTML page

Now that we've been through a discussion of typical text formatting elements, we will review an example of a finished page demonstrating many of the elements we've covered. First we'll provide the code, and then we'll show the page in Fig. 2-3.

Here's the code:

```
<html>
<head>
<title>The Title</title>
<meta http-equiv="Content-Type" content="text/html;
charset=iso-8859-1">
<meta name="keywords" content="text, formatting, bold,
italics, paragraphs">
</head>
<body bgcolor="#CCFFFF">
<h2>Welome to the Example Web page!</h2>
<p>Here is the beginning of a paragraph. Notice there is no
automatic indentation, and the words wrap in the browser,
rather than being forced by some automatic HTML formatting.
```

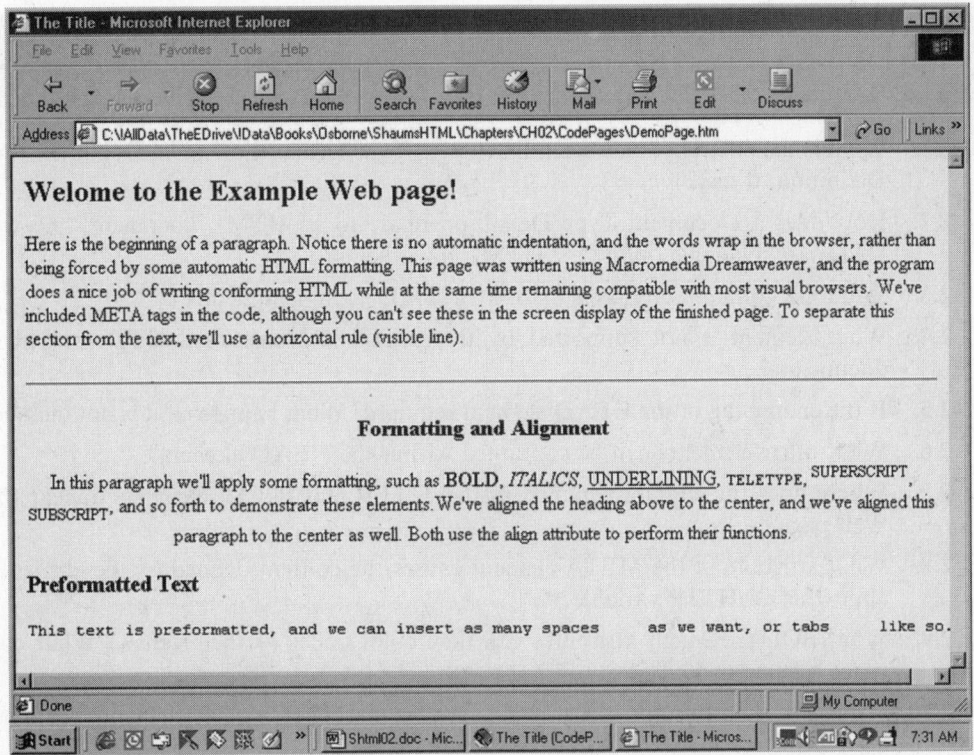

Fig. 2-3.   The demo page.

```
This page was written using Macromedia Dreamweaver, and the
program does a nice job of writing conforming HTML while
at the same time remaining compatible with most visual
browsers. We've included META tags in the code, although
you can't see these in the screen display of the finished page.
To separate this section from the next, we'll use a horizontal
rule (visible line).</p>
<hr>
<h3 align="center">Formatting and Alignment</h3>
<p align="center">In this paragraph we'll apply some
formatting, such as <b>BOLD</b>, <i>ITALICS</i>,
<u>UNDERLINING</u>, <tt>TELETYPE</tt>,
<sup>SUPERSCRIPT</sup>, <sub>SUBSCRIPT</sub>, and so forth
to demonstrate these elements. We've aligned the heading
above to the center, and we've aligned this
paragraph to the center as well. Both use the align
attribute to perform their functions.</p>
<h3 align="left">Preformatted Text</h3>
<pre align="left">This text is preformatted, and we can insert
as many spaces   as we want, or tabs   like so.</pre>
</body>
</html>
```

Review Questions

2.1. What is the difference between a Document Type Declaration and a Document Type Definition, if any?

2.2. How does a Document Type Definition relate to an HTML document, and what DTDs are available online for HTML documents?

2.3. What are common components of an HTML document element?

2.4. What element is not supported by the strict and transitional DTD for HTML documents?

2.5. Is the ending tag of the HEAD element required? What happens if it is not included?

2.6. What other elements can be contained within the HEAD element?

2.7. Where does the content supplied in the TITLE and BODY elements appear on a Web page?

2.8. What attribute of the META element causes the content defined by the element to appear as an HTTP variable?

2.9. What BODY element attributes can take color codes as their values? What color space scheme is used?

2.10. What is the purpose of block-level elements in HTML? What elements are block-level elements?

2.11. What is the primary difference between the DIV and the SPAN elements?

2.12. What is an attribute, and what relation does it have to an HTML element? How does an attribute work?

2.13. What is an intrinsic event, and how is it different from an attribute?

2.14. What purpose does the *lang* attribute serve?

2.15. What purpose does the *dir* attribute serve?

2.16. How many white spaces will a browser display between words? Will a browser show tabs?

2.17. What is a character entity reference? What character entity reference displays a non-breaking space?

2.18. What does the P element do? When is it necessary to include an ending P tag with the P element?

2.19. What are Phrase elements? Give several examples, and tell what do they do.

2.20. What effect does the BLOCKQUOTE element have on displayed text?

2.21. What is the default alignment for text and images in an HTML document? What values can the *align* attribute take for text?

2.22. How would a smooth, unbroken background image be generated in an HTML document, if image size was an issue?

2.23. What attribute sets the color for visited links in an HTML document. What element does this attribute belong to? Are there any caveats on its behavior in a given browser?

2.24. What is the purpose of the clear attribute?

2.25. What effect is produced by inserting the TT element into a section of text?

Solved Problems

2.1. What delimiters are used to denote HTML tags?

The less-than (<) and greater-than (>) signs, also called angle brackets.

2.2. Suppose there is a requirement to assign a document to the transitional DTD. Where does this DTD reside? What code would accomplish this?

The DTD resides at the location indicated by the URL in the DOCTYPE tag at the beginning of the HTML document, as illustrated in the following code:

```
<!DOCTYPE HTML PUBLIC "-//W3C//DTD HTML 4.01 Transitional//EN"
"http://www.w3.org/TR/html4/loose.dtd">
```

2.3. You need to create an HTML document with the least possible number of elements. What code would accomplish this?

```
<HTML><HEAD><TITLE>The Title</TITLE></HEAD></HTML>
```

2.4. Search engines deploy software agents called spiders to index Web pages within their databases. What element could you include in your documents to assist spiders in properly indexing the contents of your Web pages, and how is the element coded?

The META element can assist spider software in the process of indexing Web pages, by providing information about the contents of the Web page. The code can be written as follows:

```
<META NAME="keywords" CONTENT="searchterm1, searchterm2">
<META NAME="description" CONTENT="A short description of the
site">
```

2.5. To define the color for the background of a Web page as gray, what color code would be used. How would the shade of gray produced be made lighter or darker?

Gray can be generated by any combination of color values in which the Red, Green, and Blue values are equal, and not the highest or lowest values of each. For example, all three of the following color codes would produce a shade of gray, from lightest to darkest:

```
<BODY bgcolor="#111111">
<BODY bgcolor="#888888">
<BODY bgcolor="#EEEEEE">
```

2.6. What method can be used to convert a hexadecimal number to a decimal number, for HTML color codes?

HTML color codes consist of a two-character hexadecimal color code for each color in the RGB color space. The alphabetical characters represent numbers beyond the standard 0 to 9. The letter "A" is equivalent to the decimal number 10, while "F" is equivalent to the decimal number 15. The decimal value of a hexadecimal number can be derived by multiplying the decimal value of the number by 1, 16, 256, and so forth, depending upon the position of the character.

For example, if the first character in a two-character hexadecimal number is "B", and "B" is equivalent to decimal 11, then the first part of the value would be $(11*16) = 176$. If the second character is also "B", then the second part of the value would be 11. The decimal value of the two-character hexadecimal number "BB" would be the first and second values added together $(176 + 11) = 187$.

2.7. What code could be used to align a paragraph to the right or center? Show more than one way to perform such alignment.

```
<P align="right">The paragraph</P>
<DIV align="right"><P>A paragraph</P><P>Another
  paragraph</P></DIV>
<CENTER><P>A paragraph</P></CENTER>
```

2.8. What code would be used to initiate a scripting language function in response to the BODY element of an HTML document being loaded into a browser?

The onload intrinsic event is triggered when the BODY element of an HTML document is loaded into a browser. The following code illustrates how this would be written in HTML, using the made-up function name myfunction:

```
<BODY onload="myfunction">
```

2.9. Give an example of code that would produce a very large heading, boldfaced, with blank lines before and after the heading.

The H element will produce headings, boldfaced, with blank lines before and after the heading. The size of an H element is determined by a numerical value following the letter "H" in the starting and ending tags, the largest being 1 and the smallest being 6, as shown in this example:

```
<H1>This is the largest heading</H1>
```

 # Supplementary Programming Problems

2.10. To cause a browser to break a line of text at a specified point, what code would be used, and to cause a browser to continue a line without breaking it (even past the right side of the displayed window) what code would be used?

To break a line of text, the following code would be used:

```
The line of<BR> text.
```

To force a line of text to continue, the following code would be used:

```
<NOBR>The line of text, going on and on and on and on</NOBR>
```

2.11. Written dates make up part of the content of an HTML document. Show the code for an element that can make text smaller and superscripted, such as that following the numerical date (21st, for example).

The SUP element can make text smaller and superscripted, as shown here:

```
Today is January 21<sup>st</sup>, 2000.
```

2.12. Write code to separate blocks of text onscreen with a visible line 9 pixels high, centered, and unshaded.

The HR element produces visible lines across the display screen of a browser, and can assume values for shading, height, and width, as shown here:

```
Here is a block of text.
<HR noshade height="9" align="center">
```

2.13. You have provided contact information in a Web page, and wish to ensure that it is identified as an address. What tags could be used to perform this function?

The ADDRESS element identifies content as an address (even though it is not well supported and causes no discernible change in the way text is rendered in most browsers):

```
<ADDRESS>John Doe<BR>Street Address<BR>City, ST,
Zip</ADDRESS>
```

2.14. To display a background image repeatedly until it covers the entire display screen in a browser window, what code would be used? Demonstrate using the image name "myimage.jpg".

```
<BODY BACKGROUND="myimage.jpg">
```

2.15. Code the following section of text properly in HTML, use the second largest heading size for the heading:

Welcome to my Web Page!

This Web page is devoted to the study of HTML elements and their tags, such as the < HTML > tag. The delimiters of HTML tags (< and >) are **very** important.

```
<H2 align=center>Welcome to my Web Page!</H2>
<P>This Web page is devoted to the study of HTML elements and their
tags, such as the &lt; HTML&gt; tag. The <I>delimiters</I> of HTML
tags (&lt; and &gt;) are <B>very</B> important<>.</P>
```

Answers to Review Questions

2.1. A Document Type Declaration goes in an HTML document to reference the proper Document Type Definition for the HTML document being created or read, while the Document Type Definition is the online code defining the elements and attributes acceptable for use with the document.

2.2. The DTDs used with HTML specify the elements used in an HTML document, and the appropriate syntax for each element. There are three DTDs used with the HTML 4.01 recommendation: strict, transitional (loose), and frameset.

2.3. Typically, each HTML element consists of the beginning and ending tags (which may be optional), the attributes that element may allow, and the events that can affect the element.

2.4. The FRAMESET element.

2.5. The starting and ending tags of the HEAD element are not required, and nothing happens in your browser if they do not appear on a page.

2.6. The META element, for one.

2.7. The content of the TITLE element appears in the title bar of your browser, and the content within the BODY element appears on the main screen of the browser window.

2.8. The http-equiv attribute.

2.9. The BODY element allows use of colors values with the bgcolor, text, link, vlink, and alink attributes.

2.10. The DIV and SPAN elements are block-level elements, and one of their primary functions is to identify sections of content by name, and that attributes can be applied to the entire block, rather than to just a specific section of text, for example.

2.11. The DIV element defines a section of content as block-level, while the SPAN element defines a section of content as inline.

2.12. An attribute, in relationship to an HTML element, modifies the display or behavior of the element, or identifies the element for reference. For example, the bgcolor attribute, when included in the BODY element, applies a color to the background screen display. The name attribute, when applied to the DIV element, gives the section delimited by the starting and ending DIV tags a name that can be used to reference the section via the DOM.

2.13. An intrinsic event, such as onclick, can be assigned to an element much like an attribute, but does not directly modify the element or give it an identification. Instead, an intrinsic event provides a mechanism by which an element may trigger scripting code within an HTML document, in response to specific action or occurrence on or to the Web page. For example, if the onclick intrinsic event is assigned to a button and the button is clicked by the user, the function associated with the intrinsic event is activated.

2.14. The lang attribute specifies the language in which the document is written. Specifying the correct language with the lang attribute may be helpful to search engines indexing the document, to browsers displaying the document, and to spelling or grammar checkers editing the document.

2.15. The dir attribute specifies whether text flows across a page left-to-right or right-to-left. It may also be used to specify directionality in tables.

2.16. Browser have some control over word-wrapping, and part of that control comes from the fact that browsers only display one white space between words. If more than one white space is entered in plain text in an HTML document, the browser will ignore (not display) the additional space characters. Browsers also ignore (do not display) tabs.

2.17. Character entity references are numerical or abbreviated codes that cause the browser to display the character referenced. Character entity references begin with the ampersand and end with the semi-colon (;). For example, the character entity reference for a non-breaking space   in HTML.

2.18. The P element is the paragraph element, and it places a blank line across the displayed screen of the browser. It is used to separate text and other elements on the screen into blocks that serve as paragraphs. Although the ending tag is optional, it must be included when the P element is being used to align objects on the screen, to mark the ending point of the alignment effect.

2.19. Phrase elements apply structure and formatting to text sections within an HTML document. Whereas the I element (italics) specifically causes browsers to render text in italics, the EM element causes browsers to render text with emphasis. In a screen display the EM element may cause the same effect as the I element, but in a speech-synthesis browser the effect may be that the affected text is actually spoken with emphasis.

2.20. The BLOCKQUOTE element causes the browser to display text indented from the left-hand side.

2.21. The default alignment for text and graphics is to the left and to the top. The *align* attribute can be set to a value of *left*, *center*, or *right*.

2.22. Background images can be tiled (repeated over and over by the browser, starting at the top, left corner of the display screen) onto the background of an HTML document using the *background* attribute of the BODY element. To display a smooth, unbroken background the image file must be created with a smooth transition at the edges.

2.23. The *vlink* attribute sets the color of visited links in an HTML document, and it belongs with the BODY element. If a user sets certain browser options or preferences, links will be displayed in that browser according to those options or preferences rather than according to the setting of the attribute.

2.24. The *clear* attribute specifies where text begins again following a line break when wrapping words next to a floating element such as an image.

2.25. The text is rendered in a Teletype font.

CHAPTER 3

Advanced Web Page Formatting

3.1 The FONT and BASEFONT Elements

A tremendous amount of the information we consume daily takes the form of written words. The size, color, font face (the style of the letters or characters), and other formatting characteristics play a significant role in the effectiveness of written communications. As you might expect, some font sizes, faces, and formatting work better then others in certain situations.

HTML contains the FONT and BASEFONT elements for setting and managing font properties, and they are still widely used despite being deprecated in favor of style sheets. The BASEFONT element establishes basic font properties for text on a Web page, while the FONT element sets font properties for a specific character, word, phrase, sentence, paragraph, or section of text. The DTD for these elements is:

```
<!ELEMENT BASEFONT - O EMPTY      -- base font size -->
<!ATTLIST BASEFONT
  id        ID         #IMPLIED   -- document-wide unique id --
  size      CDATA      #REQUIRED  -- base font size for FONT
                                     elements --
  color     %Color;    #IMPLIED   -- text color --
  face      CDATA      #IMPLIED   -- comma-separated list of
                                     font names --
  >
<!ELEMENT FONT -- (%inline;)*     -- local change to font -->
<!ATTLIST FONT
  %coreattrs;                      -- id, class, style, title --
```

```
%i18n;                                 -- lang, dir --
size       CDATA      #IMPLIED  -- [+|-]nn e.g. size="+1",
                                       size="4" -
color      %Color;    #IMPLIED  -- text color --
face       CDATA      #IMPLIED  -- comma-separated list of
                                       font names --
>
```

The BASEFONT element does not have an ending tag since it contains all the information required to perform its function within the starting tag. Using the BASEFONT element to set font properties is not required, but if it is used the attributes it contains apply properties to all text on the page. For example, the following code sets the basic font size (4) and face (Arial) for a Web page (notice that the BASEFONT tag is written just below the starting BODY tag of the Web page, but before any FONT tags):

```
<HTML>
<HEAD>
<TITLE>The Title</TITLE>
</HEAD>
<BODY>
<BASEFONT SIZE="4" FACE="ARIAL">
This text is size 4 and displayed in the Arial font face.
</BODY>
</HTML>
```

While the BASEFONT element only supports the *id* attribute as a core attribute, the core attributes of the FONT element are *id*, *class*, *lang*, *dir*, *style*, and *title*. Additional attributes supported for both elements are *color*, *size*, and *face*. The *color* attribute can be set using the RGB color coding scheme discussed in Chapter 2, while the *face* is a comma-separated list for font face names such as Arial, Times New Roman, and so forth. The browser will search the user's computer for font faces, starting with the first font in the list, and if none of the listed font faces is loaded the browser will use a default font. Therefore, it is good practice to use fairly common font faces so that your font formatting will not be lost on the majority of your audience.

The *size* attribute sets the size of the font on a scale from 1 to 7, the actual screen size depending upon the screen resolution and how the browser interprets the size. The FONT element can set sizes directly, like this:

```
<FONT SIZE="4">This text is size 4</FONT>
```

The FONT element can also set font size in relation to the BASEFONT size, like this:

```
<FONT SIZE=+2>This text is 2 sizes larger than the BASEFONT
size</FONT>
```

If the BASEFONT element is not used, the text size will default to 3.

3.2 Lists and the UL, OL, and LI Elements

Another pleasant and useful text formatting technique is the numbered or bulleted list. HTML provides for lists with the UL and OL elements, *unordered* and *ordered* lists, respectively. Both of these elements use the same basic structure to accomplish their tasks, starting with the <UL> or <OL> tag (both starting and ending tags required), each bulleted or numbered item starting with the <LI> tag (the starting List Item or <LI> tag is required, and the ending </LI> tag may be used but is not required), and ending with the ending </UL> or </OL> tag. The DTDs for the UL, OL, and LI elements are:

```
<!ELEMENT UL -- (LI)+      -- unordered list -->
<!ATTLIST UL
  %attrs;                  -- %coreattrs, %i18n, %events --
  >
<!ELEMENT OL -- (LI)+      -- ordered list -->
<!ATTLIST OL
  %attrs;                  -- %coreattrs, %i18n, %events --
  >
<!ELEMENT LI - O (%flow;)* -- list item -->
<!ATTLIST LI
  %attrs;                  -- %coreattrs, %i18n, %events --
  >
```

These lists support the core attributes *id*, *class*, *lang*, *dir*, *style*, *title*, and the standard intrinsic events (onmouseover, onclick, and so forth). There are also a number of other supported attributes (all deprecated):

- *Type* – Allows the author to set the style of the symbol beginning the list item. For example, the UL symbol may be rendered as a disc, square, or circle, while the OL numerical value may be rendered as number (1), alphabetical characters (A for uppercase and a for lowercase), or roman numerals (I for uppercase and i for lowercase). Some aspects of the rendering are dependent upon the browser.

- *Start* – Sets the starting value for ordered list items, so that a list will start at the specified number, character, or roman numeral. While the value is a number (6, for example) the actual symbol rendered depends upon the setting of the *type* attribute (if the *type* value is III then a *start* value of 5 would produce VI in roman numerals).

- *Value* – Sets the value of the current LI item, so that you can change numbering midstream. For example, if you wanted to jump from 3 to 12 in your numbered list (as shown in Fig. 3-1) you could do that by setting the *value* attribute to 12.

- *Compact* – Tells the browser to display the list in a more compact way, but how it is rendered is up to the browser.

3.3   Definition Lists and the DL Element

A *definition list* is a structure for presenting terms followed by their definitions, with the definitions indented. This structure may be used in any case where the author wishes to present a single term or phrase followed by content related to the term, but the recommendation suggests using style sheets instead of this structure where the only desire is to produce indentation. The DTD of the DL element is:

```
<!-- definition lists - DT for term, DD for its definition -->
<!ELEMENT DL - - (DT|DD)+  -- definition list -->
<!ATTLIST DL
  %attrs;                 -- %coreattrs, %i18n, %events --
  >
```

Within the DL element the DT and DD elements produce the *definition term* and the *definition description*. For the DL element the starting and ending tags are required, but for the DT and DD elements only the starting tag is required. The DTD for the DT and DD elements is:

```
<!ELEMENT DT - O (%inline;)*  -- definition term -->
<!ELEMENT DD - O (%flow;)*    -- definition description -->
<!ATTLIST (DT|DD)
  %attrs;                 -- %coreattrs, %i18n,
                             %events --
  >
```

No unusual attributes are supported, but the core attributes of *id*, *class*, *lang*, *dir*, *style*, and *title* are, as well as the standard intrinsic events. Following is the code for a series of lists, including ordered and unordered lists and a definition list, and Fig. 3-1 shows the lists as they are rendered in a browser.

```
<html><head><title>Untitled Document</title>
<meta http-equiv="Content-Type" content="text/html;
charset=iso-8859-1">
</head>
<body bgcolor="#FFFFFF">
<p><font size="5">Unordered and Ordered Lists</font></p>
<ul >
  <li>This is the first item in an unordered list</li>
  <li>This is the second item</li>
  <li>and so on</li>
</ul>
<ul>
  <li type="circle">Here is the circle</li>
</ul>
<ul type="SQUARE">
```

```
    <li>Here is the square</li>
</ul>
<ol>
    <li>Here is an ordered list in numbers</li>
    <li>and the number 2</li>
    <li>and the number 3</li>
    <li value="12">This number is different</li>
    <li>and this number follows the last, rather than from the
        beginning of the list</li>
</ol>
<p>Here is a definition list:</p>
<dl>
    <dt><b>Term 1</b></dt>
    <dd>The description for the first term</dd>
    <dt><b>Term 2</b></dt>
    <dd>The description for the second term</dd>
</dl>
</body></html>
```

Note that the bold font style for the definition list terms was added, and is not part of the formatting of the definition list itself.

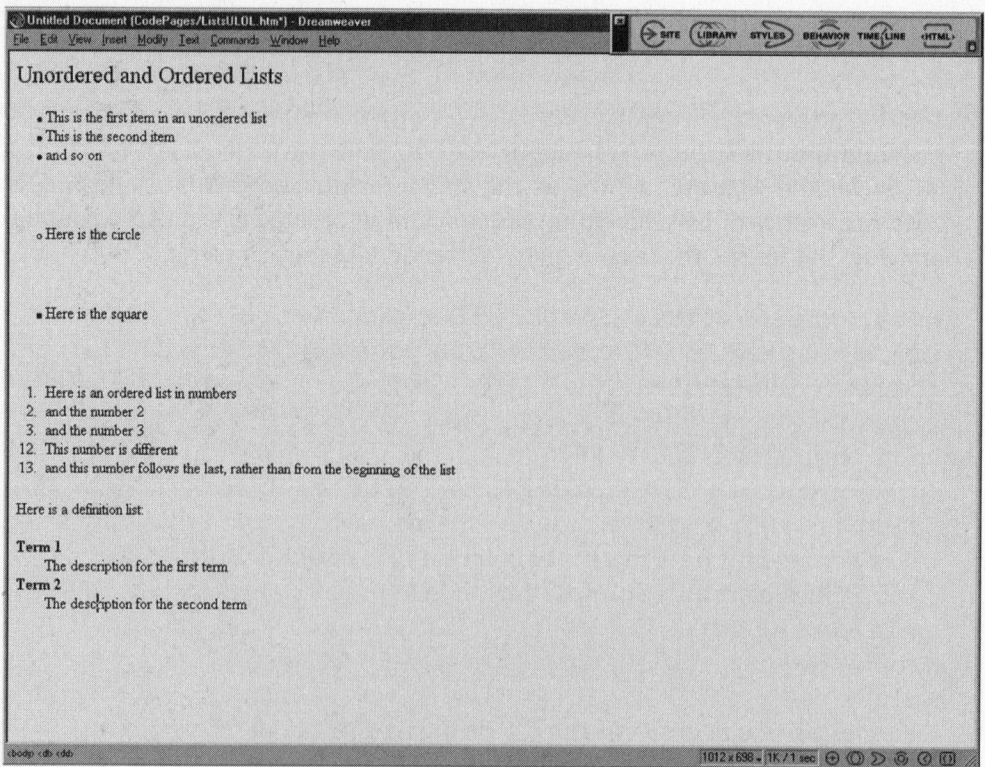

Fig. 3-1.   List elements.

3.4   Preformatted Text and the PRE Element

As we discussed earlier, browsers allow only one white space between words, and eliminate any additional white spaces. If you happen to have a document that is formatted with white spaces for readability, such as text output from a database program containing columns of names, addresses, and phone numbers, inserting this text directly into an HTML page will result in a completely unreadable Web page, because the spacing that maintains the columns will be eliminated, except for one space between each word.

To prevent the browser from ignoring additional spaces, the PRE element may be used. Following the starting PRE tag, the browser respects all white spaces, tabs, and so forth. Browsers will also render the text in a mono-spaced font such as Courier, often not a very palatable choice, and will prevent automatic word-wrapping. Realistically, a better way to include columnized text is to use table structures, as then the text remains columnized but is not converted to a mono-spaced font.

The DTD of the PRE element is (notice the elements, such as IMG, that may not be included within a PRE element):

```
<!ENTITY % pre.exclusion "IMG|OBJECT|BIG|SMALL|SUB|SUP">
<!ELEMENT PRE - - (%inline;)* -(%pre.exclusion;)
                        -- preformatted text -->
<!ATTLIST PRE
  %attrs;                 -- %coreattrs, %i18n, %events --
  >
```

Both the starting and ending tags are required, and the PRE element supports the standard attributes such as *id*, *class*, *style*, *title*, *lang*, *dir*, and the standard events. The PRE element also supports the attribute *width*. This attribute specifies the desired width of the section (in number of characters), but is not widely supported.

3.5   HTML Hypertext Links

The ability to connect directly to other documents or HTML resources by clicking content (text, images, and so forth being browsed) is an extraordinarily powerful feature of HTML, particularly since so many documents and other resources are now a part of the Internet. The concept has roots going back many years (well before the Internet and the World Wide Web entered the mainstream), and even ordinary footnotes and citations illustrate how important this kind of document connection capability has always been.

Within HTML the A (anchor) element serves to provide hypertext links, as well as several other useful features. Technically, the code providing the link to be clicked is considered the *source* anchor, and if there is code at the other document or resource providing a place to link to, it is considered the *destination* anchor.

However, it is not necessary for anchor code to be present at the destination in order to complete the link. Simply including the URL of the destination within the source anchor code is enough.

Destination anchors use syntax similar to the source anchor, but must include a name. Names can be set with the *name* attribute. When a destination anchor is used, the name must be included within the source anchor URL. The following code shows source and destination anchors using the A element, including the name attribute at the destination:

```
<a href="nextpage.htm">This text is clickable.</a>
<a href="nextpage.htm#otherpagename">Goes to a named
   anchor.</a>
<a name="otherpagename">
```

The first link is a common one having no destination name included. The page it refers to ("nextpage.htm") will appear in the normal fashion when the text message is clicked. Browsers render the clickable text blue and underlined, easily identifiable as a link. The second link is the same as the first but includes the name of the destination anchor, "otherpagename". The final line of code is not a link but only an anchor, containing the name "otherpagename". Note that when the second link is clicked not only will the document named "nextpage.htm" appear, but also the document will automatically scroll to the location of the named destination within the page. One key point to keep in mind; you must have control over the document linked to in order to create a destination anchor. By the way, when creating links within a document to other places in the same document, simply including the pound sign and the destination name is enough to create a working link.

Although most links connect HTML documents to other HTML documents, any file type can be linked to. If the user's browser is capable, the file type will be opened. If not, the browser typically offers the user the opportunity to retrieve and save the resource to storage (such as a Hard Disk Drive). In practice, this means users can open Web pages, image files, video and audio, multimedia, and many other common file types, without trouble. In addition, there are *plug-in* modules, freely available software that extends browser capabilities to open proprietary file types. One very common plug-in is used for Macromedia Flash. Macromedia distributes the plug-in free, to encourage sales and use of the Flash application for creating multimedia Web content.

3.6 The A and LINK Elements

The A element is the most commonly used element for forming links to other resources on the Web. The LINK element, in fact, does not form links but instead provides information to the browser as to the author's intended relationship between documents. For example, the LINK element may be set to show which document is the previous page and which is the next page, as shown here:

```
<HEAD><TITLE>The Title</TITLE>
<LINK rel="prev" href="page2.htm">
<LINK rel="next" href="page4.htm">
</HEAD>
```

The DTD for the LINK element is:

```
<!ELEMENT LINK - O EMPTY -- a media-independent link -->
<!ATTLIST LINK
    %attrs;                              -- %coreattrs, %i18n,
                                            %events --

    charset     %Charset;       #IMPLIED -- char encoding of
                                            linked resource -

    href        %URI;           #IMPLIED -- URI for linked
                                            resource --

    hreflang    %LanguageCode;  #IMPLIED -- language code --
    type        %ContentType;   #IMPLIED -- advisory content
                                            type --

    rel         %LinkTypes;     #IMPLIED -- forward link
                                            types --

    rev         %LinkTypes;     #IMPLIED -- reverse link
                                            types --

    media       %MediaDesc;     #IMPLIED -- for rendering on
                                            these media --
>
```

The starting tag for the LINK element is required but an ending tag is forbidden, and the LINK element may only be coded inside the HEAD element of a document. The standard attributes (*id*, *class*, *lang*, *dir*, *style*, and *title*) and the intrinsic events are supported. In addition, the following attributes are also supported:

- *Charset* – Allows the author to specify the character set to be used to interpret the characters of the document being linked to.

- *Href* – Specifies the URL of the resource being linked to.

- *Hreflang* – Specifies the language of the document being linked to.

- *Type* – Allows the author to provide an indication of the content type of the content at the other end of the link. For example, there may be an audio file at the end of the link, rather than text.

- *Rel* and *Rev* – Indicate the next and previous documents in a series of documents, *rel* indicating a forward link and *rev* indicating a reverse link. However, their values can become any of the currently recommended link types, such as alternate, start, next, prev, contents, index, glossary, and so forth. Their primary function is to assist the author with organizing content in a familiar (book-like) style.

- *Media* – Intended to provide the browser information concerning what media the content is suitable for. For example, assigning the value "aural" to this attribute indicates the content is meant for a speech-synthesizer.

- *Target* – Can be used to specify the name of a frame in which to open the link. Of course, the author must give the frame a name in the code before a targeted link can be opened in it. Frames will be discussed in greater detail in Chapter 6.

Unlike the LINK element, the A or anchor element does form displayed links within an HTML document (or else a named anchor or destination that may be linked to). The A element DTD is:

```
<!ELEMENT A - - (%inline;)* -(A) -- anchor -->
<!ATTLIST A
  %attrs;                        -- %coreattrs, %i18n, %events --
  charset     %Charset;          #IMPLIED -- char encoding of
                                             linked resource --
  type        %ContentType;      #IMPLIED -- advisory content
                                             type --
  name        CDATA              #IMPLIED -- named link end --
  href        %URI;              #IMPLIED -- URI for linked
                                             resource --
  hreflang    %LanguageCode;     #IMPLIED -- language code --
  rel         %LinkTypes;        #IMPLIED -- forward link types --
  rev         %LinkTypes;        #IMPLIED -- reverse link types --
  accesskey   %Character;        #IMPLIED -- accessibility key
                                             character --
  shape       %Shape;            rect     -- for use with client-
                                             side image maps --
  coords      %Coords;           #IMPLIED -- for use with client-
                                             side image maps --
  tabindex    NUMBER             #IMPLIED -- position in tabbing
                                             order --
  onfocus     %Script;           #IMPLIED -- the element got the
                                             focus --
  onblur      %Script;           #IMPLIED -- the element lost the
                                             focus --
  >
```

The starting and ending tags are required for the A element (you'll know if you leave off the ending tag, because everything in your document will become clickable, in some browsers). The *id, class, lang, dir, style,* and *title* attributes are all supported, as well as the intrinsic events, and quite a few other attributes and a couple of other events are also supported. They are:

- *Shape* and *coords* – Both of these attributes work with client-side image maps, to be discussed in further detail in Chapter 5.

- *Hreflang, rev, rel, target, type,* and *charset* – These attributes all work the same way as with the LINK element.

- *Name* – This attribute gives the link a name (required if the link is going to serve as a destination anchor).

- *Tabindex* – This attribute allows the author to specify a tab index, meaning the author can decide what element will be focused upon in what order as the user tabs through the document.

- *Accesskey* – This attribute can be assigned a value equivalent to a key on the keyboard, and when that key is pressed (or the key combination, depending upon the user's operating system) the link will be activated.

- *Onfocus* – This event occurs when the element in question receives focus. *Focus* means the element, whether it is a link, a button, or some other element, is currently active upon the user's screen. For example, if a button has focus, it will have a dotted line around its caption on the Windows operating system.

- *Onblur* – This event is the opposite of focus, and it occurs when an element loses focus.

3.7 Absolute and Relative URLs

Places on the Internet (connected computers, websites, and so forth) can be found using Internet Protocol (IP) Addresses. In IP version 4 (the fourth version of the Internet Protocol specification) IP addresses are made from a series of four numbers ranging from 0 to 255, for several billion possible combinations. Domain names map IP addresses to easy-to-remember names. Domain names and IP addresses are related to Uniform Resource Locators (URLs) in that the domain name or IP address of a Website is the second portion of a URL. URLs also contain other information allowing specific resources (files) to be found on the World Wide Web. URLs consist of four parts:

- The *protocol*, such as http.
- The *host computer name* or *domain name*, such as e4free.com, that represents the assigned IP address of the Website.
- The *path* to the resource, meaning the folder (and any subfolders) in which the file resides.
- The *filename and extension* of the resource.

Authors can use the entire or absolute URL to specify a resource within a hypertext link, or a relative URL. A *relative* URL takes its name from the fact that the resource is found by the browser relative to the location at which the browser found the current document (the default URL). For example, it is very common to create a link from one HTML document to another by specifying only the file name of the file being linked to, when that file is in the same folder as the HTML document being linked from. The browser will assume the protocol, the domain name, and the path to be identical as those of the document currently being displayed, and attempt to find the file being linked to in the same place. If a folder name is included in the *href* value, then the browser looks for the resource in a subfolder relative to the one in which the current document is found. Here is an example of absolute and relative *href* values:

```
<a href="http://www.e4free.com/mypictures.htm">This is an
absolute reference, and works from a document located anywhere
on the Web.</a>
<a href="mypictures.htm">This is a relative reference, and
works when the linked to document is located in the same folder
as the current document.</a>
<a href="pictures/mypictures.htm">This is a relative
reference to a subfolder, and works when the linked to document
is located in a subfolder named pictures beneath the folder of
the current document.</a>
```

3.8 The BASE Element

By default, the base URL from which relative links are calculated is the URL of the current document. If an author wishes to specifically set the base URL for a document, that can be accomplished with the BASE element. The BASE element must be placed in the HEAD element, and must come before any other element that refers to an external resource. The base URL specified applies only to the current document and affects any resources specified within it.

There is a starting tag for the BASE element, but an ending tag is forbidden. The DTD for the BASE element is:

```
<!ELEMENT BASE - O EMPTY                    -- document base URI -->
<!ATTLIST BASE
  href          %URI;            #REQUIRED -- URI that acts as base
                                            URI --
  >
```

The only attribute supported by the BASE element, *href*, can contain as a value an absolute URL. This URL becomes the base from which any relative URLs specified within the document are calculated, regardless of the actual location of the current document.

3.9 Placing Objects in Web Pages; the OBJECT Element

Practically anyone who has seen a Web page knows that images can be included in the pages, but not everyone knows how this is done. From a programming standpoint, the data composing the image could be included along with the code forming the page, but this would be messy and inconvenient. Instead, HTML allows for the inclusion of images via the IMG element. The limitation, of course, is that the IMG element works well only for image file formats, and there are many types of objects besides images that authors would like to include within Web pages. For example, suppose an author wants to include a calendar that displays the correct day and date. If the calendar could be created with a Java applet, then the APPLET element could be used to insert it into the Web page. However, for applications and objects that are not Java based there was no support within HTML until the introduction of the OBJECT element in HTML version 4.0.

Because the OBJECT element supersedes the APPLET element, the APPLET element is *now* deprecated. Both elements function in a similar way, with similar attributes defining essential parameters of their functions, but the OBJECT element is generic, meaning current and even future applications will have a mechanism by which they may be inserted into Web pages.

The starting and ending tags for the OBJECT element are required, and the DTD for the OBJECT element is:

```
<!ELEMENT OBJECT -- (PARAM | %flow;)*
                                 -- generic embedded object -->
<!ATTLIST OBJECT
  %attrs;                               -- %coreattrs, %i18n,
                                           %events --
  declare    (declare)    #IMPLIED -- declare but don't
                                       instantiate flag --
  classid    %URI;        #IMPLIED -- identifies an
                                       implementation --
  codebase   %URI;        #IMPLIED -- base URI for classid,
                                       data, archive --
  data       %URI;        #IMPLIED -- reference to
                                       object's data --
  type       %ContentType; #IMPLIED -- content type for
                                       data --
  codetype   %ContentType; #IMPLIED -- content type for
                                       code --
  archive    CDATA        #IMPLIED -- space-separated
                                       list of URIs --
  standby    %Text;       #IMPLIED -- message to show while
                                       loading --
  height     %Length;     #IMPLIED -- override height --
  width      %Length;     #IMPLIED -- override width --
  usemap     %URI;        #IMPLIED -- use client-side
                                       image map --
  name       CDATA        #IMPLIED -- submit as part of
                                       form --
  tabindex   NUMBER       #IMPLIED -- position in tabbing
                                       order --

>
```

The core attributes (*id*, *class*, *lang*, *dir*, *style*, and *title*) are supported, as well as the intrinsic events. The OBJECT element also includes a number of parameters that assist the object in displaying itself, in finding starting data, and in working with other objects and elements on the page. The other supported attributes are:

- *Declare* – Allows the author to declare but not instantiate the object, and simply including the word *declare* in the tag performs this function (no value is set).

- *Data* – Specifies the location of data used by the object to perform its function. For example, if a calendar application loads appointment data for an individual, the value of the *data* attribute may be a URL pointing to the location where data for this individual is stored.

- *Type* – Specifies the content type of the data to be received from the location specified in the *data* attribute. Content types (or media types) specify the type of formatting (such as text/html, image/gif, and so forth) of the data.

- *Standby* – Can be set to a value which is displayed as a message to the user while the object is loading.

- *Classid* – Can be used to specify a location from which an object may be implemented, as a URL.

- *Codebase* – Similar to the BASE element, in that it specifies a base URL from which relative URLs may be calculated. For example, if the *classid* attribute is set as a relative URL, the *codebase* attribute will be used as the base URL from which to calculate the path to the *classid* location. If the *codebase* attribute is not set then the base URL of the document will be used for this purpose by default.

- *Codetype* – Sets the content type for data when the *classid* attribute is used.

- *Archive* – Can contain a space-separated list of URLs of resources which may be used by the object, as some objects work with more than one data set.

- *Tabindex* – Can be set to a number that specifies the order, in relation to other objects/elements on the page, to which focus will go as the user tabs through the page.

- *Usemap* – Used with client-side image maps, and will be discussed further in Chapter 5.

- *Name* – Allows the author to assign a name to an object, so that it may be referenced by scripts and its contents submitted if it is within a FORM element. This attribute will receive further attention in Chapter 7.

- *Align*, *width*, *height*, *border*, *hspace*, *vspace* – These attributes provide data for rendering the display of the object. They will be discussed in greater detail in Chapter 5, as they are used frequently with images.

As we have discussed, authors appreciate the ability to include many objects other than images in HTML documents. While images can usually be rendered by the browser without assistance, other types of objects may need help, not only to be rendered properly but also to function correctly. For example, an object may need initial values applied when the object is first instantiated, or a stream of data to be processed. And because the OBJECT element gives authors control over an object's implementation, the OBJECT element may require information concerning the location of the object's executable files. These data can be set using the attributes *data*, *archive*, *codetype*, *codebase*, and so forth.

Because some browsers do not support some object types, not only can a text message be included, but additional objects can be included as well. For example, if an author wishes to include objects that can be displayed using either Internet Explorer or Netscape Navigator, but wants to use an ActiveX control as the primary object, then an image file OBJECT element that takes the place of the ActiveX control can be nested inside the first OBJECT element.

Objects can be declared in the HEAD element if the authors wishes, but authors should ensure that the object contains no data to be rendered because browsers generally don't render objects placed in the HEAD of a document. Objects declared in the HEAD element may be referenced by scripts, however, if they are assigned names via the *name* or *id* attribute.

3.10   Initializing Objects with the PARAM Element

Objects declared with the OBJECT element may be initialized with the PARAM element. Initialization means they are given initial operating values. For example, suppose a calendar object is included in a Web page. If the author wants a particular date displayed each time the calendar opens, then that date could be specified with the PARAM element. The value in the PARAM element could be a fixed date value, or it could be a location at which the current date (or some offset from the current date) could be found. The attributes of the PARAM element provide the capability to insert the appropriate data, and tell the browser what kind of data is being provided.

The PARAM element has only a starting tag, and the ending tag is forbidden. The DTD for the PARAM element is:

```
<!ELEMENT PARAM - O EMPTY -- named property value -->
<!ATTLIST PARAM
  id         ID               #IMPLIED   -- document-wide
                                            unique id --
  name       CDATA            #REQUIRED -- property name --
  value      CDATA            #IMPLIED   -- property value --
  valuetype  (DATA|REF|OBJECT)  DATA    -- How to interpret
                                            value --
  type       %ContentType;    #IMPLIED   -- content type for
                                            value when
                                            valuetype=ref --
>
```

Although the *id* attribute is supported, no other core attributes are, and no events are either. Additional attributes are:

- *Name* – Gives the parameter (or property) a name, so that the object knows to which property of itself to apply the value given.

- *Valuetype* – Indicates the type of value being supplied. For example, the *valuetype* may be *data* (this is the default *valuetype*), meaning that the data in the *value* attribute will be evaluated (calculated, if necessary) and the result passed to the object as a string. The *valuetype* could also be *ref*, meaning the value contains a URL that points to a resource where the actual value or values are stored. Finally, the *valuetype* could be *object*, meaning the name of a declared object has been supplied.

- *Value* – Supplies the value for the property, and is interpreted according to the type of value it is (as specified in the *valuetype* attribute).

- *Type* – Specifies the content type (image/gif, text/HTML, and so forth) but is only used when the *valuetype* is set to *ref*.

The following code is provided to illustrate how an object can be inserted into a Web page. The page was constructed with Microsoft FrontPage 2000, using an ActiveX Control called the Calendar Control 9.0. Interestingly (and not surprisingly), while Internet Explorer 5.0 displays the control without problem, Netscape Navigator 4.74 displays only the alternate text description of the control.

```
<html><head>
<meta http-equiv="Content-Type" content="text/html;
charset=windows-1252">
<meta name="GENERATOR" content="Microsoft FrontPage 4.0">
<meta name="ProgId" content="FrontPage.Editor.Document">
<title>New Page 1</title>
</head>
<body>
<object classid=
   "clsid:8E27C92B-1264-101C-8A2F-040224009C02"
   id="Calendar1" width="288" height="192">
 <param name="_Version" value="524288">
 <param name="_ExtentX" value="7620">
 <param name="_ExtentY" value="5080">
 <param name="_StockProps" value="1">
 <param name="BackColor" value="-2147483633">
 <param name="Year" value="2000">
 <param name="Month" value="10">
 <param name="Day" value="3">
 <param name="DayLength" value="1">
 <param name="MonthLength" value="2">
 <param name="DayFontColor" value="0">
 <param name="FirstDay" value="1">
 <param name="GridCellEffect" value="1">
 <param name="GridFontColor" value="10485760">
 <param name="GridLinesColor" value="-2147483632">
 <param name="ShowDateSelectors" value="-1">
 <param name="ShowDays" value="-1">
```

```
<param name="ShowHorizontalGrid" value="-1">
<param name="ShowTitle" value="-1">
<param name="ShowVerticalGrid" value="-1">
<param name="TitleFontColor" value="10485760">
<param name="ValueIsNull" value="0">
The calendar control alternate text
</object>
</body></html>
```

Notice all the PARAM elements containing what are clearly starting values for the control. Notice also that this control uses the *classid* attribute in the OBJECT element to tell the browser how to find the implementation of the control. Finally, notice the default name (*id* attribute) assigned to the control by FrontPage: Calendar1. Like many of the other PARAM element values automatically supplied, this value can be modified by the author. Additional PARAM elements and values can be supplied if desired, so long as the control supports them. Figures 3-2 and 3-3 show screen shots of the control in Internet Explorer and Netscape Navigator, respectively.

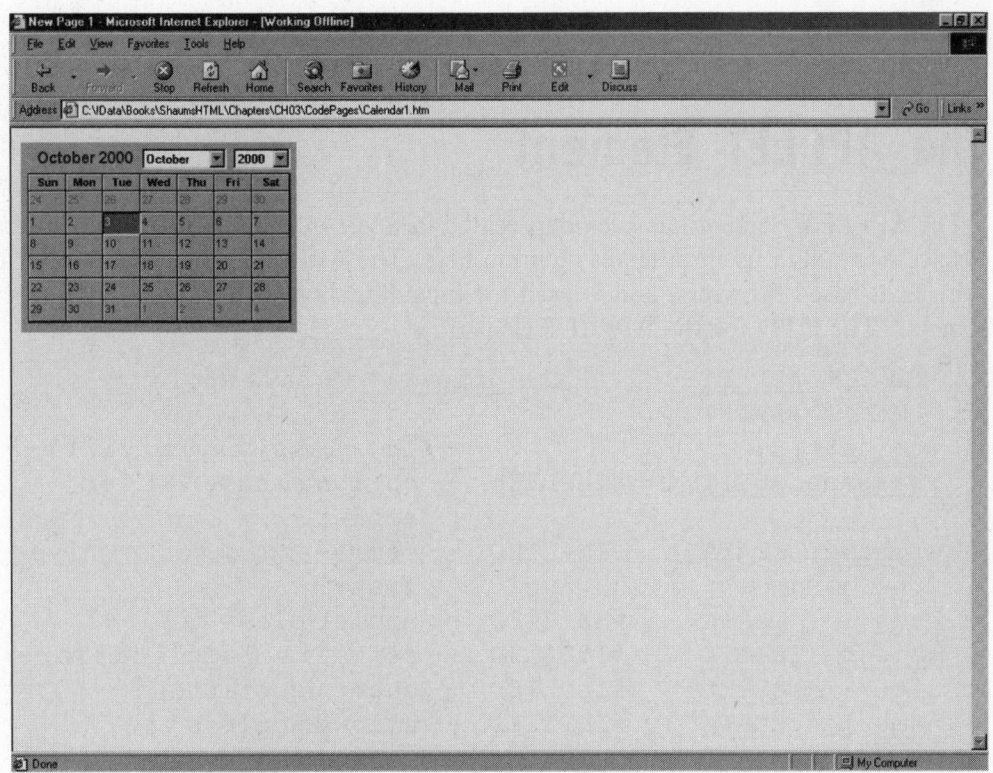

Fig. 3-2.   The Calendar Control in Internet Explorer.

Fig. 3-3. The Calendar Control in Netscape Navigator.

3.11 The APPLET Element

The APPLET element has been deprecated in favor of the OBJECT element, but since it is still in use it deserves mention here. The APPLET element is supported by Java-based browsers, and is used for including Java applets in HTML documents. The DTD for the APPLET element is:

```
<!ELEMENT APPLET - - (PARAM | %flow;)* -- Java applet -->
<!ATTLIST APPLET
  %coreattrs;                    -- id, class, style, title --
  codebase  %URI;     #IMPLIED  -- optional base URI for
                                   applet --
  archive   CDATA     #IMPLIED  -- comma-separated archive
                                   list --
  code      CDATA     #IMPLIED  -- applet class file --
  object    CDATA     #IMPLIED  -- serialized applet file --
  alt       %Text;    #IMPLIED  -- short description --
  name      CDATA     #IMPLIED  -- allows applets to
                                   find each other --
  width     %Length;  #REQUIRED -- initial width --
```

```
height    %Length;  #REQUIRED -- initial height --
align     %IAlign;  #IMPLIED  -- vertical or horizontal
                                 alignment --
hspace    %Pixels;  #IMPLIED  -- horizontal gutter --
vspace    %Pixels;  #IMPLIED  -- vertical gutter --
>
```

As you can see, the core attributes *id*, *class*, *style*, and *title* are supported (but only in the transitional DTD) and also the display attributes (*width*, *height*, *align*, *hspace*, and *vspace*). In addition, the *codebase*, *archive*, *code*, *object*, and *name* attributes are supported, and perform similar functions as in the OBJECT and PARAM elements. To provide an alternate means of displaying the presence of an applet for non-supporting browsers, the *alt* attribute is offered.

Review Questions

3.1. Regarding elements covered so far in this book, with what HTML elements can color for text be set? What differences are there in the way these elements set text color, and what are their consequences?

3.2. Why is there a FONT and a BASEFONT element? How do the two differ in use?

3.3. How is text size set with the FONT and BASEFONT elements? What size will text appear as when the size attribute is set to +3? +5?

3.4. What fonts are available for use with Web pages? What fonts should be used, and why?

3.5. What elements are available for creating bulleted and numbered lists in HTML? What syntax do they use, and what attributes can they contain?

3.6. What does the DL element do? What kind of list does it make?

3.7. What is word-wrapping?

3.8. How is word-wrapping accomplished on Web pages? What are some of the consequences of this methodology?

3.9. What element preserves white spaces and tab characters? Should it be used whenever the author desires columns or other types of spacing?

3.10. Data is all around us, and we have developed interesting ways of conveying it. Traditional books provide information in a linear format, meaning we progress from the simple to the more complex, or from the past to the future, or from the beginning of a story to the end, as we read a book. How do hypertext links change the format by which we convey information?

3.11. What elements provide hypertext links and other support? How do they work in relation to each other? Are they all required to provide links?

3.12. How are documents retrieved by the browser? What is a URL?

3.13. What is the difference between an absolute and a relative URL?

3.14. The base location of a Web page is by default the location from which it was retrieved. How can this be changed to suit the purposes of the author? What effect will this have on links within the document?

3.15. If a link contains a file name, this is considered a relative URL, and when clicked will provide the resource located at the URL, in this case a file. What mechanism can be used to not only retrieve the file, but scroll to a certain place within the file (if it is an HTML file)?

3.16. What is dot-notation?

3.17. What is an object (in the context of HTML documents)?

3.18. What element is used to insert images? Objects? How are they different?

3.19. Why might an author wish to declare an object, rather than simply instantiating the object whenever necessary?

3.20. An author can provide initialization data directly to an object, or can provide the object a URL to data, via the *value* attribute. What element provides this data? How does the object know what the contents of the *value* attribute contain?

3.21. Within the OBJECT element the author can specify a unique name for the object using the *id* attribute, and the location of the implementation of the object (the executable files) using the *classid* attribute. What attributes specify display characteristics of the object?

3.22. How does the *codebase* attribute affect an object as it retrieves data or is instantiated?

3.23. What element is specifically designed to include Java applets within an HTML document? How does it work?

Solved Problems

3.1. What code can be used to display text in green and hypertext links in red?

The BODY element can be used for this function, with the code:

```
<BODY text="#00FF00" link="#FF0000">
```

3.2. For an individual section of text, what code can be used to set text color to white, size to 3, and font face to sans-serif, or to Arial if sans-serif is not available on the user's computer?

For this exercise the FONT element performs the tasks. Setting the size attribute is not necessary (assuming that no BASEFONT element has been included in the document) because the default text size is 3, and the face attribute can contain a comma-separated list of fonts to use starting with the first one. Note that if Arial is not available either, the browser will use the default font available on the user's computer.

```
<FONT color="#FFFFFF" face="sans-serif,Arial">
The text</FONT>
```

3.3. An author creates a Web page for distribution across many Websites. Within the page are links containing relative URLs to other pages in the author's Website. What method could be used to ensure that the links all still work, regardless of what other Website the page ends up on?

The BASE element could be set as follows:

```
<HEAD>
<TITLE>The Title</TITLE>
<BASE href="http://www.e4free.com">
</HEAD>
```

Using this method, with the BASE element present in the HEAD element of the document, ensures that all links are calculated as though they had come from http://www.e4free.com, rather than the default base location from which the document is retrieved.

3.4. What code produces a numbered list with three items in the list, where the numbers are upper-case roman numerals starting at 12?

```
<OL type="I" start="12">
<LI>Item twelve in the list
<LI>Item thirteen in the list
<LI>Item fourteen in the list
</OL>
```

3.5. What code would produce a bulleted list with three items in the list, with squares for the bullets, and with a numbered list starting before the second item in the bulleted list, with two items in the numbered list?

```
<ul type="square">
  <li>First item in bulleted list</li>
  <ol type="a">
  <li>The first item in the numbered list
  <li> The second item in the numbered list
  </ol>
  <li>Second item in bulleted list</li>
  <li>Third item in bulleted list</li>
</ul>
```

3.6. What code would create four even columns of text, without using the TABLE element or style sheets or dynamic HTML?

```
<PRE>
      Name        Address            Phone      FAX
      Dave        11123 Vermont St.  555-1212   444-5353
      Marty       22213 State St.    444-3232   555-1314
      John        33324 Ohio St.     333-5252   777-7272
</PRE>
```

3.7. What code will create a link to another Website, with the domain name www.servata.com?

```
<A href="http://www.servata.com">The clickable text goes
here</a>
```

3.8. What code will create a link to www.servata.com, so that the file retrieved is about.htm, and the page automatically scrolls to the bottom?

The following code creates the link:

```
<A href="http://www.servata.com/about.htm#bottom">
Click here to go to the bottom of the about page</a>
```

The following code creates the destination anchor in the about.htm page, and must be inserted towards the bottom of the page:

```
<A name="bottom">
```

3.9. What code would insert an ActiveX component in an HTML document, with the classid value of clsid:22D6F312-B0F6-11D0-94AB-0080C74C7E95, an id value of MediaPlayer1, a width of 286 pixels, and a height of 225 pixels?

```
<object classid=
"clsid:22D6F312-B0F6-11D0-94AB-0080C74C7E95"
id="MediaPlayer1" width="286" height="225">
</object>
```

Supplementary Programming Problems

3.10. What code would add a parameter named AutoStart with a value of −1? Where should the code be placed?

> The following code should be placed inside the starting and ending OBJECT tags:

```
<param name="AutoStart" value="-1">
```

3.11. What code would display a message while an object is loading, and what code would serve as the alternate text to be displayed if the object was not supported by the browser?

> To display an alternate text message if the browser does not support the object, insert text after the PARAM elements, as shown:

```
<object classid=
"clsid:22D6F312-B0F6-11D0-94AB-0080C74C7E95"
id="MediaPlayer1" width="286" height="225">
Your browser does not support this player.
</object>
```

> To display a message while the object is loading, enter the text string as the value for the standby attribute, as shown:

```
<object classid=
"clsid:22D6F312-B0F6-11D0-94AB-0080C74C7E95"
id="MediaPlayer1" width="286" height="225"
standby="Loading Player, please wait...">
```

3.12. Write the HTML code to produce the following effect:

> ● *Large, red-colored text, in an interesting font face*

```
<UL type="square">
<LI><FONT SIZE=+3 COLOR="#FF0000" FACE="Brush Script
MT">Large, red-colored text, in an interesting font face
</FONT>
</UL>
```

3.13. Create a hypertext link to www.e4free.com/books/new/support.htm, using a relative URL, from a Web page at www.e4free.com/classes/index.htm.

```
<A href="../books/new/support.htm">The clickable text goes
here</A>
```

3.14. Using the code included in this chapter, what code will change the month displayed on the ActiveX Calendar Control from October to November?

> The following code sets the month displayed to October:

```
<param name="Month" value="10">
```

> Replacing that code with the following code sets the month displayed to November:

```
<param name="Month" value="11">
```

3.15. Write code that will display a Calendar Control (but for the sake of brevity, do not include the PARAM elements), and if that is not supported, will display a picture of a calendar (named TheCalendar.jpg), and if that is not supported will display a text message reading "The Calendar".

```
<object classid=
"clsid:8E27C92B-1264-101C-8A2F-040224009C02"
```

```
id="Calendar1" width="288" height="192">
  <object data="TheCalendar.jpg" type="image/jpeg">
    The Calendar
  </object>
</object>
```

Answers to Review Questions

3.1.   So far, we have covered the BODY, the BASEFONT, and the FONT elements, any of which can be used to set text color. Text color is set using the *text* attribute in the BODY element, and with the *color* attribute in the FONT and BASEFONT elements. When text color is set in the BODY element, setting a different text color with the FONT or BASEFONT elements overrides the color set in the BODY element.

3.2.   Although color can be set for text within the BODY element, there is no support in this element for size or face properties. The BASEFONT element provides support for setting these characteristics for an entire page, while the FONT element allows the author to set these attributes for individual sections of text.

3.3.   Because Web pages are built with HTML for presentation across the Internet, authors have few means available to determine screen resolution or printing parameters. Therefore, sizing text is done relative to the default font size the browser displays. Setting text size with the size attribute is performed by simply setting the size attribute equal to the size the author wished to use, on a scale of 1 to 7. The default text size is 3 (if the BASEFONT element contains a size setting, the size setting in the FONT element will be in relation to that rather than the default text size), so a size of 1 is two sizes smaller than 3, and a size of 7 is four sizes larger than 3. Setting the size to +3 gives 6 (default of 3 plus 3 = 6) but setting the size to +5 gives 7 (because the largest size is 7, and the default 3 plus 5 = 8 which then defaults to 7).

3.4.   When creating Web pages, authors can use all the fonts available on their computers, and this can be misleading because users may not have the same fonts installed. Therefore, it is advisable to use widely installed fonts, such as Arial, Times New Roman, sans-serif, and so forth. If the user still does not have the chosen font installed, the browser uses whatever default font is available.

3.5.   Bulleted lists can be created with the UL element, and numbered lists can be created with the OL element. Both use the LI element to designate the contents of each item in the list. OL stands for Ordered List, because it can produce not only numbers but letters and roman numerals as well, depending upon the setting of the type attribute. For the UL element, the type attribute designates the shape and look of the bullet. The starting number or symbol for an ordered list can be set with the start attribute, and the current value or number can be set or changed with the value attribute. All the core attributes are also supported for list elements.

3.6.   The DL element is the container element for defined terms, and it makes a list of terms and their definitions. The primary displayed structure is a series of terms followed by definitions, with the definitions indented. This element is deprecated in favor of style sheets, and the recommendation warns against using it solely to indent text.

3.7.   Word-wrapping is the term used to describe the effect produced when sentences are truncated and continued on a new line. The beginning of a new paragraph does not qualify, because word-wrapping ends a sentence only when available space on a line runs out.

3.8. By default, the browser decides at what point to wrap sentences, leaving the document's author little choice in presentation. For example, browsers only recognize one white space between words, and if additional spaces or tab characters are included they are ignored by the browser.

3.9. The PRE element (PRE stands for preformatted) preserves white spaces and tab characters. However, browsers usually render text within the PRE element in a mono-spaced font that is not visually appealing.

3.10. Hypertext links allow authors to provide more in-depth information, or multiple paths to more information, throughout a document. One of the significant values of this approach is that it allows the user to chart their own course through the information, picking and choosing what subjects deserve more investigation and what areas can be ignored or covered lightly. Another significant value is the ease with which additional data can be included and retrieved.

3.11. The A element, the BASE element, and the LINK element provide hypertext links and other support. The A element can make links directly, the BASE element assists the browser in calculating where to retrieve other resources, and the LINK element does not provide links but instead gives the browser information as to the relationship of documents one to the other.

3.12. Technically, when a user enters a URL in the address bar of a browser, the browser first sends the URL to a Domain Name Server (DNS) that translates the URL into the appropriate IP address. The request is then sent to that IP address, where it is used to find the first document of that Website (or a specific file, if the file name was included), and the server at the Website sends a copy of the document back to the user. The URL consists of the name of the protocol (usually http), the domain name (www.e4free.com, for example), any folders in the path (separated by slashes), and the file name, unless the user wants to open the site at the first page, in which case the server looks for an appropriately named file to offer. Interestingly, a common beginning mistake is to neglect to name one of the Web page files with the correct name for first pages (traditionally index.html, but may also be index.htm, default.html, default.htm, and a few others).

3.13. An absolute URL contains all parts required to retrieve the appropriate resource when starting from any location on the World Wide Web (WWW). For example, http://www.e4free.com is an absolute URL, as is http://www.e4free.com/books/new/support.htm. Although the first contains only the protocol and the domain name, that is enough to retrieve the resource desired from any location on the WWW. The second contains the protocol, the domain name, several folders in the path, and a specific file name to retrieve.

A relative URL contains only enough information to allow the resource to be retrieved relative to the base location of the current document. For example, if a document is opened at http://www.e4free.com/books/new/, then a link containing only a file name will cause the browser (when the link is clicked) to look for the file in the same location as the current document was found. If additional information is provided with the file name, then the browser will use the additional information in calculating the link.

3.14. The BASE location can be set to any location desired by the author when the BASE element is used. When a link within the document, containing a relative URL, is clicked, the browser will calculate the location of the resource specified based on the URL in the BASE element, rather than the actual location at which the current document was found.

3.15. The A element is the Anchor element, and anchor refers to source and destination anchor. If no destination anchor is provided, the page retrieved will automatically be displayed starting at the top. However, if the author knows of or can insert a destination anchor, then the author can specify not only the page to retrieve, but also the location within the document to go to.

3.16. Dot notation refers to the practice of placing dots before a path name, to specify how far up or down the path from the root directory to go before following the path specified. For example, suppose an author wants to insert a relative URL specifying a folder off the root folder, while the base location is three folders down from the root along a different path. The author could place two dots before the path and file name of the resource desired (../books/new/support.htm) and the browser would calculate the URL as beginning in the same location as the current file, but following the path specified directly from the root folder, rather than from the folder in which the current file resides.

3.17. Regarding HTML documents, objects are executable applications, images, and applets that can be placed and run inside the Web page they are called from. They appear as part of the page, but carry with them their application-like capabilities.

3.18. The IMG element can be used to insert images in HTML documents. The OBJECT element can also be used to insert images, and in addition supports the inclusion of many other types of application-like entities. Although the IMG element is very useful for most image display purposes, the OBJECT element is much more flexible and represents a growth path for current and as-yet-undeveloped object types.

3.19. An object that has been declared is available from within the page or from within related pages (if frames are used). The start values of the object are downloaded but not executed when the object is declared, possibly saving download time. Additional instantiations of the object are therefore quicker.

3.20. The PARAM element can provide starting values to an object. The valuetype attribute informs the object what type of data resides within the value attribute. The valuetype attribute can be ref (a reference to data), object (a reference to another object that provides the data), or simply data (the default, provides data directly).

3.21. The *height*, *width*, *align*, *border*, *hspace*, and *vspace* attributes all contribute to the display of objects, when defined by the author.

3.22. The codebase attribute performs the same function for objects as the BASE element performs for hypertext links. It provides a base location from which relative URLs in the *code* and *data* attributes can be calculated.

3.23. The APPLET element inserts a Java applet within an HTML document. It works by specifying the location, initial code, executable code, and display properties for the Java applet within the element. PARAM elements can be used to provide additional values, as with the OBJECT element.

CHAPTER 4

Web Graphics Basics

4.1   Web-safe or Browser-safe Colors

Although this chapter deals mainly with images, it is important to distinguish between the ways browsers deal with color in HTML and in images themselves. Colors in images are limited only by the color resolution of the user's video card and video driver (as well as the setting used). Colors in HTML are limited in another way, explored here.

As we've discussed, colors can be created on Web pages with HTML using either numeric values (in hexadecimal, such as #FFFFFF) or as simply a color name (because browsers recognize the names of quite a few colors). The recommended color values and names are:

Table 4-1   Recommended color values and names

Black – #000000	Silver – #C0C0C0	Gray – #808080	White – #FFFFFF
Maroon – #800000	Red – #FF000000	Purple – #800080	Fuchsia – #FF00FF
Green – #008000	Lime – #00FF00	Olive – #808000	Yellow – #FFFF00
Navy – #000080	Blue – #0000FF	Teal – #008080	Aqua – #00FFFF

These color values are listed and the color space sRGB discussed in detail at www.w3.org/Graphics/Color/sRGB. For any individual browser there are hundreds of color names supported (although not always exactly the same ones, unfortunately). Web-safe (or browser-safe) colors are those that are supported by both Netscape Navigator and Microsoft Internet Explorer on either the Windows or Macintosh systems, when they are set to 256-color mode.

Although many people think there are 216 common Web/browser-safe colors (comprising the value-pairs 00, 33, 66, 99, CC, and FF), some authorities make the case that only 212 of these colors are Web/browser-safe. HTML-editing applications such as Macromedia's Dreamweaver allow choices from these 212 colors (Dreamweaver also allows direct editing of HTML so that any color can be used).

4.2   Images and Image File Formats

As discussed in Chapter 3, section 3.9, images can be included within HTML documents with the IMG element. While any image type can be included only certain types are supported by browsers, and these types are: Compuserve Graphics Interchange Format (GIF), Joint Photographic Experts Group (JPEG or JPG), and Portable Network Graphics (PNG). In practice, other file types are not used except in very special circumstances.

Image file types suitable for the Internet are commonly compressed, meaning the file type takes up less space than the full-resolution original. For two of the supported image file types (GIF and JPEG) the compression is called *lossy* compression, because some data is lost when the image is converted to the supported file type. Unlike most file types (such as executable files), where the loss of bits can render the file unusable, these image file types often appear much the same to the human eye, and therefore the data loss is acceptable. Lossy compression is desirable because smaller file sizes mean faster downloads, and for many users communication on the Internet is still constrained by file size.

4.3   The Graphics Interchange Format (GIF)

Images in the GIF image file format have been used for years and the format is still popular, but recently there has been a movement away from this format because of the problems raised by patent disputes over the algorithms used to achieve compression. According to an announcement released by Compuserve in January, 1995, Compuserve had incorporated into the GIF format (which it developed) the Lempel-Ziv-Welch algorithm for compressing files, and Unisys corporation independently obtained a patent for this technology (the primary patent rights to expire in 2003). Once Unisys had the patent rights to the algorithm, Compuserve made a licensing agreement with Unisys, and proceeded to charge application developers a small one-time fee and a per-copy fee for applications using the algorithm to compress image files. Unisys itself is now requesting additional (rather large) licensing fees from Website operators under some situations. Since the GIF image file format was disseminated and used for quite a few years with the understanding that there were no charges for using it, developers are understandably upset that patent rights were granted and fees are now being requested. Part of the reason for the development of the PNG format is that it is intended (as a replacement for the GIF file format) to be and remain free.

In any case, the GIF format is useful because it compresses well and in more recent revisions of the format it supports interlacing, background transparency, and animation. *Interlacing* is the capability of the format to be broken into lines and transmitted across the Web, so that the image will begin to appear (as lines of gradually increasing sharpness) before all the data is received.

Transparent backgrounds are achieved by having the ability to designate a single color as having no color, and when this effect is applied to the background color, it makes the background appear transparent. Note that only one color can be designated as transparent, so if you make the background of a GIF image transparent make sure each pixel of the background has the exact same color value, or your image background will look only partially transparent.

Animation is supported by the capability to incorporate multiple-image files into a single file, with playback data (such as file order, speed of frames, and so forth) included. Animated GIFs are produced by making a starting frame in an image editing program, saving the first image as the first frame, and then moving the objects making up the image around on the screen, stopping at selected intervals to take "snapshots" of subsequent frames. The "snapshots" are actually additional saved files. The final step is to "stitch" the individual images together into a single animated GIF file, set parameters such as playback speed for each frame, and then save the file under its own name. Once the animated GIF file is created it can be inserted into an HTML page using code identical to the code for inserting an ordinary image. All playback work is performed by the browser, with no special HTML tags or coding required.

Images saved as GIFs are compressed in two ways; the first algorithm is called Lempel-Ziv encoding. This algorithm counts pixels having the same colors in rows and simply notes the row, the location, and the number of pixels. GIF images are also limited to a maximum of 256 colors, and for each multiple of half this number or less colors a lower number of bits is used to save the color values. For example, 128 or fewer colors are saved with 7-bit data; 64 or fewer with 6-bit data; down to 2 colors or less as 1-bit data.

4.4 The JPEG Image File Format

The Joint Photographic Experts Group (JPEG) developed the JPEG image file format. As the name implies, it is suitable for photographic images containing many colors, and supports over 16.7 million colors (with 24-bit color). Images are compressed by recording each pixel's brightness and the average hue. JPEG supports multiple compression levels, and the quality of the image depends upon the level of compression applied.

4.5 The PNG Image File Format

The Portable Network Graphics (PNG) image file format was developed in response to several needs: a more efficient format and the compression algorithm patent controversy associated with the GIF format. PNG uses *lossless* compression, and therefore image quality does not degrade during the compression process. PNG supports interlacing and transparency, but not animation. There are related formats that do support animation, primarily Multiple-image Network Graphics (MNG).

The PNG specification is considered to be stable and is being standardized by the ISO. Knowledge and use of PNG is taking hold among technical users, and users have come to expect all new versions of the major browsers and image-editing programs to support it, although support remains somewhat spotty and not all applications or browsers support all the features offered by PNG.

4.6   Creating Images

When an image is captured with a scanner, the images captured are called *raster* images, signifying that each pixel is assigned individual values. *Vector* images use equations to calculate the appropriate values for each part of an image. Raster and vector images are the two basic image types computers can use (not to be confused with file types such as .tiff, .bmp, and so on, which will be discussed later). Raster images record color and brightness data as pixels (picture elements, or dots on the screen) while vector images are mathematical representations of the lines and shapes making up an image. Raster images cannot be scaled well, and lose quality with significant scaling, while vector images scale quite well.

Microsoft Image Composer is a workhorse image-editing application usually provided with Microsoft FrontPage at no charge, although other Microsoft image-editing programs are now beginning to replace it. It has the basic scanning, drawing, effects, and editing capabilities required for most graphics work, but is not a high-end program like Adobe Photoshop. It also contains a utility for converting GIF images into animated GIFs, called Microsoft GIF Animator.

Adobe Photoshop is a high-end image-editing tool known as *the* tool for graphics professionals, although it should be noted that there are many software tools in use, no single one of which does everything.

Images used in Web pages tend to fall into several distinct categories because they have a variety of uses, rather than being limited to just photographs, for instance. Some images are used to help define the layout of the page, other serve as buttons, and others inform and communicate. The basic categories of images are:

- Structural – Bars, backgrounds, buttons, arrows, and so forth. They assist the designer with page layout, look, and navigation, and come in an enormous variety. Clear, simple, unobtrusive buttons and backgrounds are more important in the vast majority of uses than fancy, flashy buttons.

- Icons – Symbols that are meant to visually communicate directions, intentions, and sometimes more complex messages such as the information contained on a particular page. Some icons already have meaning or convey their meaning easily to many people, but too many icons or obscure icons detract from ease of use and should be avoided.

- Marketing – These actually include bars and backgrounds, but here the term marketing graphics refers to trademark symbols, banner ads, logos, and other graphics that directly communicate a marketing message, usually in cartoon or billboard type fashion. Marketing graphics can also include photographs, but usually only in an indirect way, such as the feathered-in graphics often found in brochures and magazine ads.

- Informational – Here the term refers to charts, graphs, flow charts, organization charts, and so forth. These graphics typically represent data, and may be static or dynamic (dynamic meaning the data from which they spring are changing, so that each user may see a different graphic).

- Photographic – Photographic image refers to the use of scanned or digitized photos of real things (although they may be retouched or heavily modified, depending upon the intended use). Often, photographic images are portraits, landscapes, stills, or some other traditional image composition of a real thing, and are given labels on the page (rather than being an integral part of the page layout). In addition, it is not uncommon to provide thumbnail versions of photographic images, so users can pick which ones they wish to download.

4.6.1 CAPTURING IMAGES

Quality scanning and color printing devices are now much less expensive then they were several years ago, and there are more applications for them than ever. As prices have dropped, more people are buying them and the price-performance ratio continues to improve. Getting good performance from image capture devices is something of an art, and there is some knowledge involved. One of the objectives of this chapter is to provide enough information so that Web page authors can get the most out of today's excellent scanners and digital cameras, and use them to produce high-quality graphics for the Web.

Scanners capture images in a format your computer and software can work with. Basically, scanning devices shine light on a subject, then focus that light on a sensor. The sensor reads the light values and records them as digital data, the familiar 1s and 0s. Inside the computer, image-processing software can be used to manipulate the scanned images and store the finished product as a file in an appropriate format.

One of the first basic steps to excellent scanning is the language of scanning. Scanning actually refers to the process of *image acquisition*, also known as digital input or digitization. Frequently, image processing software (such as Microsoft Image Composer, Corel Photo Paint, or Adobe Photoshop) will include a means of connecting the software directly to the scanner, and the menu option may be "Acquire Image".

In the best case, image capture using a flat-bed scanner is a fast, easy, simple process that doesn't require much effort on the author's part. Just put the picture on the glass, close the lid, hit the switch (or click the button), then choose File| Acquire Image and the scan is complete, with a beautiful image waiting to be inserted into a Web page. Unfortunately, the color, brightness, contrast, resolution, or some other factor is frequently not quite right, and the results can't be used. Or perhaps some other effect is desired, but the proper settings are a mystery. To create high-quality graphics for the Web, it is necessary to understand the devices used and the parameters involved.

4.6.2 IMAGE CAPTURE DEVICES

There are a multitude of scanning devices other than the familiar flatbed scanners, such as digital cameras. This section covers the other kinds of image digitizing devices, how they work and how they fit in to a scanning system.

4.6.2.1 Drum Scanners

Only large and well-financed professional color printing houses used to use rotary drum scanners, mainly because of the cost of owning and operating them. Recently, baby drum scanners have come onto the market and their use is now more widespread, but they still appeal to a much more limited market than flatbed scanners.

To use a rotary drum scanner, artwork is affixed to a plastic cylinder (the drum) and then the drum rotates at high speed (over 1000 RPM in some cases) just a short distance from the sensing unit (which remains in a fixed, stable position). A very bright light source shines upon the artwork in a tiny spot, sampling the color and brightness values one pixel at a time.

Drum scanners can accommodate either reflective artwork (such as a picture) or transmissive media (such as a slide or negative) because they can produce light from inside the plastic drum or outside it. Once the image is scanned, Analog to Digital (A/D) converters then convert the signal to a stream of digital data for storage as a file.

Today's technology enables drum scanners to offer excellent color depth and dynamic range, as well as the ability to magnify small images many times without loss of quality. This is due to extremely high dots-per-inch (dpi), up to 8000, depending on the make and model.

4.6.2.2 Flatbed Scanners

Flatbed scanners are very common these days, thanks to falling prices and improved quality. They work by moving the light source and sensors past the artwork lying on a glass platen. A very bright light falls on the original and then is split into three color channels using filters. The color and brightness values are converted into a stream of digital data by A/D converters and stored as a file in your computer.

Flatbed scanners can be divided into three categories:

- High-end – Approaching drum scanners in performance.
- Midrange – 600 dpi and up, 30 to 36 bit color depth.
- Low-end – 300 dpi, 24 bit color depth.

It is now possible to purchase a 600–1200 dpi optical resolution flatbed scanner with 36 bit color for only $120 (a few years ago these same scanners would have been over $2000). A midrange scanner these days would probably have nearly the same optical resolution and color depth, but provide much more flexibility in other areas, such as the ability to perform batch scans and set separate prescan adjustments on each image.

4.6.2.3 Film and Transparency Scanners

Without a good drum scanner, scanning films and transparencies requires a special transparency adapter for flatbed scanners. Dedicated film and transparency scanners are designed to produce output with quality near that of drum scanners, but at a fraction of the price. A good dedicated transparency scanner can be purchased for around $1000 and up.

A film and transparency scanner should accept at least 35mm slides and negatives, and better ones also accept other media sizes. Important characteristics to look for include special software and controls that make scanning negatives easier, as well as high optical resolution and excellent color depth and dynamic range.

4.6.2.4 Sheetfed and Multipurpose Scanners

Sheetfed scanners are much like flatbed scanners except the originals are fed into the unit. Normally lower priced, they are also lower-end in terms of quality, but they can be very handy for day-to-day office use.

Frequently, several devices are combined into one, such as the printer, copier, fax, and scanner machines that have appeared in the last few years. Not capable of producing the highest quality, but useful for lower-end scanning purposes, these scanners may be all that is needed for many Website design jobs. Consider these devices when there are lots of lower quality scans to do, or compact and multiple-use machines fit the budget best.

4.6.2.5 Hand-held Scanners

Sales of hand-held scanners are declining because flatbed scanners have become so cheap, but they still have their uses. They work like other scanners, only the light source and sensors are moved over the original by hand (hence the term hand-held). They take some getting used to, because the device must be moved steadily at just the right speed to get a good scan. Most of them come with "stitching" software that "stitches" two separately scanned images into one full-page image.

Typically, hand-held scanners are black-and-white (perhaps 256 grayscale) and cost under $100. They are best whenever there is a need to scan something (such as a large book) that won't fit in a flatbed or drum scanner and high quality is not necessary.

4.6.2.6   Digital Cameras

Digital cameras excel at digitizing odd-shaped things. A digital camera works just like a regular camera except the image is captured by a Charge-Coupled Device (CCD) after passing through the lens, rather than by a photo sensitive emulsion on film.

The primary advantage of digital cameras is the speed and ease with which they can take pictures, and that the images can be downloaded or erased quickly. There is no film purchasing or processing charge (unless the images are printed). The primary disadvantage is that they are more expensive than analog 35mm cameras and the resolution is somewhat lower. As usual, though, the price/performance ratio is constantly improving.

Because digital images have so many uses other than just color printing (such as for Web pages, electronic postcards, and so on) digital cameras make an excellent addition to any imaging setup. Good models start under $500 these days.

4.7   Processing Images for the Web

Before the actual scanning process begins some important subjects deserve discussion. There is a lot to learn about color and resolution, and this section covers the basics.

Color vision lets people see a broad range of colors, but people tend to think of colors in terms of the most familiar color names: red, blue, green, yellow, brown, purple, white, black, and so on. In fact the human eye can distinguish between millions of colors, all the subtle variations that make up the rich color experience we perceive.

Color is actually electromagnetic waves (light) falling upon the retina after being focused by the eye's lens, stimulating special receptor cells in the retina, and the resulting signal is transmitted to the brains by nerve cells. The range of light waves humans perceive is only a small part of the entire electromagnetic spectrum. In order to accurately communicate color values to another person, color needs to be defined in an objective way.

4.7.1   COLOR SPACES

Color *spaces* (or color models) are used to describe color values in precise, standard terms. Color spaces specify colors:

- Without reference to any particular device.
- Using the gamut (or range) of the included colors.
- By the color-influencing properties of *reflection*, *absorption*, and *perception*.

The Commission Internationale de l'Eclairage (CIE) three-dimensional color space describes the billions of colors the human eye can perceive in terms of *luminance* (brightness, but not hue) and *color value*. Artists and designers usually use *hue*, *saturation*, and *brightness* to specify colors. These systems rely on perception to define the range of colors possible.

Computers and scanners use the Red, Green, Blue (RGB) color space, which is an *additive* system for reproducing color values. Additive systems generate color by transmitting light. For instance, computer monitors produce colors on the screen when electron beams cause the red, green, and blue phosphors to glow. The combination of the three colors in varying amounts displays the correct color. Colors produced using the additive process are always brighter than the colors that make them up.

Printers use the Cyan, Magenta, Yellow, and blacK (CMYK) color space, which is a *subtractive* system for reproducing color values (incidentally, the K stands for key color, but the "k" in the word black is a reminder of the color it represents). Subtractive systems generate color by absorbing some light and reflecting the rest. For instance, when a printer prints a color document, mixing the inks generates additional colors by absorbing some and reflecting others. The reason a printer needs a fourth color (black) is that colored inks contain small amounts of impurities that will not produce a "real" black when mixed. The fourth color is a very pure black that helps the printer produce more realistic shades of black in shadows and darker areas of an image. Colors produced using the subtractive process are always *darker* than the colors that make them up.

Because computers and scanners use RGB while printers use CMYK, and these color spaces do not overlap completely and are darker or lighter than their counterparts, the colors on a Web page will not look exactly the same when printed, especially because authors have no control over the settings on users' printers and browsers.

4.7.2 FILE SIZES

Higher-end scanners will allow scanning at a variety of color depths:

- 1 bit. Black and white (bitmapped or line art mode).
- 8 bit. Grayscale or indexed color mode.
- 24 bit. RGB color mode (8 bits in three channels).
- 32 bit. CMYK color mode (8 bits in four channels).
- 36 to 48 bits. High-bit RGB color mode (12 to 16 bits in three channels).

Obviously, a hard copy original will produce larger file sizes the more colors and channels are used to digitize the image. For example, a 48-bit RGB color mode file will be almost 48 times larger than the same original scanned at 1-bit line art mode.

4.7.3 CALIBRATION

Calibration is an important part of the scanning and printing process because each device in the chain, from the scanner to the monitor to the color printer, may interpret color values differently. Also, the color values these machines display or output will change through constant use.

You can perform calibration on your equipment using an industry standard color target, but that's only part of the job. The full process is:

- Adjust the lighting and colors in your work area to a standard, constant level.
- Calibrate each device individually, then as a group.
- Print a color proof and readjust as necessary.
- Color Management Systems (CMSs) assist in the calibration process by describing and recording the color reproduction characteristics of different devices in a standard way, and then translating those values from one device to another.

4.7.3.1 Monitor Calibration

Monitor calibration tools adjust the monitor back to the manufacturer's original specifications. In order to get the best results, leave the monitor on for at least 30 minutes. Make sure to run the calibration frequently.

Monitor calibration systems can be software-based (usually part of an image-editing package), hardware-based, or monitor profiles included with a CMS. Only use one system at a time, since they can affect each other if used simultaneously.

Image-editing software may include a monitor calibration utility that lets you adjust such monitor display parameters as:

- The representation of gray shades.
- The brightest and darkest shades a monitor can display.
- The gamma curve of the monitor (even tone distribution).
- Color balance.

Hardware calibration devices have a sensor that attaches physically to the front of the screen to measure and correct the white color temperature as well as color balance and gamma curve. Color temperature is measured in degrees Kelvin (K), with the standard for viewing color print work at 5000 K (roughly equal to white as seen under the bright noonday sun). Uncalibrated monitors, on the other hand, usually have a color temperature of 6300 to 9300 K, so it's easy to see why calibration is important.

4.7.4 RESOLUTION

The term resolution refers to the amount of information contained in an image. It's important because the quality of the output, whether on paper or on a computer screen, depends heavily upon the amount of information utilized at each stage of the overall process.

Typically, people think of resolution as pixels, or dots of color data. Formally defined, resolution is the amount or density of digital information. Analog photos can also be thought of in terms of resolution. A 35mm picture contains millions of grains of photographic chemicals, each exposed to light and producing a different color or grayscale. In fact, the resolution of a 35mm picture is many times higher than that of the best digital scanners.

4.7.5   PIXELS

The word *pixel* originally came from two words, picture and element. When you scan a photo, the colors and grayscales over the entire image are digitally sampled by separating the image into a pattern of dots, each dot being a pixel. The pixels in a raster image contain data about four properties:

- Size – The size of each pixel is directly related to the number of pixels scanned. For instance, if scanning at 300 dpi, a 1 inch square of the image will produce 90,000 pixels, with each pixel being 1/300th of an inch on a side. Higher resolutions produce more pixels per inch, and each pixel is smaller. More pixels per inch means more data is being captured for the same image size, and therefore better detail and more continuous-appearing images are the result.

- Tonal Value – Tonal value is a function of the dynamic range of a scanner. Think of the visible spectrum versus the entire spectrum to understand dynamic range. With a small dynamic range, a scanner can only pick up a small portion of the visible spectrum. With a broad dynamic range, a scanner can pick up most of the visible spectrum. Regardless of how many colors the scanner can assign, a smaller dynamic range will produce less detail, because there will be less differentiation between the individual colors.

- Color Depth – Color depth refers directly to the number of colors that can be assigned to each pixel. If your scanner can only assign two colors (black and white, or 1-bit) obviously you wouldn't be able to produce any other colors or even grayscale, but of course your file sizes would be much smaller; the reverse is true with higher color depths.

- Location – Location data in a pixel refers to the X-Y coordinates of the pixel within a raster image. Each pixel has a location on the image, measured by the pixels themselves. A location of 5,5 means the pixel is located 5 pixels from the left (along the X axis) and 5 pixels from the top (along the Y axis). This information can be compressed within the image file by assigning a line number and then picking out the location of the pixel based on its sequence within the file.

4.7.6   CHANGING RESOLUTION

As the scanning process is conducted, the resolution of each device and the resolution required at each stage in order to produce high-quality output must be addressed. Here are the most important resolution terms to remember:

- Input or Scanning Resolution – Input resolution is set at scan-time. Although a scanner may be capable of 600 dpi, scans may be made at a lower resolution in order to speed things up. Whatever resolution is set becomes the input resolution for that particular image. Input resolution is very important because everything else has to use that resolution.

- Optical Resolution – Optical resolution refers to the maximum resolution a scanner can sample. For instance, a 300×600 dpi scanner has an optical resolution of 180,000 pixels per square inch.

- Interpolated Resolution – Interpolated resolution is frequently advertised because it makes a nice, high-sounding number (9600 dpi, for instance, is common on 600×1200 dpi optical resolution scanners). Pixels can be interpolated (averaged) to create new pixels between the scanned pixels by using interpolation software. This can be done either during the input scan or during the output process. Because no new image information is obtained quality is reduced, so interpolation is best avoided wherever possible.

- Image Resolution – Image resolution is the total number of pixels contained within an image at any stage during the process. It is different from input resolution because it can change as the image is processed. Maintaining proper image resolution is important in order to make sure there is enough for proper output at the end of the process.

- Monitor Resolution – Monitor resolution refers to the display resolution a monitor is capable of. Monitor resolution is typically much less than optical or interpolated resolution, and will frequently be less than input or image resolution. Higher-resolution monitors are important when fairly fine control over the image editing process is required, but the resolution of a monitor has no effect on the resolution of the image itself.

- Output Resolution – Output resolution is only applicable to print projects, and refers to the final image file resolution when the image is sent to the printer. It is just a special case of image resolution, but it is identified specifically because the print process, halftoning, and printer resolution must be taken into account to get the correct output resolution. If the image is to be used on the Web, resolution is referred to as *image resolution*.

- Printer Resolution – Printer resolution is a measure of the dpi the printer that outputs the image is capable of. The higher the resolution, the finer the detail the printer can create.

4.7.7 HALFTONING

Halftoning doesn't mean half a tone is used to make a color, although that description isn't too far from the mark. For example, the artwork in a comic book uses halftoning to create many of the shades used. In practice, commercial printing presses can't create continuous colors, so they use a few inks together in a pattern of dots to fool the eye.

It works like this. Ink is sprayed onto the paper in dots of different sizes in a pattern of equal spacing. The patterns are rotated slightly to avoid generating *moiré* patterns. The different-size dots make the eye think it is seeing different shades of colors, and the multiple inks combine to create a rich variety of colors.

This is important when using a laser or bubblejet printer, because these printers can only produce dots of a single size. Therefore, they create what's called a *halftone cell*, made up of a number of single size dots. The halftone cell could be a small grid of 268 tiny dots. A lighter color might have a halftone dot consisting of 12 dots' worth of color, while a very dark color may have 84 dots' worth of color. When these grids are arranged on paper they resemble the correct size halftone dots, and perform the same function of fooling the eye. The number of halftone dots per inch is referred to as the *halftone screen frequency* or *line screen*. The lower the line screen the less detail will be visible. Scanners often include software tools that reduce the effects of halftoning on scans.

4.7.8   CONTROLLING RESOLUTION

Resolution affects quality at every step throughout the scanning process. While it is important to ensure that scans are at a high enough resolution to get excellent quality in the end, it is also important to limit resolution to only what is really required. One thing affected by high resolution is file size, and files that are too large can be expensive and time-consuming to process, not to mention tougher to upload and download.

Here's an example of calculating file size for a typical scanned image (ignoring the overhead of location data and so forth). Assume the original image is 4 inches by 4 inches in size. Next, assume scanning at 300 dpi. Finally, assume scanning in RGB mode (3 colors). The calculation would proceed as follows:

$$[4'' \times 4'' \times (300 \text{ dpi})^2 \times 3 \text{ colors}] = 4{,}320{,}000 \text{ bits or over 540 KB}$$

Now watch what happens when you increase the resolution to 600 dpi:

$$[4'' \times 4'' \times (600 \text{ dpi})^2 \times 3 \text{ colors}] = 17{,}280{,}000 \text{ bits or over 2.16 MB}$$

As you can see, *doubling resolution doesn't just double the file size, it quadruples it*. The name for this phenomenon is geometric progression. Tripling the resolution will cause the file size to increase nine times, and quadrupling the resolution will cause the file size to increase by a factor of 16. Clearly it's very important to know the proper resolution for the output quality you need, and scan at only that resolution.

As a contrast to scanning for the Web, the following section discusses scanning for print purposes. Scanning for print output takes several variables into account:

- Is the output device a halftoning device or continuous-tone?
- If halftone, does it use FM Screening?
- If not FM, what is the screen frequency?
- What is the final enlargement factor?

4.7.9 CONTINUOUS TONES

If the device is a continuous-tone printer, the enlargement factor (by what percentage is the size of the final image going to be increased or decreased over the original) and the printer's resolution must be known. For instance, if the printer resolution is 300 dpi and the enlargement factor is 2, then the scanning resolution should be set at 600 dpi.

4.7.10 HALFTONING DEVICES

If the device is a halftoning device, you must know the enlargement factor, the quality factor, and the halftone screen frequency. For instance, if the halftone screen frequency is 150 lpi (lines per inch), the enlargement factor is 2, and the quality factor is 1.5, then scanning resolution would be 450 dpi. By the way, the quality factor is required to make sure correct halftone dots are produced by the output device, and if FM halftoning is used, a factor of roughly 1.2 may be used instead of 1.5. In each case, the scanning resolution should be a number that is an integral of the scanner's optical resolution.

4.7.11 RESIZING AND RESAMPLING

For display output (images to be displayed on computer monitors in Web pages, for instance), if the number of pixels in an image is changed, the size is changed. For instance, if an original that is 4 inches × 4 inches is scanned at 100 dpi, on a video screen it will appear 400 pixels × 400 pixels. The original size in inches doesn't matter, because the image's pixels will match those provided by the screen resolution. The same image scanned at 50 dpi will appear half the width and half the height (200 pixels × 200 pixels).

For printing, the number of dpi doesn't make the difference, but the scaling resolution does. If the image is scanned at 100 dpi with the resolution set to 200%, the scanner creates an image file at 200 dpi with the scale set twice as high. Therefore, the final image will be twice as big, but the number of dots per inch when printed will still be 100.

For an image that is 750 pixels high by 600 pixels wide, if the output (printed) resolution is 300 dpi, that means the final image may be 2.5 inches high by 2 inches wide with no loss of quality. If a smaller image size is desired it must be downsampled to remove pixels. To increase output image size, pixels must be added.

Removing pixels may not degrade the quality of an image much, since it will be printed at a smaller size. Adding pixels, however, means interpolation, and using this technique can result in a loss of sharpness and detail. Some sharpness can be regained with a sharpening filter, but use this approach sparingly. The best way to increase size is to increase the enlargement factor in the original scan.

4.8   Inserting Images with the IMG Element

The IMG element inserts an image into a Web page at the point in the code where it is inserted, by default, unless the author uses x index, y index, and z index coordinates to place the image on the page. The use of these coordinates is supported only in the version 4.0 and above browsers of the major manufacturers, and will be discussed in more detail in Chapter 8.

The IMG element has only a starting tag; an ending tag is forbidden. This makes sense, as all the information required to insert an image is contained in the attributes of the starting tag. The DTD of the IMG element is:

```
<!ELEMENT IMG -- O EMPTY -- Embedded image -->
<!ATTLIST IMG
  %attrs;                            -- %coreattrs, %i18n,
                                         %events --
  src       %URI;     #REQUIRED -- URI of image to embed --
  alt       %Text;    #REQUIRED -- short description --
  longdesc  %URI;     #IMPLIED  -- link to long description
                                    (complements alt) --
  name      CDATA     #IMPLIED  -- name of image for
                                    scripting --
  height    %Length;  #IMPLIED  -- override height --
  width     %Length;  #IMPLIED  -- override width --
  usemap    %URI;     #IMPLIED  -- use client-side image map --
  ismap     (ismap)   #IMPLIED  -- use server-side image map --
  >
```

As you can see from the DTD, the core attributes (*id*, *class*, *lang*, *dir*, *title*, *style*) and the intrinsic events are supported, as well as a few other helpful attributes. The *src* attribute value is the URL to the image file, and can be an absolute or relative path. By the way, even though not a part of the recommendation, there is an attribute called *lowsrc* that is supported by the major browsers. The *lowsrc* attribute can be set to reference another image file that is smaller than the primary image, and should therefore load very quickly to provide both a space for the final image but also a quick peek at the image being downloaded.

One attribute in particular should always be set, and that is the *alt* attribute. This attribute can contain a text message telling the user the contents of the image. Because users may have images turned off in their browser preferences (or may even be unable to display images if, for example, they are using a wireless device) an indication of the contents of an image can be very helpful. The *longdesc* attribute can be set to retrieve a longer description of the image in text form (and has other uses as well, which will be discussed in Chapter 5).

There are also attributes that apply to images that are not included directly in the DTD shown. In the recommendation they are defined elsewhere. In this chapter we cover the *border* attribute; in Chapter 5 we cover the rest. The *border* attribute sets the size of a border around the image, in pixels. This attribute is deprecated, and the default size depends upon the browser in use. An important

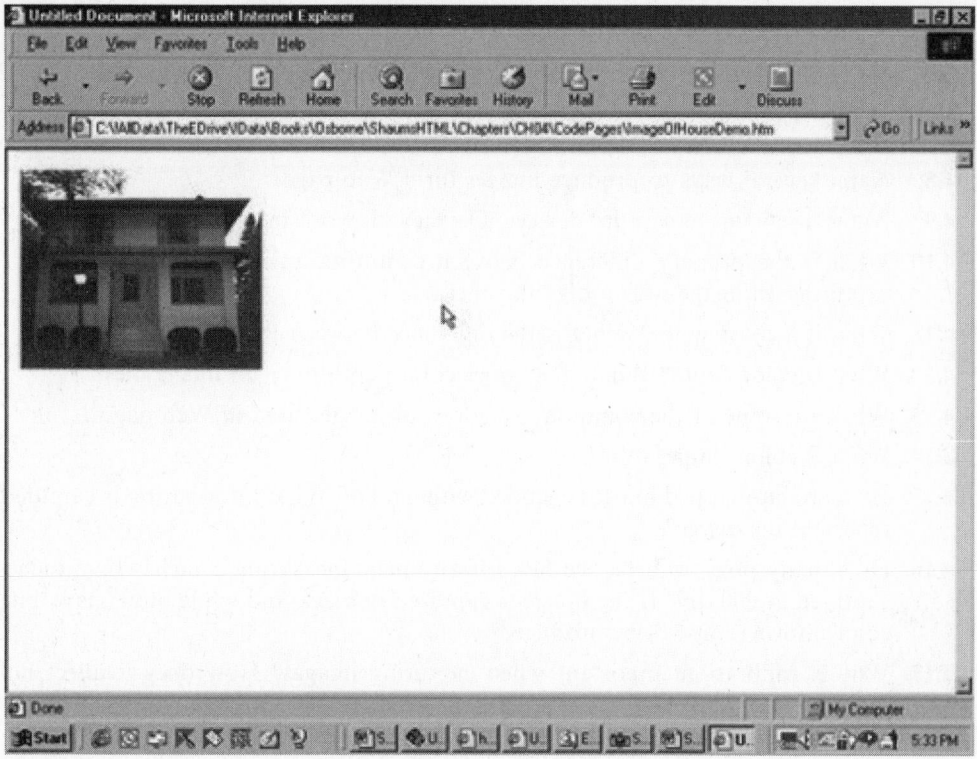

Fig. 4-1.   Image of house on Web page.

design note: if the image is used as a link, browsers typically display a blue border around the image by default. This border will have a negative effect on most graphic schemes, so it is best to set border equal to zero or none in this situation. Chapter 5 covers the use and manipulation of images in detail, but here is an example (also shown in Fig. 4-1) of the code for inserting an image and setting the *alt* and *border* attributes:

```
<IMG alt="Image of House" Border="0" SRC="ImageOfHouse.gif">
```

Review Questions

4.1. How many colors are supported by HTML? Are all of these colors supported by the major browsers? If not, how many colors are supported by the major browsers?

4.2. What does it mean that only 16 color names are supported by HTML? How does this affect color coding using color names in HTML documents?

4.3. What image file formats are supported by the major browsers? Which ones have the broadest range of support?

4.4. Why is file format important? What characteristic do the supported image file formats share that makes them useful for the Web?

4.5. What is lossy compression? What effect does it have on image files?

4.6. What is the difference between raster and vector image? What type is currently supported natively by browsers?

4.7. How is an animated image created? What effect does this have on file size?

4.8. Name several ways to produce images for a Web page.

4.9. Name a few image capture devices. Do they all work in the same manner?

4.10. What is the primary difference between capturing an image with a scanner and capturing an image with a digital camera?

4.11. What is a color space? What is the difference between RGB and CMYK?

4.12. What is color depth? What effect does color depth have on image files?

4.13. What are some of the common categories of images used in Web pages?

4.14. What is color temperature?

4.15. How are bit-mapped images encoded within a file? What information is captured to represent the image?

4.16. How many pixels will be produced if an image measuring 5 inches by 5 inches is captured at 600 dpi? If the image is captured in black and white, how many bits of color information will be produced?

4.17. Why is calibration important when capturing images? How does it affect image quality?

4.18. If an image is scanned at 5 inches by 5 inches at 300 dpi, what size will the image be displayed when printed? When displayed on a monitor?

4.19. Where does an image element fall on the page by default?

4.20. What content is contained in the ending IMG tag?

4.21. What *image* attribute should always be set? Why?

4.22. How does the *lowsrc* attribute work? Is it supported?

4.23. What is the effect of the *border* attribute? Under what circumstances does it appear? How can it be removed?

4.24. What is the purpose of the *longdesc* attribute?

4.25. What content does the *src* attribute contain? What values are acceptable?

 # Solved Problems

4.1. What hexadecimal color codes will always produce some shade of gray?

From pure black to pure white, color codes that produce some shade of gray are called grayscale. They can be produced by using the same values for red, green, and blue. For example, #111111, #565656, and #FAFAFA will all produce some shade of gray.

4.2. What hexadecimal color codes would produce some shade of red? Blue? Yellow?

Any shades of pure red will be produced by any values in the red characters of the code, such as #220000, #2D0000, #990000, and so forth. The same is true of blue (#000033, #0000BB, and so forth), and green (#005500, #00EE00, and so forth). To produce a yellow shade, mix equal amounts of red and green (#222200, #999900, and so forth).

4.3. You have a requirement to produce an image file of a photograph, without losing any image quality. What file format would you most likely use?

Portable Network Graphics (PNG) is a lossless compression format, and supports up to 48-bit color depth.

4.4. You have a requirement to produce an animated banner ad that can be displayed on most browsers. What file format would you most likely use?

The GIF format is suitable for animated graphics, and it is supported widely among browsers. The chief limitation is the low number of colors supported (256).

4.5. For an animated image, you need to create 22 frames, each of which is 14 KB in size. What size will the animated image file be?

If each frame is 14 KB, the final image file size will be 14×22, plus a little overhead for playback information, or a total of 308 KB.

4.6. You have a requirement to produce a background for a Web page that smoothly shifts from blue to red from left to right across the screen, but must download quickly. What method might be useful?

A large graphic image could be produced that covers the entire background, but it would likely take quite a while to download. A better method is to use the fact that background images are tiled across the background, from left to right and from top to bottom. Producing an image that is a few pixels high but very wide, and shifts from blue to red across the screen, would give you a small image size, but, because it tiles, would cover the entire screen properly.

4.7. What image file type would you use to create images that scale smoothly larger or smaller? Is this type supported on the Web?

Vector images can be smoothly scaled, because vector images are rendered by mathematical formulas representing the objects in the image. When they are resized, the formulas rebuild the image at larger or smaller sizes. Vector images are not supported on the web under most conditions. In contrast, raster images are made up of a fixed number of pixels. Resizing these images means adding or subtracting pixels, therefore degrading image quality. *Pixelation* is the name for the effect that occurs when raster images are resized so that the loss in quality is noticeable.

4.8. You have an image file containing 50 pixels per inch, measuring 1.5 inches by 1.5 inches. You have a requirement for the same image, but with a screen size of 3 inches by 3 inches. What can you do to achieve this objective? What will the effect be on the image quality? Why?

You can resize the image from 50 pixels per inch to 100 pixels per inch, and this will double the size of the image on screen. However, doubling is accomplished by interpolation, which adds pixels but adds no data. Therefore the image will most likely look pixelated, and probably be unsuitable for use. A better method would be to rescan the image at a higher resolution, if possible.

4.9. Your monitor is set to 800×600 resolution. The size of each pixel on your monitor is 0.25 mm. On it is displayed an image measuring 3 inches by 3 inches. How many pixels per inch are included in the image file?

Since monitors show one pixel on the screen for every pixel in the image, you can determine the answer by dividing 3 inches by 0.25 mm to get the total number of pixels across (or down), and then dividing that number by 3 to get the number of pixels per inch. However, you must first convert inches to millimeters so you are working with like units. One inch contains 2.54 centimeters, or 25.4 millimeters. Three inches contains 76.2 millimeters (25.4×3). If the image is 3 inches wide it must be taking up 304.8 pixels (76.2/0.25). Dividing 304.8 by 3 gives about 102 pixels per inch.

Supplementary Solved Problems

4.10. What code would place an image on a Web page located in a folder named "content" underneath the root folder, if the image file, named logo.gif, is located in a folder named "images" underneath the root folder of the Website?

```
<IMG SRC="../images/logo.gif">
```

4.11. What code would give the image mentioned above a description as follows: "Corporate Logo Image"?

```
<IMG ALT="Corporate Logo Image" SRC="../images/logo.gif">
```

4.12. What code would give the image mentioned above a border 2 pixels wide?

```
<IMG BORDER="2" ALT="Corporate Logo Image" SRC="../images/
logo.gif">
```

4.13. You have a requirement to display an image that is quite large (in file size) on a Web page. What three techniques could you use to display the image in a reasonable manner, and what code would you use to accomplish them?

One technique for displaying large images in a reasonable manner is to make the image interlaced. Interlacing means that the image is broken up and transmitted as lines which are gradually reassembled in the browser. The effect looks as if the image is coming into focus, and although it takes just as long to download, it generally fools the user into thinking the download was faster. No special coding is required.

Another technique is to use the *lowsrc* attribute, and include a very low resolution image to be displayed first. Although this actually takes longer, it can be a more satisfying experience because the user will get a look at a complete image quickly, and therefore be more willing to wait for the finished image to appear. The code to accomplish this would resemble the following:

```
<IMG lowsrc="lowresimage.gif" src="image.gif">
```

Finally, a thumbnail image can be used, meaning a very small (height and width) version of the final image is placed on the page, and if the user clicks the thumbnail image then the full-size image appears. The code to accomplish this would resemble the following:

```
<A HREF="fullsizeimage.gif"><IMG BORDER="0" SRC="thumbnail.
gif"></A>
```

4.14. What code would place an image in a Web page on a line of text?

Images are treated as inline elements, meaning they automatically fall on lines of text by default. Therefore, to place an image on a line of text the only requirement is to have some text on the page, as shown here:

```
Here is some text in a Web page, and here is an image <IMG
SRC="animage.gif">
```

4.15. What code could be used to ensure an image falls on the very next line after some text?

To force an image to the next line of text after some existing text, use a line break, as shown here:

```
Here is some text, and the line break will force the image to
the next line<BR><IMG SRC="animage.gif">
```

Answers to Review Questions

4.1. HTML supports over 16.7 million colors, as defined by the RGB color scheme, meaning 256 shades each of red, green, and blue. Of these, only 216 are supported by major browsers, and some browsers only support 212 of the 216.

4.2. Using color names rather than numerical, hexadecimal color codes in HTML documents is convenient, because color names are easier to remember than color codes. Although HTML supports only 16 color names in the recommendation, major browsers support hundreds of color names. However the major browsers do not necessarily agree on the color names they support, using the color names can be problematic, and it is best to refer to supported color lists before using color names on pages intended for more than one browser.

4.3. The Compuserve GIF format, the Joint Photographic Experts Group (JPEG) format, and the Portable Network Graphics (PNG) format have support of the major browsers, but GIF and JPEG have the broadest support across all versions of these browsers.

4.4. Some file types are very high resolution, and tend to be very large. GIF, JPEG, and PNG are compressed file formats, and therefore images produced with these formats tend to be smaller and easier to download.

4.5. Lossy compression refers to the loss of data when a file is compressed. Although for many file types loss of data is fatal, for image files and many other digitizations of analog things, compression with loss of data is not only acceptable but is required for practical use. In fact, some levels of compression achieve dramatically smaller file sizes without noticeable effect on the displayed or rendered file.

4.6. Raster images have individual values assigned to each pixel. Vector images use a mathematical representation of computer image element values. Vector images can be easily scaled, while raster images lose quality as they are scaled.

4.7. An animated image is often made using the GIF file format, although support for other file formats is growing. It is created by the saving of single images, which are then added to a single file along with playback information, such as sequence and playback speed. File size ends up larger than any single one of the individual frame image files.

4.8. Images can be produced using a drawing program, by scanning, and by taking a digital photograph. In each case the result is a file containing the digitized information representing the image.

4.9. There are a variety of scanners, each suited to a particular purpose. For example, flatbed scanners are popular for capturing images for Web pages, while drum scanners are more suited to high-end printing work (because they capture images at a very high resolution that won't work well for most Web applications).

4.10. An image captured with a scanner (whether sheetfed, drum, handheld, or flatbed) must be relatively flat, but an image captured with a digital camera can be any shape.

4.11. A color space is the range of colors represented by a particular color definition scheme. For example, RGB represents all the colors that can be derived using red, green, and blue. The formal definition of RGB encompasses some 16.7 million colors. The primary difference between RGB and CMYK is that RGB is an additive color definition scheme, meaning that the colors are added together to produce all the shades available. Additive color schemes work where colors are displayed, in such devices as monitors and scanners. CMYK, on the other hand, is a subtractive color scheme. When ink is sprayed on paper, colors are gradually subtracted until black is reached.

4.12. Color depth refers to the amount of color information gathered during the scanning or digitization process. For example, a black and white image contains only two colors (black and white) and is considered to have very low color depth, while an image captured with a full range of colors has a high color depth. Higher color depths produce more realistic images, but the tradeoff is a much larger file size.

4.13. Some images are structural, such as bars and backgrounds. Structural images help build the page layout and general look. Photographic images generally are used to directly convey the information in the image itself, such as a portrait of a person. Cartoon-like images, such as banner ads, are often used for marketing purposes. Button images add style to a page, as well as assisting with navigation. Icons usually represent a concept, the idea being that they will make it easier for users to work with the features of the site once they are familiar with the icons.

4.14. Color temperature refers to the shade of white produced when a substance is heated. For example, the sun produces white light from the radiation of its gaseous material at a high temperature. Shades of white are graded according to the temperature a material would have to be heated to in order to produce that shade of white. The sun at noon gives off light with a shade of white roughly corresponding to 5000 K.

4.15. Bit-mapped images are encoded in a raster format, meaning separate areas of the image are sampled for location, brightness, and color values. Each area is a pixel.

4.16. The number of pixels per square inch is derived by multiplying the dpi by itself ($600 \times 600 = 240,000$). The number of square inches is derived by multiplying the width in inches by the height in inches ($5 \times 5 = 25$). The total number of pixels can then be derived by multiplying the pixels per square inch by the number of square inches ($240,000 \times 25 = 6,000,000$). Six million bits of color information would be produced because a single bit can convey black or white color data.

4.17. Calibration is important because there can be differences in color value among the various pieces of hardware used to produce images. Color that looks correct on one piece of hardware may look much different on another piece of hardware. Calibration minimizes color value differences among hardware, and therefore improves the final product.

4.18. If no scaling resolution factor is set, the image will be printed at 5 inches by 5 inches, with 300 dpi. On a monitor, the image will appear at 300 dpi, and its size in inches will be determined by the screen resolution (how many dpi the screen displays).

4.19. If an ordinary image element is placed on a Web page, it will be rendered to the left and to the top as far as it can go, until it runs into some other element on the page. If it appears towards the end of a line of text, it may be wrapped to the next line (just like text) if its width exceeds the width of the page in the browser.

4.20. There is no ending IMG tag (it is forbidden) because all the data needed to display the image is contained within the starting tag.

4.21. The *alt* attribute should always be set, because it gives a description of the image in text form. Having a description of the image is important for viewers who have images turned off in their browser, or whose browser is not capable of displaying images.

4.22. The *lowsrc* attribute is not supported in HTML, but is supported by the major browsers. It is intended to provide a quick image download as a placeholder image, while the primary image takes its time finishing. Of course, this implies that the author has created a second, low resolution image that has a much smaller file size than the primary image.

4.23. The *border* attribute creates a border around an image, the width of which can be defined in pixels. It will appear when the attribute is explicitly set to a pixel value, or when the image is used as a hyperlink. Image borders are in most cases unwanted, and setting the border to "none" or "0" makes the border vanish.

4.24. The *longdesc* attribute is intended to point to a longer description of the image (in text format) than would be practical to provide with the alt attribute. The value of the *longdesc* attribute is a URL to the file containing the longer description.

4.25. The *src* attribute contains the URL to the image file intended to be displayed in the IMG element, and it can contain either an absolute or relative URL. Technically, Web page images can come from any source on the Web.

CHAPTER 5

Advanced Web Graphics

5.1 Manipulating Images with IMG Element Attributes

Stylistically, images are one of the most popular elements included with HTML documents. Only text is more common. Images greatly assist in the efficient communication of information (no need to restate the old cliché). Although most image editing is done within the image-editing application of choice, HTML offers a few useful utility attributes within the IMG element to make authoring easier and faster.

For example, the displayed (meaning these attributes have no effect on file size or downloading time, only size as rendered) width and height of images can be manipulated with the *width* and *height* attributes. If only one or the other of these attributes is assigned a value, the image is automatically scaled so that the ratio of height to width remains the same. Otherwise, the image takes on the scaling dictated by both attribute assignments. Note that one of the advantages of assigning width and height parameters, even when there will be no difference between the actual dimensions and the assigned dimensions, is that browsers will render the finished document only once rather than once when the HTML arrives and again when the images finish downloading.

Both the *width* attribute and the *height* attribute can be assigned values in pixels or as a percentage of the screen. If a value of 50 is assigned, then the width or height is 50 pixels, but a value of 50% means half of the screen. Using pixel values tends to be imprecise, because there is little support available telling the author what screen resolution the user is running, and therefore pixel size bears little relationship to actual screen size when the image is rendered. Assigning a percentage is not necessarily more precise, but it tends to make the size of the image stable in relationship to other elements rendered.

5.2 Image Alignment and Word-wrapping

The *align* attribute is deprecated, but still in common use. Images (as well as other objects) can be aligned both horizontally and vertically, offering authors the ability to place objects on the page with a limited degree of control. Interestingly, aligning an image gives the appearance of having more effect on surrounding text than on the image itself. While an image defaults to the left side of the screen by default, setting the *align* attribute to "left" makes nearby text wrap around the image. The settings of the *align* attribute and their effect are as follows:

- Left – Forces the image to the left and wraps text (if any is near) around the image. Technically, the image is "floated" to the left, meaning it becomes part of the left margin, and text flows around the right side of the new margin as defined by the image. The *clear* attribute of the BR element controls where new lines start in text around "floated" images.
- Right – Does the same as left (including the "floating" aspect), but with the image to the right margin.
- Middle – Centers the image vertically on the text baseline (the text goes to the middle of the image).
- Top – Places the image top vertically at the text baseline (the text goes to the top of the image).
- Bottom – Places the image bottom vertically at the text baseline (the text goes to the bottom of the image).

Some HTML editing programs and browsers support additional values for the *align* attribute, such as:

- Absmiddle – Centers the image vertically on the text middle.
- Abstop – Centers the image vertically on the text top.
- Absbottom – Centers the image vertically on the text bottom.

5.3 Spacing Around Images

Another device helpful in presenting images in a pleasing way is the use of horizontal and vertical spacing. Both the *hspace* and *vspace* attributes can contain numerical values for pixels, and if they are set the number of pixels assigned is divided half on one side and half on the other (right and left or top and bottom, respectively). The effect produced is the inclusion of white space around the images, making a separation between the image and other elements on the page, including text. This effect is often used in magazines to set images apart from text, and generally looks very good.

5.4 Making an Image into an Image Map

The *usemap* attribute assigns a MAP element (via the MAP element's name attribute) to an image, so that the image becomes an image map according to the shapes and coordinates defined in the MAP element. The *ismap* attribute takes no value; it simply makes the image a clickable map, meaning that when the image is clicked the relative image coordinates are appended to the URL and sent to the server for processing. We will discuss how both of these attributes work in greater detail later in this chapter, in section 5.6, "Image Maps Basics".

5.5 Creative Graphics Usage

Many creative techniques for page formatting and design have been devised over the years, using images in unusual ways to accomplish stunning effects. Depending upon the capabilities of the user's browser, images may make possible effects that can be achieved no other way. Among these effects are near-pixel placement of on screen elements for older browsers, use of images for consistent spacing, and basic animations.

Because GIF images can be created with only one color, and that one color can be transparent, and the displayed size of the image can be anything the authors desires, single-pixel image files (or image files with a very small number of pixels) are useful as "shims". A single, small, transparent image is downloaded once, and used over and over again to provide close-tolerance spacing wherever needed on the Web page.

For example, using plain HTML alone (without tables) the following example shows consistent indenting and other effects (see Fig. 5-1):

```
<html>
<head>
<title>Untitled Document</title>
<meta http-equiv="Content-Type" content="text/html;
charset=iso-8859-1">
</head>
<body bgcolor="#FFFFFF">
<p>Here is a line of text, without tables or any other spacing
elements.</p>
<p><img src="SmallTransparent.gif" width="256"
height="8"> Here is a line of text inserted after a small,
transparent image made up of 9 pixels (3 by 3) that has been
changed to render at 256 pixels wide by 8 pixels high. The total
file size of the image is 1KB.</p>
<p><img src="SmallTransparent.gif" width="69"
height="74" align="left">Here is more text<br> wrapping
around the<br>
same image time and<br>
```

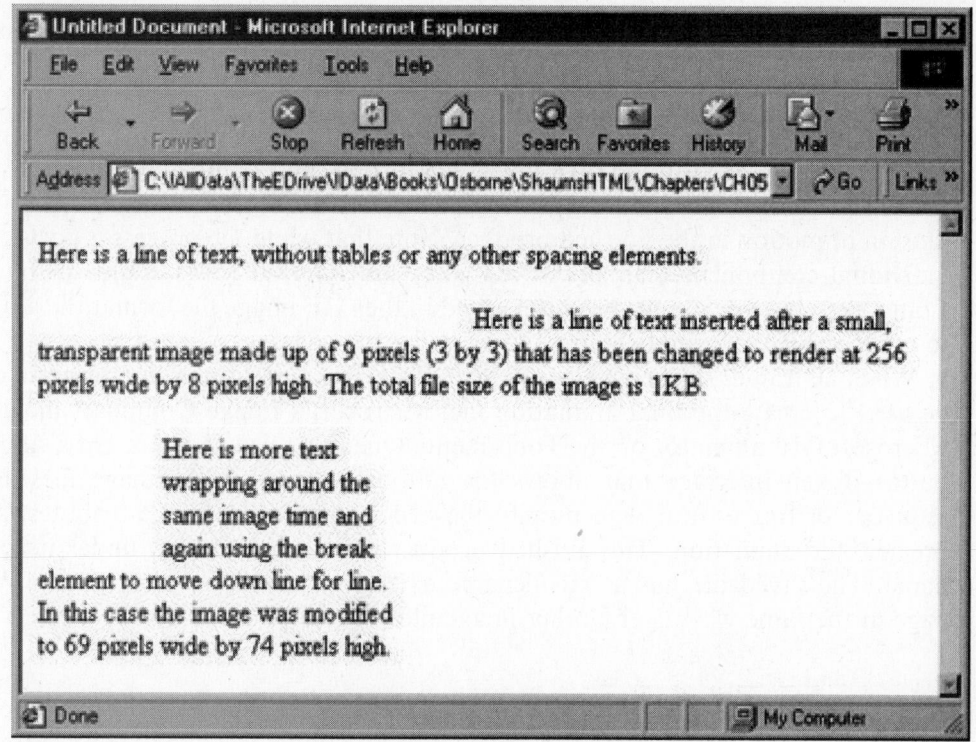

Fig. 5-1.   This Web page in Internet Explorer.

```
again using the break<br>
element to move down line for line.<br>
In this case the image was modified<br>
to 69 pixels wide by 74 pixels high.</p>
</body>
</html>
```

5.5.1   BUILDING ANIMATED GRAPHICS

As discussed in Chapter 4, the GIF image file format supports not only static images, but animated images as well. In this section the process for using common image-editing tools (such as Microsoft's Image Composer) to create animated GIF image files is discussed.

The first step in the process is to decide the size the finished image is going to be. For example, a banner ad might be 300 pixels wide by 75 pixels high. Image-editing applications allow the author to set these parameters before starting the image-building process. Next, the background color for the image should be chosen and set. Image-editing applications make this easy with a choice of colors suitable for the Web.

While it is easy to generate images from here for an animated GIF, a prudent step is to storyboard the concept, to assist in the process of deciding what objects will be animated and how they will move from frame to frame. Text, clip art, drawn objects, and other components should be assembled and checked for color and size before inserting them into the working space.

Once a simple storyboard is complete and the components are in the working space, the author places them in their initial starting position and saves the first file. Each file is saved in the GIF image file format, and numbered consecutively. From file to file the components of the animation are moved about, creating the illusion of motion in the finished product. Note that while the process is occurring individual components can be moved (they are referred to as *sprites* in Image Composer), but when a file has been saved in the GIF image file format the ability to move sprites separately is lost.

When all frames (files) have been created, a GIF animation utility program can be used to create the final animation file. Microsoft's Image Composer includes Microsoft GIF animator on the Tools menu. Opening this utility present a simple, button-driven interface that allows the author to insert GIF image files as a sequence of frames and then modify the order, adjust playback attributes, and preview the animation. The finished product can then be saved under its own name. The saved file has a .gif filename extension, and is inserted into a Web page in the same way as any other image file.

5.6　Image Map Basics

Image maps, while in a sense examples of somewhat fluffy Web design, are actually quite useful in certain situations. Originally, the structures used were designed to add additional functionality to images, and although there may (from a programming standpoint) be more elegant ways to achieve the same results, image maps have a solid place in any Website designer's toolbox.

Image files consist of rows (or lines) of pixels, and each pixel has a unique location on the user's screen. Because this location can be determined within the browser, in relationship to the mouse doing the pointing, mouse clicks within a region can be identified. Therefore, actions can be performed in accordance with the location found when the mouse is clicked, by default the action of retrieving a file (like a hyperlink). An image map element allows regions of the image to be specified in the shape of circles, rectangles, and polygons (shapes consisting of many points connected by lines). Examples of common uses include actual maps, images of groups of people, and other groupings of individual items.

Image maps work by providing the information that associates regions of an image with the action to be taken. The first image maps to be run depended upon *server-side* programs to direct the browser as to the action to take when a location on an image was clicked, but that functionality has become a part of the browser, so that *client-side* image maps are now the norm (although both types can still be used). For client-side image maps the browser detects and processes the region coordinates, but for server-side image maps the coordinates are sent to the server with the *href* attribute of the A element. Use of client-side image maps is preferred because processing is performed by the browser, rather than adding load to the server, and the user can (in most cases) tell what file will be retrieved when they place the mouse over an active region.

5.7   Client-side Image Map Coding

To create an image map on the client side requires an image, of course, and the image can be inserted with an image element (the IMG tag). To direct the browser to image map coordinates, the *usemap* attribute is used. Setting the usemap attribute to the name of a MAP element (in which an AREA element may reside) starts the process. The MAP element contains the active region and shape definitions, either as part of A elements (along with URLs) or within AREA elements. Using the DOM and events such as onclick are not necessary to make the image map work, although they can be used if the author desires.

Starting and ending tags are required for MAP elements, while for the AREA element a starting tag is required and an ending tag is forbidden. The DTDs for the MAP and AREA elements are as follows:

```
<!ELEMENT MAP -- ((%block;) | AREA)+  -- client-side image
                                         map -->
<!ATTLIST MAP
  %attrs;                             -- %coreattrs, %i18n,
                                         %events --

  name       CDATA        #REQUIRED -- for reference by
                                         usemap --
  >
<!ELEMENT AREA -- O EMPTY              -- client-side image map
                                         area -->
<!ATTLIST AREA
  %attrs;                             -- %coreattrs, %i18n,
                                         %events --
  shape      %Shape;      rect       -- controls
                                         interpretation
                                         of coords --
  coords     %Coords;     #IMPLIED   -- comma-separated list
                                         of lengths --
  href       %URI;        #IMPLIED   -- URI for linked
                                         resource --
  nohref     (nohref)     #IMPLIED   -- this region has no
                                         action --
  alt        %Text;       #REQUIRED  -- short description --
  tabindex   NUMBER       #IMPLIED   -- position in tabbing
                                         order --
  accesskey  %Character;  #IMPLIED   -- accessibility key
                                         character --
```

```
onfocus      %Script;      #IMPLIED  -- the element got the
                                        focus --
onblur       %Script;      #IMPLIED  -- the element lost the
                                        focus --
>
```

The core attributes (*id*, *class*, *lang*, *dir*, *title*, *style*) and the intrinsic events apply to the MAP and AREA elements. Both the MAP and AREA elements must be assigned a name using the *name* attribute, so they can be referenced from the image to which the image map will be applied in the client.

5.7.1 ASSIGNING SHAPES AND COORDINATES TO CLIENT-SIDE IMAGE MAPS

The *usemap* attribute must be included in an IMG element to turn it into an image map. It can be set to the value of the name assigned to the MAP element. Within the MAP and AREA elements, naturally enough, image map regions can assume a variety of standard shapes, set by the *shape* attribute. The shapes are:

- Default – Specifies the entire image, except areas defined by other shapes.
- Rect – Defines a rectangle in terms of its four corners.
- Circle – Defines a circle in terms of its center and radius.
- Poly – Defines a polygon in terms of its starting and ending points, and the points in between.

The *coords* attribute supplies the coordinates of the points determining the actual area covered by a region in an image map. The x and y coordinates are measured from the top left of the image, and the coordinates must be specified in a particular order, because they are interpreted in that order. For example, the coordinates of a rectangle must be specified as left-x, top-y, right-x, bottom-y. The following code produces (in the BODY element of a Web page) a rectangular image map region centered on the state of Wyoming within an image of the United States:

```
<body bgcolor="#FFFFFF">
<div align="center"><img src="map.gif" width="401"
height="241" border="0" usemap="#states"></div>
<map name="states">
<area shape="rect" coords="152,58,190,89"
href="http://www.e4free.com/Wyoming/">
</map>
</body>
```

The first point is the left-x, top-y point, located 152 pixels (left-x) from the left side of the image and 58 pixels (top-y) from the top of the image. The second point is the right-x, bottom-y point, located 190 pixels (right-x) from the left side of the image and 89 pixels (bottom-y) from the top of the image. The coordinates of the other two points can be inferred from these coordinates, assuming a rectangular shape.

To make a circular image map region, only the center point and the radius are required, because the location of the circle is given by the center, and the size of the circle is given by the radius, or distance from the center to the edge. To specify the center two dimensions are used, the x and the y points (from the left in the x dimension and from the top in the y dimension), and the distance from the center in pixels or as a percentage. The code looks like this:

```
<area shape="circle" coords="314,86,14"
href="http://www.e4free.com/Ohio/">
```

The circle created by this code has a center that is located 314 pixels from the left side of the image and 86 pixels from the top of the image, and the edge extends 14 pixels from the radius in all directions. The recommendation indicates that browsers should calculate the radius, if it is expressed as a percentage, based on the image's height and width, but using the smaller of the two. For example, if an image is 400 pixels wide and 300 pixels high, and the radius of a circular image map region is 20%, then the circle should have a radius of 20% of 300, or 60 pixels.

To make a polygonal image map region, the coordinates are expressed in groups of two as x-y pairs, for as many points as the author desires. Ideally, the ending pair should be identical to the beginning pair, to close the polygon. If not, the browser should assume an additional pair of coordinates to close the polygon. The following code example shows how a polygonal image map region is specified:

```
<area shape="poly"
coords="142,231,94,154,201,198,175,236"
href="http://www.e4free.com/Hawaii">
```

Each set of points represents an x-y point on the image (from the left-top of the image), and these points outline the area of the image in which the island of Hawaii is depicted. The image on the page takes on no unusual appearance, as shown in Fig. 5-2.

A region may be set to no hypertext reference using the *nohref* attribute. Simply including this attribute in the element sets it, so there is no value to assign to it. With the *href* attribute, of course, the resource to which they will be taken is assigned as a URL. The *target* attribute allows the author to specify the frame in which to open the referenced document. The *alt* attribute is used to specify an alternate message for users (similar to the *alt* attribute for images) for an image map region, and the *tabindex* attribute is used to set the order in which image map regions are reached when the user tabs through a document. The *accesskey* attribute assigns a key (from the document character set) to a region, and when the key is pressed the hypertext reference will be followed.

As we mentioned, the MAP element content of hypertext references, coordinates, and shapes can be presented to the browser in the form of AREA elements, A elements, or both. Older browsers will respond to AREA elements, whereas newer browsers can ignore the AREA element in favor of the A element's content. The order in which shapes and their coordinates are assigned has importance as well,

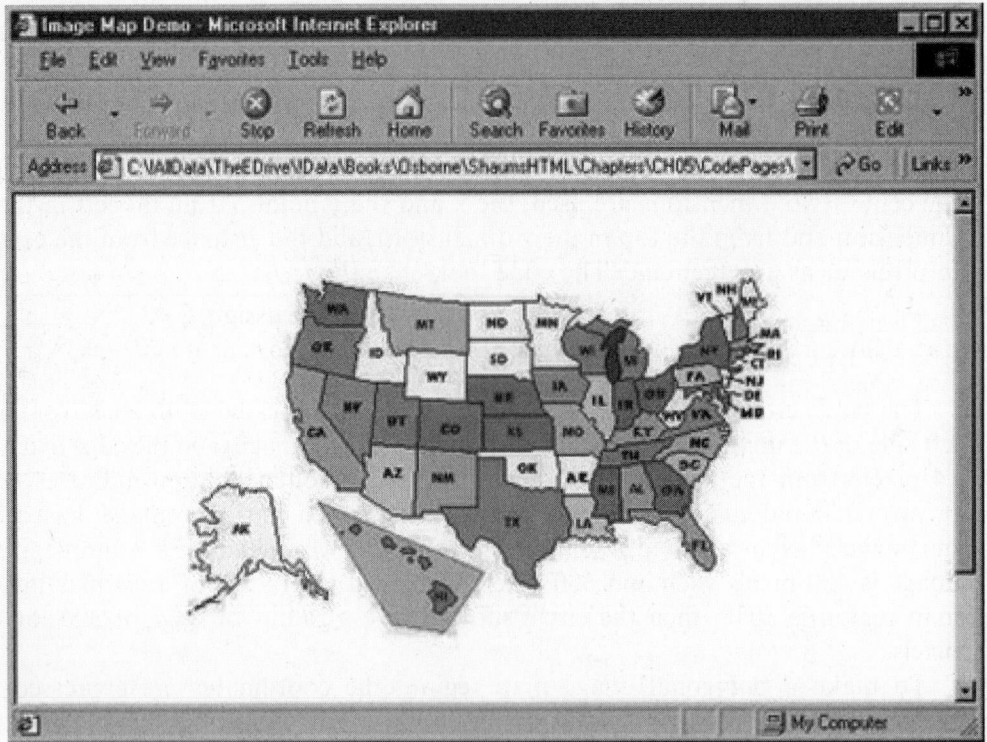

Fig. 5-2.   A mapped image in Internet Explorer.

because browsers activate regions according to their sequence. For example, if one region overlaps another, the first region takes precedence. This leads to the ability to set one region as inactive (say, perhaps a small box) and then create a larger box around it with an active region. In this case, only the edge of the box, when clicked, will lead to a particular URL.

5.8   Server-side Image Map Coding

Server-side image maps were at one time the only method by which image maps could be utilized. They rely on a special map file (stored on the server, and written as plain ASCII text) containing the shapes, coordinates, and URL destinations for each region. On the server, there must exist an application capable of decoding the contents of the map file and carrying out the action specified. The URL of this application must be the URL assigned to the link to which the pixel coordinates are sent.

Adding the *ismap* attribute (no value is assigned to this attribute) to the IMG element causes the pixel coordinates clicked upon to be appended to the URL sent back to the browser, thus providing enough information to activate a particular hypertext link based on the data contained in the special map file. Of course, the A element must be used to define a link around the IMG element in the first place.

An example of the code that could be used to produce a server-side image map is shown next.

Within the Web page sent to the user, the hypertext reference and the image element are coded as follows:

```
<A HREF="http://www.yourdomain.com/cgi-bin/ImageMapApp/
mapfile.map">
<IMG ismap SRC="mapimage.gif"></A>
```

For this implementation a default location must be assigned. Defining shapes and their coordinates works in much the same way as for client-side image maps. The special map file could be coded as follows:

```
default http://www.yourdomain.com/homepage.html
rect http://www.yourdomain.com/firstpage.html 27,71,
144,145
circle http://www.yourdomain.com/secondpage.html 262,114,
295
poly http://www.yourdomain.com/thirdpage.html
389,64,440,64,465,105,365,105
```

In this map file, default is activated when the user clicks on a region for which no coordinates are specified, and in this case takes the user to the home page. On the second line, rect corresponds to the coordinates set after the URL, and if the user clicks on the image in an area inside these coordinates, the first page will be retrieved. The remaining lines follow this pattern.

Review Questions

5.1. When a browser begins to display a Web page, in what sequence are the elements usually rendered, and what effect might this have on rendering times?

5.2. What can be done to assist browsers in correctly rendering Web pages before images are completely downloaded?

5.3. What happens to the rendered dimensions of an image inserted into a Web page if no width or height is specified? Width only? Height only? Both?

5.4. What image attribute affects the way text is displayed in relationship to an image?

5.5. What image attributes can be set to create space around an image? How do they accomplish their work?

5.6. What is an image map?

5.7. What image attribute makes the image into an image map? What kind of image map does this attribute specify? What values can be assigned?

5.8. How are image map coordinates calculated?

5.9. How are shapes generated from pixel coordinates?

5.10. What methods can be used to process image map coordinates and the resulting URL request? What are the benefits or drawbacks of each method?

5.11. What methods can be used to define image maps?

5.12. How does a server-side image map work?

5.13. What is the purpose of the default region in an image map?

5.14. What attribute of the AREA element allows the author to specify a particular frame in which to open a URL?

Solved Problems

5.1. What code inserts an image into an HTML page and also reserves space for it? Of what benefit is this effect?

The code to insert an image in an HTML page and reserve space for it makes use of the ordinary IMG element plus the attributes width and height. For example:

```
<IMG width="100" height="200" SRC="myimage.gif">
```

This code inserts an image named myimage.gif in the standard way. It also tells the browser to set aside a space 100 pixels wide by 200 pixels high, in which to insert the image when it is finished downloading. If width and height parameters are not given, the browser only knows to set aside a small space (displaying the broken image icon) until the image is completely downloaded and the size is known. Then the browser must re-render the page to account for the actual size of the image. If space is set aside for the image, re-rendering is avoided, thus displaying the finished page a bit faster.

5.2. An image 100 pixels high and 200 pixels wide is to be inserted into an HTML page with the *width* attribute set at 100. What effect, if any, will this have on the height of the image as displayed? On the file size?

When only width or height (but not both) is set, browsers automatically scale the other attribute so that the two values maintain the same ratio. In this case, because the true width of the image is 200 pixels, and the *width* attribute is to be set at 100 pixels (the same as dividing in half), the height of the image will be scaled from 100 to 50 pixels. There is no effect on file size.

5.3. What code will insert an image into an HTML page so that it floats to the top left of the document? To the top right? To the top center?

By default, images float to the top left using only the basic IMG element, as shown:

```
<IMG SRC="myimage.gif">
```

To place an image at the top right, the align attribute is used:

```
<IMG align="right" SRC="myimage.gif">
```

To place an image at the top center, the align attribute doesn't help. Therefore any of the several centering elements or center alignment attributes of other elements may be used. For example:

```
<CENTER>
<IMG SRC="myimage.gif">
</CENTER>
```

5.4. When an image is inserted into an HTML page with the following code:

```
<IMG SRC="myimage.gif">This text follows the image
```

where will text that follows it appear? Why?

If the image takes up less space horizontally than the first word of the text needs to display itself, then the first word (and as many other words as can fit) will display by default next to the image, on the same line as the image, at the bottom of the image.

If the image takes up so much space horizontally that there is no room for even the first word of the text to display, then the text will drop down to the next line and begin there.

The reason for this is that images are inline elements, and compete with text for space. They are wrapped in the same way text is, the primary difference being that they extend the height of lines to their own height.

5.5. When an image is inserted into an HTML page with the following code:

```
<IMG align="middle" SRC="myimage.gif">This text follows the
image
```

what effect does this have on the text? On the image?

Setting the *align* attribute to "middle" centers the image vertically on the baseline of the current line. What this means is that the image is placed so that its vertical center (a line drawn horizontally across its middle) is flush with the line upon which the text sits. In practice, the appearance is more that the text has been raised to the center of the image, although it is actually not the text that has moved.

5.6. What code would insert an image into an HTML page on the right side, with 7 pixels of space between the left edge of the image and text wrapping next to it?

```
<IMG align="right" hspace="14" SRC="myimage.gif">
```

5.7. Using a single transparent GIF image and HTML only, what code would produce an effect such as that shown in Fig. 5-3?

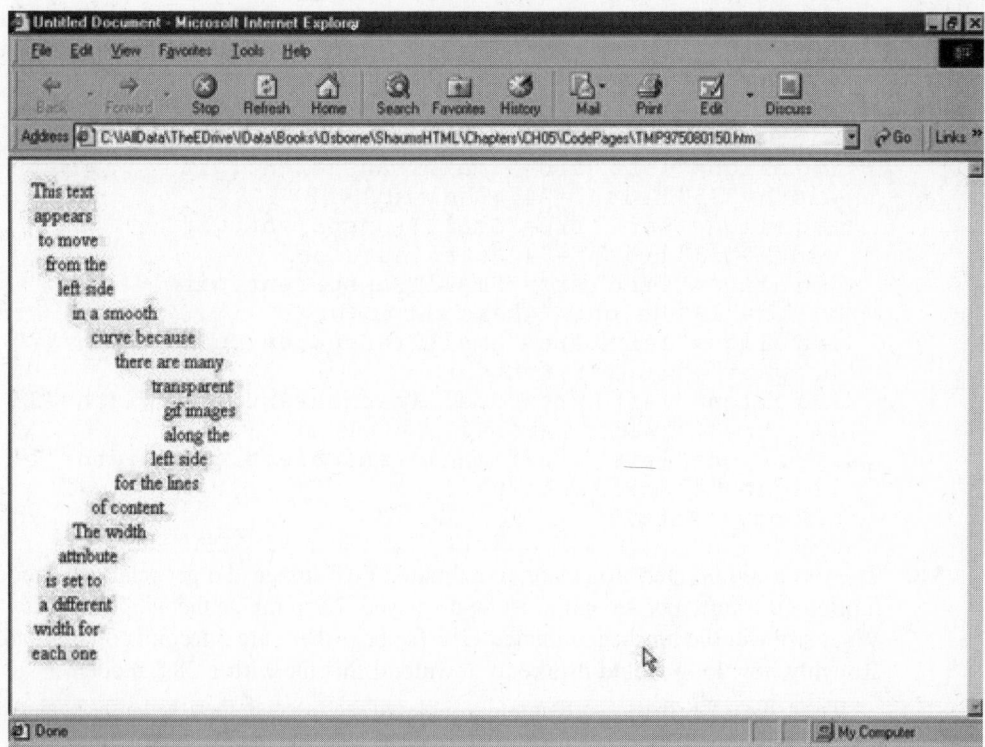

Fig. 5-3.   An unusual column of text.

```
<html><head><title>Column of Text</title>
<meta http-equiv="Content-Type" content="text/html;
charset=iso-8859-1">
</head>
<body bgcolor="#FFFFFF">
<p><img align="left" src="SmallTransparent.gif"
width="1" height="4">This text<br>
  <img align="left" src="SmallTransparent.gif"
    width="3" height="4">appears<br>
  <img align="left" src="SmallTransparent.gif"
    width="7" height="4">to move<br>
  <img align="left" src="SmallTransparent.gif"
    width="13" height="4">from the<br>
  <img align="left" src="SmallTransparent.gif"
    width="23" height="4">left side<br>
  <img align="left" src="SmallTransparent.gif"
    width="35" height="4">in a smooth<br>
  <img align="left" src="SmallTransparent.gif"
    width="50" height="4">curve because<br>
  <img align="left" src="SmallTransparent.gif"
    width="70" height="4">there are many<br>
  <img align="left" src="SmallTransparent.gif"
    width="100" height="4">transparent<br>
  <img align="left" src="SmallTransparent.gif"
    width="110" height="4">gif images<br>
  <img align="left" src="SmallTransparent.gif"
    width="110" height="4">along the<br>
  <img align="left" src="SmallTransparent.gif"
    width="100" height="4">left side<br>
  <img align="left" src="SmallTransparent.gif"
    width="70" height="4">for the lines<br>
  <img align="left" src="SmallTransparent.gif"
    width="50" height="4">of content.<br>
  <img align="left" src="SmallTransparent.gif"
    width="35" height="4">The width<br>
  <img align="left" src="SmallTransparent.gif"
    width="23" height="4">attribute<br>
  <img align="left" src="SmallTransparent.gif"
    width="13" height="4">is set to<br>
  <img align="left" src="SmallTransparent.gif" width="7"
    height="4">a different<br>
  <img align="left" src="SmallTransparent.gif" width="3"
    height="4">width for<br>
  <img align="left" src="SmallTransparent.gif" width="1"
    height="4">each one</p>
<p></body></html>
```

5.8. There is a requirement to create an animated GIF image. To get relatively smooth motion 10 frames per second must be displayed. Each image file will be 5000 bytes. What size will the finished animated GIF file be if there are 5 seconds of animation? Roughly how long would it take to download this file with a 28.8 modem?

   If each file is 5 K bytes and 10 must be displayed each second, then the finished animation file will be 250 K bytes (5000 × 10 × 5). It could take almost 2 minutes to download the entire animation, not to mention everything else on the page, much too long for the typical user.

5.9. Define a rectangular shape within an image 250 pixels in height and 430 pixels in width, where the shape is 50 pixels by 50 pixels and begins 50 pixels from the top and 50 pixels from the left, in terms of x-y coordinates for an image map.

For image maps, the x dimension runs along the horizontal from left to right, while the y dimension runs along the vertical from top to bottom. Therefore, a rectangular shape 50 pixels by 50 pixels can be defined as two sets of x-y coordinates, starting with the top left and ending with the bottom right. For the rectangle required in this problem, the starting point would be 50,50, and the ending point would be 100,100.

Supplementary Solved Problems

5.10. Define a circular shape in an image 250 pixels in height and 430 pixels in width, where the center point begins 100 pixels from the top and 100 pixels from the left, and the diameter is 100 pixels, in the x-y coordinates required for an image map.

A circular shape can be defined based on a center point and an edge. The starting point would be 100,100, and the ending point would be half the diameter in any direction away from the center. Half the diameter is 50 pixels, and simply adding this number to either the x or y coordinate of the center point will produce an edge of the correct distance. Therefore, the edge point is either 150, 100 or 100, 150. The coded coordinates would be 100, 100 (the x and y of the starting point), 100 (the diameter).

5.11. What code causes an image to be treated as a client-side image map?

When the usemap attribute is set, it causes the image within which it resides to be treated as an image map. For example, if there were map coordinates set within a MAP element named "NavBar", then the following code would cause the browser to refer to the map coordinates when the image is used:

```
<IMG usemap="NavBar" SRC="navbar.gif">
```

5.12. Show the code that would make a client-side image map MAP element, using AREA elements, in which there are five buttons, one each for About, Contact, Home, Order, and Privacy, each button is 20 pixels high and 40 pixels long, and there are no default areas (the buttons comprise the entire image). Use appropriate names for the links.

```
<map name="NavBar">
<area shape="rect" coords="0,0,40,20"
              href="http://www.e4free.com/About.htm">
<area shape="rect" coords="0,0,80,20"
              href="http://www.e4free.com/Contact.htm">
<area shape="rect" coords="0,0,120,20"
              href="http://www.e4free.com/Home.htm">
<area shape="rect" coords="0,0,160,20"
              href="http://www.e4free.com/Order.htm">
<area shape="rect" coords="0,0,200,20"
              href="http://www.e4free.com/Privacy.htm">
</map>
```

Answers to Review Questions

5.1. The browser will begin to render the Web page as the HTML is downloaded. Therefore, if an image or series of images takes longer to download than the HTML, the browser may render the page twice with differing configurations, once for the HTML without images (showing only broken image icons) and again with the images when they arrive.

5.2. If the width and height parameters are set for an image, the browser will "reserve" space for the images and render a Web page correctly, inserting images into their assigned spots when download is complete.

5.3. If no width or height is specified the image is rendered at the width and height specified in the image file itself. If width or height alone is specified, the image is proportionally scaled so that it is rendered to the width or height specified, and the missing dimension is calculated by the browser. If both are specified, the image is rendered at the width and height specified.

5.4. The *align* attribute, while it aligns the image, has the appearance of altering the way text is displayed next to an image. For example, if the *align* attribute is set to "right", the image floats to the right and text wraps around it as though it were part of the right margin. If the *align* attribute is set to "middle", the image is vertically centered on the line of text in which it appears. The appearance is that the text has been elevated to the center of the image, even though it is the image that has moved.

5.5. The *hspace* and *vspace* attributes can be set for an image to provide horizontal and vertical spacing around an image. They can be assigned numerical values representing pixels, and the number of pixels assigned will be divided in half and applied equally to both sides or top and bottom of an image.

5.6. An image map is an image for which coordinates corresponding to geometric shapes on the surface of the image have been set. Using the appropriate HTML code, the author of a Web page can specify URLs for each geometric shape specified, and thus divide the image into separately clickable hypertext link regions.

5.7. The *usemap* and *ismap* attributes make an image into an image map. The *usemap* attribute works with client-side image maps, while the *ismap* attribute works with server-side image maps. These attributes take no values.

5.8. Image files, as displayed on a computer screen, consist of rows of pixels. For example, an image file with 100 rows of 100 pixels each contains 10,000 pixels. In addition, because the number of rows and the number of pixels in each row are identical, the image rendered will be square. If the number of rows and the number of pixels in each row are not the same, the image rendered will be rectangular.

In the example given, the image would have 100 pixels on each row, and these pixels would be counted from left to right as the x dimension. Therefore any pixel with an x coordinate of 25 would be 25 pixels from the left.

By the same token, the image would have 100 rows, counted from top to bottom as the y dimension. Therefore any pixel with a y coordinate of 25 would be 25 pixels (rows) from the top.

Each set of x-y coordinates specifies the exact location within the image as rendered for a single pixel.

5.9.   When a rectangular shape is specified, it can be defined with only two sets of pixel coordinates, one for the top left corner and one for the bottom right corner. Knowing these coordinates, the other two corners can be inferred, because the shape is identified as rectangular.

When a circular shape is specified, it can be defined with only two sets of pixel coordinates as well, one for the center and one for anywhere along the outer edge. The center point specifies the starting location for the circle, and the point along the outer edge gives the radius of the circle. All other points along the outer edge can be inferred if the radius is known.

When a polygonal shape is specified, it can be defined as a series of points in sequence, each point being defined by x and y coordinates for pixels. From the points in sequence, lines can be drawn from point to point, eventually encompassing all points of the polygon.

5.10.   Image maps can be written for processing on the client side or the server side. Either method works, although server-side image maps are now much less common. The benefit of client-side image map processing is that the processing is moved from the server to the client, therefore placing less strain on the server and improving scalability.

5.11.   The easiest way to define an image map is to use an HTML editor such as Macromedia Dreamweaver or Microsoft FrontPage. Built-in tools allow the author to map the image visually. If the shapes and sizes of the regions to be mapped (and the number of pixels in the x and y dimensions) are known, a little math can be used to calculate the regions manually. If the shapes and sizes of the regions are unknown, then some tool, such as an image-editing application, must be used to determine the appropriate pixel coordinates. Once the pixel coordinate set values are known, the code can be written.

5.12.   On the server, there must be an application that can, given enough data in the proper format, determine whether the location on the image that was clicked by the user falls into a defined region, and then by associating the defined region with a particular URL, retrieve the page or resource for that URL.

Also on the server is stored a map file, written in plain ASCII text, that contains the shape of each region, the URL associated with it (the file or resource to be retrieved), and the coordinates associated with it. This file provides the application mentioned above with the information it needs to define each region and URL.

The last piece of the puzzle is provided by the HTML code in the Web page itself. An A element is used to enclose an IMG element. The IMG element must contain the *ismap* attribute, and the URL in the A element must be that of the application on the server responsible for processing the image map, plus the rest of the path information to your map file.

When the user clicks on the image, the coordinates of the point at which they clicked are appended to the URL of the image map processing application/map file and sent to the application. The application extracts the path to the map file, examines the data contained in the map file in relation to the coordinates returned from the user, and then calculates what region corresponds to the coordinates. After determining the region, the application causes the resource or file associated with that region to appear in the user's browser.

5.13.   The default region of an image map is used to specify the URL activated when the user clicks in an area where no shape/URL has been assigned. This is useful when only certain areas of an image are used for the image map.

5.14.   The *target* attribute can accept as its value the name assigned to a particular frame, thereby allowing the author to specify a particular frame for opening the URL.

CHAPTER 6

Tables and Frames

6.1   Introduction to Tables

One of the most eagerly anticipated advancements in HTML (and the capability of browsers to support HTML elements) was the development of tables. Frames appeared a little later still. Tables not only provided a nice, neat way to display tabular data, but also offered a very precise mechanism for positioning elements on screen. The best Web designers had already achieved elegant designs using only the meager toolset available, but the advent of table structures meant an explosion of new and highly professional page layouts.

HTML tables work in a fashion similar to tables in Microsoft Word, in that authors can build columns and rows containing most of the other HTML elements and content. For example, text, images, links, forms, and even other tables can be included within table cells.

To create a simple table, all that is necessary is the following code:

```
<TABLE>
<TR>
<TH>Row 1, Column 1 Header</TH><TH>Row 1, Column 2 Header</TH>
</TR>
<TD>Row 2, Column 1 Data Cell</TD><TD>Row 2, Column 2 Data
  Cell</TD>
</TR>
</TABLE>
```

This code creates a table with four cells, the first two of which use the TH element to create table header cells. The use of the TH element denotes header information for a column or row, and is rendered in a bold-faced font in most browsers, but otherwise has no unusual properties. The TABLE element, as shown here, is rendered as an invisible table, with two rows or two cells each. The TR elements create the rows, and the TD elements create the last two cells in the table.

By default, tables float to the left-hand side of the screen, and clear the line on which they reside of any other elements.

6.2 The TABLE Element

The TABLE element contains all the other elements that make up a table, and therefore is the first tag written when a table is started, and the closing tag for the entire table. The DTD for the TABLE element is:

```
<!ELEMENT TABLE - -
    (CAPTION?, (COL*|COLGROUP*), THEAD?, TFOOT?, TBODY+)>
<!ATTLIST TABLE                       -- table element --
  %attrs;                             -- %coreattrs, %i18n,
                                         %events --
  summary      %Text;    #IMPLIED -- purpose/structure for
                                      speech output--
  width        %Length;  #IMPLIED -- table width --
  border       %Pixels;  #IMPLIED -- controls frame width
                                      around table --
  frame        %TFrame;  #IMPLIED -- which parts of frame to
                                      render --
  rules        %TRules;  #IMPLIED -- rulings between rows and
                                      cols --
  cellspacing  %Length;  #IMPLIED -- spacing between cells --
  cellpadding  %Length;  #IMPLIED -- spacing within cells --
  >
```

For the TABLE element, the starting and ending tags are required, and the core attributes and intrinsic events are supported. The *dir* attribute works a little differently in the TABLE element, though, because setting it to "RTL" (the default is left to right) makes the table display columns from right to left. Interestingly, only the TABLE element can have a reversed column order; individual table rows cannot.

An important attribute of tables is the *border* attribute, which specifies the size of the border around the table. Setting the *border* attribute to 0 (none) causes the border to disappear, and many fine page layouts have been created using invisible tables. However, it should be noted that the recommendation suggests using style sheets instead of tables for layout purposes.

The *summary* attribute allows the author to include a text message for people using browsers that don't support tables, such as speech-rendering browsers. The message summarizes the purpose of the table.

The *align* attribute is used to align the table to the center, right, or left, left being the default. This attribute is widely used, although it is deprecated. The *width* attribute is also often used, and can be set in pixels or as a percentage of the screen. Some designers make it a practice to set the width of their web pages in pixels using an initial table to encompass all content on the page, thereby ensuring that for some standard screen resolutions their pages will be sized appropriately. If no width is specified, table sizing is a function of cell content sizes (images force cells to their size, while text wraps in the ordinary manner) and screen size.

From a graphical standpoint the *bgcolor* attribute is useful, because it allows authors to set the background color of a table using color codes or color names, in the same way background colors can be set for an entire page in the BODY element. Additional table display control is possible using the *rules* attribute, because this permits the author to specify what lines of the border are visible. For example, setting the *rules* attribute to rows makes the browser show only rows but not columns (even though the content of each cell will still be confined to rows and columns correctly). All rules will be displayed if the attribute is not used, and the other values the *rules* attribute may be assigned are: "none", "groups", "rows", "cols", and "all".

The *frame* attribute, meanwhile, allows the author to specify which sides of the frame (the exterior sides of the table, not to be confused with the HTML FRAMESET element) will be visible. For example, setting the *frame* attribute to "hsides" will make the left and right side frames disappear. The permissible values for the *frame* attribute are:

- Void – No sides are shown (the default value).
- Above – The top side is shown.
- Below – The bottom side is shown.
- Hsides – The top and bottom sides are shown.
- Vsides – The right and left sides are shown.
- Lhs – The left-hand side is shown.
- Rhs – The right-hand side is shown.
- Box – All four sides are shown.
- Border – All four sides are shown.

The *cellpadding* and *cellspacing* attributes are quite useful as well. Both allow the author to specify spacing inside the table in pixels or as a percentage. The *cellpadding* attribute defines the amount of space between the content of a cell and the inside edge of the cell, while the *cellspacing* attribute specifies the spacing between cells.

6.3 Table Formatting and the CAPTION Element

The CAPTION element allows the author to provide a short description of the table structure and content as a caption with the table. However, it is deprecated, and although it is supported in Internet Explorer, Netscape Navigator does not fully support it.

The CAPTION element may only appear immediately following the starting TABLE tag, and both the beginning and ending tags are required. The DTD for the CAPTION element is:

```
<!ELEMENT CAPTION -- (%inline;)*  -- table caption -->
<!ATTLIST CAPTION
  %attrs;                        -- %coreattrs, %i18n, %events --
  >
```

As you can see from the DTD, the core attributes and intrinsic events are supported as usual. The only other attribute for the CAPTION element is the *align* attribute. This forces the caption to the top, left, or right (at the top), or to the bottom of the table. Netscape Navigator 4.7 has trouble with locating the caption to the left or right. To set a caption at the top right of a table, the syntax is:

```
<table>
<caption align="right">The caption goes here</caption>
the rest of the table tags and content follow
```

6.4   Table Groupings and the THEAD, TFOOT, and TBODY Elements

Tables, like other common document formats, are more useful when sections can be *grouped* according to function. The purpose of the THEAD, TFOOT, and TBODY elements is to allow such grouping for the TABLE element. Depending upon the browser used, these elements may be rendered at the top, in the middle, or at the bottom of the table, and can be treated as a group for the purposes of setting styles, as well as being independently scrollable. Internet Explorer appears to properly support these elements, but not Netscape Navigator.

Starting tags are required for these elements, but ending tags are optional. Each section must contain at least one row (defined by TR tags) and all should contain the same number of columns. The TFOOT element should appear before the TBODY element. The TBODY element is required except where there is only one TBODY section and there are no THEAD or TFOOT sections (as in the case of a standard table). The DTD for these elements is:

```
<!ELEMENT THEAD - O (TR)+          -- table header -->
<!ELEMENT TFOOT - O (TR)+          -- table footer -->
<!ELEMENT TBODY O O (TR)+          -- table body -->
<!ATTLIST (THEAD|TBODY|TFOOT)      -- table section --
  %attrs;                          -- %coreattrs, %i18n,
                                      %events --

  %cellhalign;                     -- horizontal alignment
                                      in cells --

  %cellvalign;                     -- vertical alignment
                                      in cells --

  >
```

The core attributes and intrinsic events are supported, as well as two other interesting attributes, *cellhalign* and *cellvalign*. These specify alignment of content within the rows/cells of the section in which they appear, and can take on typical alignment values such as "left", "center", "right", "justify", and "char" (horizontal), and "top", "middle", "bottom", and "baseline" (vertical). Following is an example of the code that might be used to create a table with sections (shown in Fig. 6-1):

```
<html><head><title>Untitled Document</title>
<meta http-equiv="Content-Type" content="text/html;
charset=iso-8859-1">
</head>
<body bgcolor="#FFFFFF">
<table rules="cols" width="75%" border="1" frame="hsides">
<caption align="bottom">This is the caption</caption>
<THEAD>
<TR><TD colspan=3>This is the Table Header Section</TD></TR>
</THEAD>
<TFOOT><TR><TD colspan=3>This is the Table Footer Section
</TD></TR>
</TFOOT>
<TBODY>
  <tr><td> </td><td> </td><td> </td>
  </tr>
</TBODY>
<TBODY>
  <tr><td> </td><td> </td><td> </td>
  </tr>
</TBODY>
```

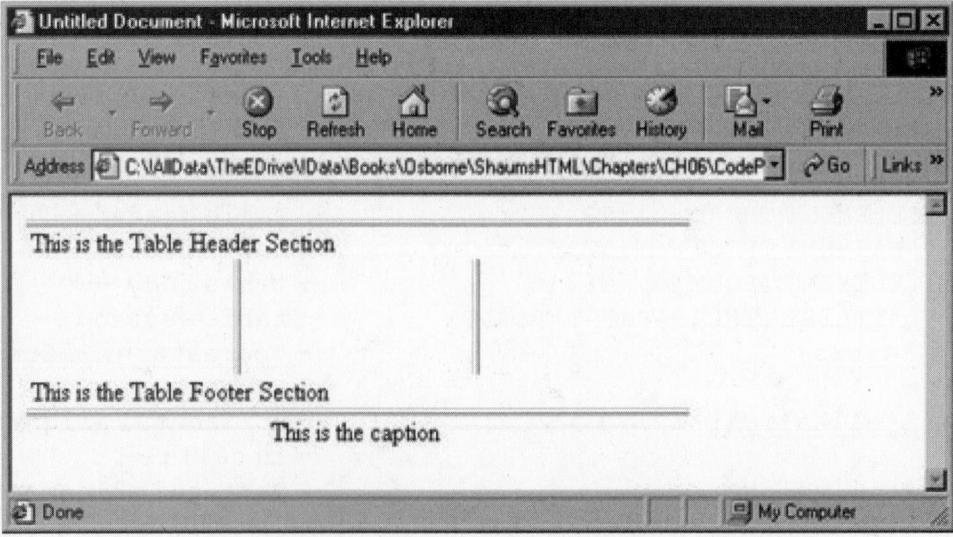

Fig. 6-1. Table with THEAD, TFOOT, caption, and frame attributes.

```
<TBODY>
 <tr><td> </td><td> </td><td> </td>
 </tr>
</TBODY>
</table></body></html>
```

6.5 Column Groupings and the COLGROUP Element

A table created without COLGROUP elements contains a single, implicit COLGROUP element, while a table with explicitly defined COLGROUP elements allows the author to define structural divisions within the table as column groupings. These groups of columns may be assigned style attributes using style sheets (more on style sheets in Chapter 8) or HTML attributes (for example, the *rules* attribute). In contrast, the COL element allows the author to assign attributes across one or more columns without implying any structural grouping.

Both of these elements may play a role in the rendering process, because HTML tables may be rendered incrementally, meaning a table may be rendered a little at a time as the HTML is received, rather than waiting for the entire table to download before rendering. If a table contains any COLGROUP or COL elements, their span attribute values will be used to calculate the number of columns to render; if none are found the row with the most cells will determine the number of columns in the table. For design purposes it is important to note that any rows containing less than the maximum number of cells will be padded with empty cells (on the right for a left-to-right table and on the left for a right-to-left table).

A starting tag is required for the COLGROUP element, while the ending tag is optional. The DTD for the COLGROUP element is:

```
<!ELEMENT COLGROUP - O (COL)*          -- table column group -->
<!ATTLIST COLGROUP
 %attrs;                                -- %coreattrs, %i18n,
                                           %events --
 span           NUMBER        1        -- default number of
                                           columns in group --
 width          %MultiLength; #IMPLIED -- default width for
                                           enclosed COLs --
 %cellhalign;                           -- horizontal
                                           alignment in
                                           cells --
 %cellvalign;                           -- vertical alignment
                                           in cells --
 >
```

Once again, the core attributes are supported, as well as the intrinsic events. For structural purposes there is a *span* attribute. If no *span* attribute is present the browser assumes a default value of 1 for this attribute. If a *span* attribute is present, the browser interprets the COLGROUP element as referring to the number of columns indicated by the *span* attribute. The value of this attribute must be an integer greater than 0. When the COLGROUP element contains COL elements, the *span* attribute of the COLGROUP element is ignored. Using the span attribute to group columns means authors need write common attribute values only once, rather than repeatedly for each COL element.

Another important attribute is the *width* attribute. The author may specify width of columns within the COLGROUP element in terms of pixels, percentage, relative values, or a special zero asterisk (0*) value. Pixels and percentages work the same way they do with images, while relative values are determined after pixels or percentages are assigned, based on relative number values. For example, columns in a COLGROUP element with a *width* attribute value of 40 will each be assigned 40 pixels width. Columns in a COLGROUP element with a *width* attribute value of 20% will each be assigned 20% of the width of the entire table. Columns in a COLGROUP element with a *width* attribute assigned a numerical value followed by an asterisk (2*, 3*, 5*, and so forth) will be given width according to the relative value of their assigned number, in this case 20%, 30%, and 50% of the available table width.

The zero asterisk (0*) value tells the browser to give only enough room to each column to contain its content. Since this minimal width will not be known until all table content is downloaded, in this case browsers are unable to render the table incrementally. And it is important to keep in mind that COL elements, if present and having a width assigned, override COLGROUP width values.

The *align* attribute allows the author to justify text to the left, right, or center, to double-justify text, or to align text around a particular character. The values the *align* attribute can take are also "left", "center", "right", "justify", and "char".

Other attributes these elements support are *char*, *charoff*, and *valign*. The *char* attribute allows the author to specify a character from which alignment will proceed backwards and forwards in a column of text. For example, if a column of numbers having two decimal places (such as currency values) appears in a table, the *char* attribute value can be set to a period (char = ".") and the values will appear all justified to the period, no matter how many characters exist to the right or left of the period. The *charoff* attribute specifies the amount of offset from the margin to the alignment character.

The *valign* attribute allows the author to specify vertical alignment of content within cells as top, middle, bottom, and baseline. Top and bottom align cell data flush with the top or bottom of the cells, while middle (the default) aligns cell data with the vertical center of the cell. Baseline aligns cell data from all cells so that the first line of text occurs on a baseline common to all cells in the row.

The code used to establish column groups and to render content at the top of the cells (Fig. 6-2 shows unaligned content in the columns, and Fig. 6-3 shows column content aligned at the top) would be something like this:

```
<html><head><title>Untitled Document</title>
<meta http-equiv="Content-Type" content="text/html;
charset=iso-8859-1">
```

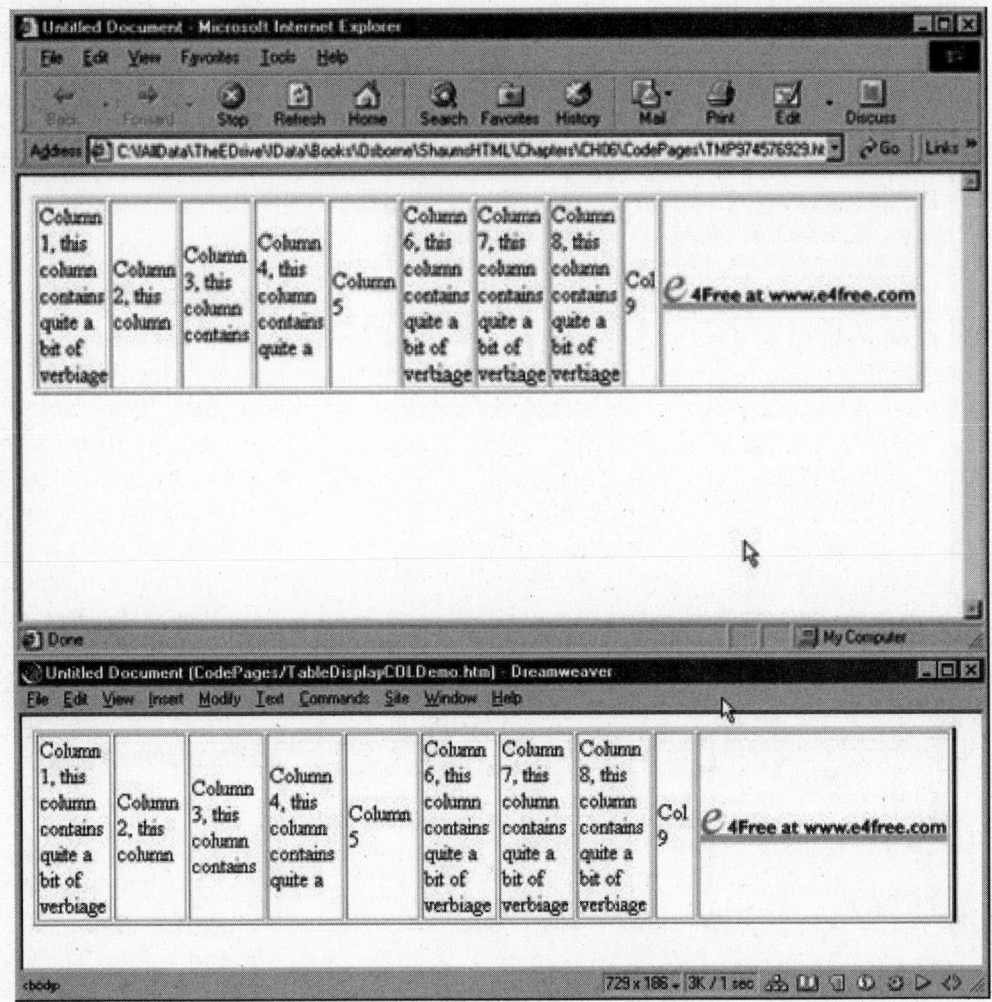

Fig. 6-2.   Columns in the default alignment.

```
</head>
<body bgcolor="#FFFFFF">
<table width="75%" border="1">
<COLGROUP span="8" width="30" valign="top">
<COLGROUP span="2" width="0*">
  <tr>
    <td>Column 1, this column contains quite a bit of
        verbiage</td>
    <td>Column 2, this column </td>
    <td>Column 3, this column contains </td>
    <td>Column 4, this column contains quite a </td>
    <td>Column 5</td>
```

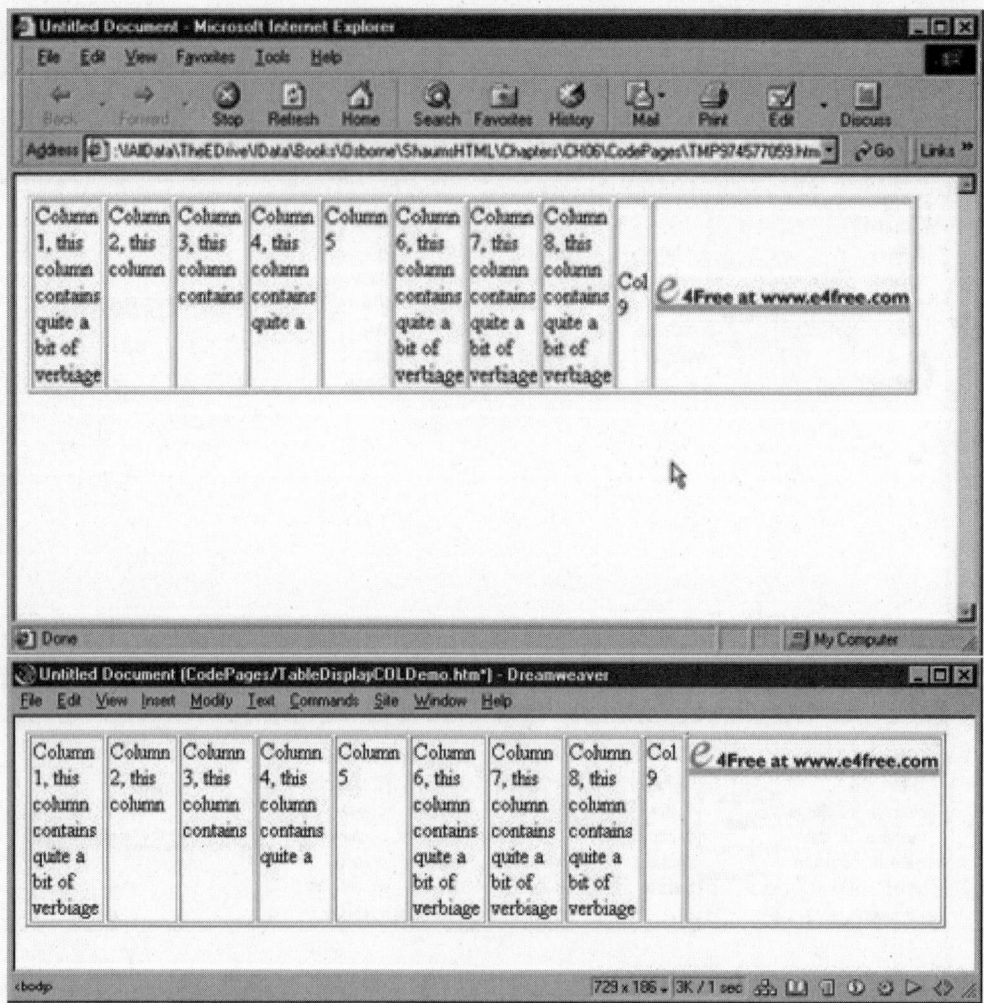

Fig. 6-3.   Columns 1 through 8 vertically aligned to top.

```
    <td>Column 6, this column contains quite a bit of
        verbiage</td>
    <td>Column 7, this column contains quite a bit of
        verbiage</td>
    <td>Column 8, this column contains quite a bit of
        verbiage</td>
    <td>Col 9</td>
    <td><img src="E4Free_Graphic.gif" width="189"
        height="29"></td>
  </tr>
</table>
</body></html>
```

6.6   Individual Columns and the COL Element

Having assigned columns to a group, there is the possibility that an author may wish to assign attribute values to an individual column within that group, and for this reason the COL element exists. The start tag for the COL element is required, and an ending tag is forbidden. The DTD for the COL element is:

```
<!ELEMENT COL     - O EMPTY               -- table column -->
<!ATTLIST COL                             -- column groups and
                                             properties --
  %attrs;                                 -- %coreattrs, %i18n,
                                             %events --
  span          NUMBER         1          -- COL attributes
                                             affect N columns --
  width         %MultiLength; #IMPLIED -- column width
                                             specification --
  %cellhalign;                            -- horizontal align-
                                             ment in cells --
  %cellvalign;                            -- vertical alignment
                                             in cells --
  >
```

The core attributes and intrinsic events are supported by the COL element, and the *span*, *width*, and *cellhalign* and *cellvalign* (horizontal and vertical) alignment attributes. The *span* attribute, if used, must be assigned a value greater than 0 (the default is 1), specifying the number of columns spanned by the COL element. Any other attributes specified in the COL element apply to all columns spanned by the element. The width attribute works the same way for the COL element as for the COLGROUP element (in fact, the *width* attribute of the COL element overrides the *width* attribute of the COLGROUP element). The remaining attributes work in the same way as their counterparts for the COLGROUP element.

6.7   Table Rows and the TR Element

Table rows are initiated with the TR element, whose starting tag is required but whose ending tag is optional. Within the TR element can be placed TH and TD elements, creating cells in a row. As we have mentioned, if the number of cells (including cells spanning more than one column) in a row is less than the total number of columns, blank cells will be added to that row until the total number of columns is reached.

Like other table elements, rows may be assigned attributes applying to elements inside them, such as table cells. They can also be grouped into headers, footers, and the body sections, as we've seen, with the THEAD, TFOOT, and TBODY elements. The DTD for the TR element is:

```
<!ELEMENT TR    - O (TH|TD)+  -- table row -->
<!ATTLIST TR                  -- table row --
  %attrs;                     -- %coreattrs, %i18n, %events --
  %cellhalign;                -- horizontal alignment in cells --
  %cellvalign;                -- vertical alignment in cells --
>
```

The core attributes are supported, as well as the intrinsic events, and in addition to the cell alignment (*align, cellhalign, cellvalign,* and *valign*) attributes and text alignment (*char* and *charoff*) attributes, the TR element also supports bgcolor, allowing the author to specify a background color for an entire row. If the author omits COLGROUP and COL elements, by default the highest number of cells in any row becomes the total number of columns for a table.

6.8   Table Cells and the TH and TD Elements

Table cells are containers for data and content within tables. While cells may be empty, and may show either as a raised surface, or as an empty, indented cell, they typically contain data. However, data is not all they can contain. Into a table cell can be placed text, images, links, forms and form element, and even whole tables. Table cells cannot be smaller than the minimum size for the content they contain. Starting tags for the elements are required, while ending tags are optional. The DTD for table cells is:

```
<!ELEMENT (TH|TD) - O (%flow;)*    -- table header cell, table
                                      data cell-->
<!-- Scope is simpler than headers attribute for common
tables -->
<!ENTITY % Scope "(row|col|rowgroup|colgroup)">
<!-- TH is for headers, TD for data, but for cells acting as both
use TD -->
<!ATTLIST (TH|TD)                       -- header or data
                                           cell --
  %attrs;                               -- %coreattrs, %i18n,
                                           %events --
  abbr       %Text;      #IMPLIED -- abbreviation for
                                     header cell --
  axis       CDATA       #IMPLIED -- comma-separated
                                     list of related
                                     headers--
  headers    IDREFS      #IMPLIED -- list of id's for
                                     header cells --
  scope      %Scope;     #IMPLIED -- scope covered by
                                     header cells --
  rowspan    NUMBER      1        -- number of rows
                                     spanned by cell --
```

```
colspan        NUMBER         1          -- number of cols
                                            spanned by cell --
%cellhalign;                             -- horizontal
                                            alignment  in  cells
                                            --
%cellvalign;                             -- vertical alignment
                                            in cells --
>
```

The core attributes and intrinsic events are supported. The *abbr* attribute allows the author to include an abbreviation for the cell's content, which could be useful for situations in which rendering the entire content of a cell may be inappropriate. The *axis* attribute can contain a comma-separated list of cell category names, and this value is useful for categorizing cells in relationship to each other.

The *headers* attribute can contain a list of cells which provide header information for the current cell, but those header cells must be named with the *id* attribute (those id values are what the headers list is made up of). The *scope* attribute has a similar function, in that it sets the scope for a particular header cell across a number of data cells. The *scope* attribute can take on the values "row", "col" (for column), "rowgroup", and "colgroup", meaning that the cell's header information applies to the row, column, rowgroup, or columngroup of which it is a part.

If a cell is meant to be rendered as spanning a number of rows or columns, the *rowspan* or *colspan* attribute may be set. These attributes take as a value an integer representing the number of rows or columns to be spanned. The default value is 1. If their value is set to 0 then the cell will span whatever rows or columns remain.

The *width* and *height* attributes recommend width and height to the browser, but it is important to note again that no cell can be smaller than its content. The *cellhalign* and *cellvalign* attributes operate in the same way they do for TR and COL elements.

Cells may have the *nowrap* attribute set, meaning text will not wrap, but this can lead to extended tables and left-to-right scrolling, something not usually desirable. What is desirable, though, in some circumstances, is the setting of the *bgcolor* attribute. When properly done, alternating one background color with another across various cells can make it much easier to read data in a table.

Following is an example of code that creates several cell types, and after that Fig. 6-4 shows how this code displays in a browser.

```
<html><head><title>Table Cell Demo</title>
<meta http-equiv="Content-Type" content="text/html;
charset=iso-8859-1">
</head>
<body bgcolor="#FFFFFF">
<table width="75%" border="1">
  <tr>
   <td width="35%"> </td>
   <td width="18%"> </td>
   <td rowspan="2" valign="top" width="47%">
    <div align="center">Text at Top</div>
```

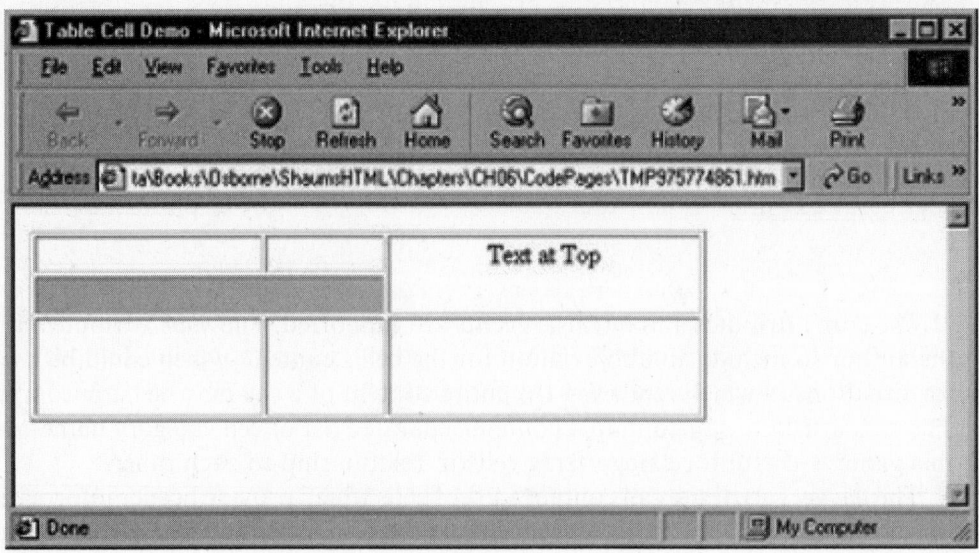

Fig. 6-4.   Illustration of a table with cells.

```
   </td>
  </tr>
  <tr>
   <td colspan="2" bgcolor="#99CCFF"> </td>
  </tr>
  <tr>
   <td height="60" width="35%"> </td>
   <td height="60" width="18%"> </td>
   <td height="60" width="47%"></td>
  </tr>
 </table>
</body></html>
```

6.9 Creating Framed Web Pages

Web pages containing frames are actually several Web pages displayed together in a framed format. The initial Web page retrieved is the framed page itself, and its primary function is to render the frames in which subsequent Web pages appear. Within the code for the initial framed page are references to other pages that appear in each frame. These are normal Web pages, but only the portion of their content that fits within the frame they appear in is displayed. Of course, if the author chooses to allow scroll bars, users can scroll to reveal other content within the Web pages appearing inside the frames.

An advantage of using frames is that multiple pages can appear in the same frame, preserving the look, feel, and layout over the overall framed page as Website content is navigated. For example, one banner and one navigation page can constantly be available to the user (typically in the top and left frames, respectively). Not only does this make it easier to navigate the Website, but the pages and code for these areas of the page need be written and maintained only once, rather than over and over again for each page in the Website.

It is possible to allow each frame in a framed Web page to be scrolled and sized independently, and frame borders can be removed. The effect is to make each area on the display screen a small window of content. This offers quite a bit of flexibility to the author, but the drawback is that a significant number of users have still not upgraded to browsers that are frames compatible, and these browsers may display little or nothing to the user when a framed page is encountered. However, the NOFRAMES element allows authors of framed pages an option for providing content to browsers that do not support frames.

6.10 The FRAMESET Element

From a structural standpoint, framed pages are different from standard pages in that they have HEAD and FRAMESET elements, rather than HEAD and BODY elements. Another difference is that, while a standard page can have only one BODY section, a framed page can have multiple FRAMESET elements. If the author wishes to place ordinary HTML content and elements in a framed page, it is important not to do so before the FRAMESET element appears, or it is possible that the FRAMESET will be ignored. It is best to use the NOFRAMES element for ordinary content.

The DTD for the FRAMESET element is:

```
<! [ %HTML.Frameset; [
<!ELEMENT FRAMESET - - ((FRAMESET|FRAME)+ & NOFRAMES?) --
window
ubdivision-->
<!ATTLIST FRAMESET
  %coreattrs;                              -- id, class, style,
                                              title --
  rows        %MultiLengths; #IMPLIED -- list of lengths,
                                           default: 100%
                                           (1 row) --
  cols        %MultiLengths; #IMPLIED -- list of lengths,
                                           default: 100%
                                           (1 col) --
  onload      %Script;       #IMPLIED -- all the frames have
                                           been loaded -
  onunload    %Script;       #IMPLIED -- all the frames have
                                           been removed --
  >
]]>
```

The recommendation does not appear to indicate whether starting and ending tags are required, but it is a good idea to include them. Only the id, class, title, and style core attributes are supported, and only the onload and onunload events are supported. Other supported attributes are *rows* and *cols*. These two can be used simultaneously, but often only one or the other is used. If a FRAMESET element uses the *rows* attribute, then the window of the browser will be broken into rows (initially); using the *cols* attribute breaks the window into columns. Using both attributes in the same FRAMESET element creates a grid.

The row or column values may be expressed as pixels, percentages, or relative values. Each type of value can be used for a similar effect, as shown in the following three code examples. In each example, a FRAMESET with four frames in columns covering one-quarter of the window is created.

Using *percentage value*:

```
<FRAMESET COLS="25%,25%,25%,25%">
```

Using *pixels* (with a screen resolution of 800 pixels wide):

```
<FRAMESET COLS="200,200,200,200">
```

Using *relative values*:

```
<FRAMESET COLS="2,2,2,2">
```

When rendered, frames start at the left and proceed to the right (if columns) and start at the top going down (for rows). If both rows and columns are used in the same FRAMESET, the order is left to right, top to bottom, essentially the same.

FRAMESET elements provide the space for individual pages of content to appear in the Web page, but it is the FRAME elements that retrieve the content pages. Each frame space created may have an associated FRAME element. If, however, another FRAMESET element is inserted into a frame space, that space can be broken down into rows and columns as well. FRAMESET elements inside FRAMESET elements are called *nested* frames. There is no limit in HTML for nested frames, but in practice there comes a point at which the resulting frame spaces will be too small to use.

6.11 Retrieving Frame Content with the FRAME Element

While the FRAMESET element lays out the spaces for frames within a framed Web page, the FRAME element does the work of retrieving content pages for each frame, as well as some formatting of individual frames. For example, the FRAME element controls resizability and scrolling characteristics for frames. The DTD for the FRAME element is:

```
<![ %HTML.Frameset; [
<!-- reserved frame names start with "_" otherwise starts with
letter -->
<!ELEMENT FRAME - O EMPTY -- subwindow -->
```

```
<!ATTLIST FRAME
  %coreattrs;                              -- id, class, style,
                                              title --
  longdesc      %URI;        #IMPLIED -- link to long
                                              description
                                              (complements
                                              title) --
  name          CDATA        #IMPLIED -- name of frame for
                                              targeting --
  src           %URI;        #IMPLIED -- source of frame
                                              content --
  frameborder   (1|0)        1        -- request frame
                                              borders? --
  marginwidth   %Pixels;     #IMPLIED -- margin widths in
                                              pixels --
  marginheight  %Pixels;     #IMPLIED -- margin height in
                                              pixels --
  noresize      (noresize)   #IMPLIED -- allow users to
                                              resize frames? --
  scrolling     (yes|no|auto) auto     -- scrollbar or none --
  >
]]>
```

No ending tag is required for the FRAME element, as all the information required for its function is contained in the starting tag. The core attributes *id*, *class*, *title*, and *style* are supported, but apparently no events. The *longdesc* attribute can be used to provide a longer description of the frame than the *title* attribute might convey. One of the most important attributes is the *src* attribute. The *src* attribute defines the URL from which the Web page displayed in a frame is retrieved. Note that the URL must not be an anchor within the same page as the FRAMESET page; all content for frames must be from separate Web page files.

Another important attribute is the *name* attribute. Frames are often given names so they can be targeted for the appearance of content linked to from other frames. For example, framed pages commonly have a "menu" frame shaped as a column on the left-hand side. This menu frame contains links to the content of the Website, and for the most part never leaves the user's screen. As links are clicked in the menu frame, their retrieved pages show up in a larger area to the right of the menu. The larger frame to the right must have a name, so that the links in the menu area know where to appear. By default, links appear in the frame in which they are clicked, but if they are targeted to a named frame they will appear in that frame. Targeting is discussed in greater detail in this chapter in section 6.13, "Targeting Frame Content".

The *noresize* attribute takes no value, but if it is present, it instructs the browser not to allow the user to resize the frame. The default value for resizing allows the user to resize frames at will. The *scrolling* attribute controls the appearance of scroll bars, and may take one of three values: "auto", "yes", and "no". The default is auto, meaning that scroll bars will appear whenever the content of a frame flows past the frame boundaries. Setting the *scrolling* attribute to "yes" tells the browser always to provide scroll bars (regardless of content dimensions) and setting this attribute to "no" means scroll bars will never be provided, again regardless of content dimensions.

The *frameborder* attribute controls the appearance of borders for frames individually. It can take a value of 1 or 0. The default is 1, meaning frame borders will appear. Setting the *frameborder* attribute value to 0 means that no frame borders will appear for this frame, although if other frames still have borders there may be no ultimate difference in the appearance of the page on screen. Interestingly, the major browsers seem to respect this attribute when it is applied to the FRAME-SET element as a whole, rather than individual FRAME elements.

The *marginwidth* and *marginheight* attributes define the number of pixels between the content of a frame and its margins. The default value is determined by the browser, and if these attributes are used they must be set to a value greater than 0.

The following code shows a simple nested frameset page, with frame names, content sources, and the noresize and scrolling attributes set:

```
<html><head><title>Nested Framesets and Frames</title>
<meta http-equiv="Content-Type" content="text/html;
charset=iso-8859-1">
</head>
<frameset rows="20%,80%" frameborder="YES" border="6"
    framespacing="6" bordercolor="#FFCCCC">
 <frame src="Frame4.htm" name="banner" noresize
    scrolling="NO">
 <frameset cols="20%,80%">
  <frame src="Frame2.htm" name="menu" noresize
    scrolling="NO">
```

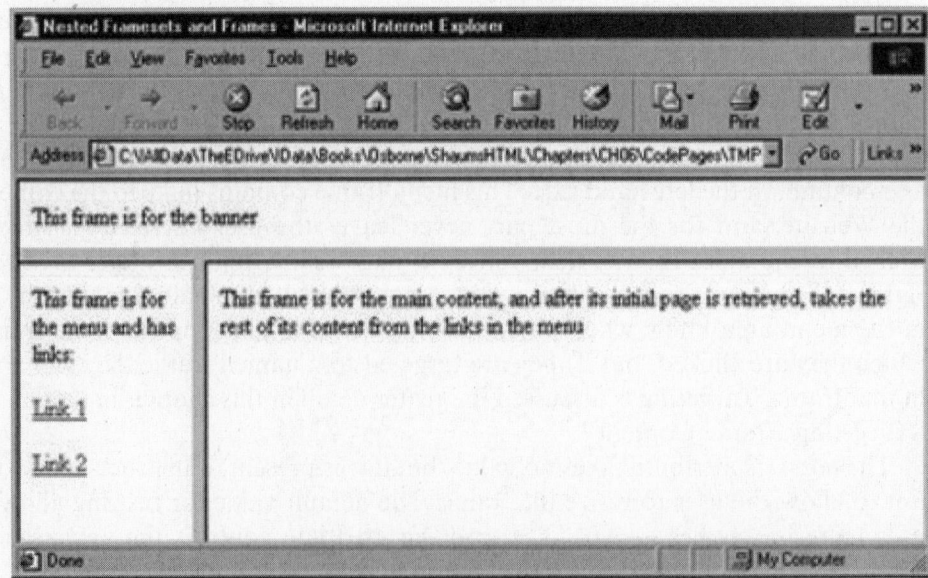

Fig. 6-5.   A nested frameset page, with borders.

```
  <frame src="Frame1.htm" name="main" noresize
    scrolling="AUTO">
 </frameset>
</frameset>
<noframes><body bgcolor="#FFFFFF">
</body></noframes></html>
```

Notice in this example that the *frameborder*, *border*, *framespacing*, and *bordercolor* attributes have been set, even though they are not noted in the DTD of the FRAMESET element. Macromedia Dreamweaver has support for these attributes expressed in this way, and Internet Explorer also displays these attributes properly, as shown in Fig. 6-5.

6.12 Sharing Data Between Frames

In an ordinary Web page scripts may be used to capture initial or changed values in one element and, based on those values, perform processing upon another element. Since framed pages consist of separate files, sharing data from one frame to another becomes more difficult, but there is a method that can be used to accomplish this function.

The method involves placing an OBJECT element in the HEAD element of the FRAMESET page, giving it a unique id via the *id* attribute, and placing some data in the object. In the HEAD element the object is not rendered, but any page retrieved within a frame in the frameset may refer to the object's data, as shown in the following code.

For the frameset page:

```
<HTML><HEAD><TITLE>A Framed Page</TITLE>
<OBJECT id="anobject" data="somedata.txt"></OBJECT>
</HEAD>
<FRAMESET cols="50%,50%">
<FRAME src="page1.htm">
<FRAME src="page2.htm">
</FRAMESET>
</HTML>
```

For page1.htm:

```
<HTML><HEAD><TITLE>Page 1</TITLE></HEAD>
<BODY>
<SCRIPT Type="text/javascript">
Parent.anobject.data
</SCRIPT>
</BODY></HTML>
```

6.13   Targeting Frame Content

A very useful feature of frames is the ability to display content in one frame based on links activated in another frame. In order for this to work, the page in which the link appears must have a means of specifying the frame in which the retrieved content is to be rendered. The *target* attribute of the link is used for this purpose. The *target* attribute works for links, image maps, and forms. The value taken by the *target* attribute is the name assigned to that frame, via the *name* attribute of the FRAME element.

The value of the *name* attribute may be anything the author desires within the character set, but it is best to use simple, descriptive, and unique names. Following is an example of a frameset file in which the frames have names, and a catalog file in which the links have assigned targets.

In the frameset file (frameset section only):

```
<FRAMESET cols="50%,50%">
<FRAME src="page1.htm" name="Page1">
<FRAME src="page2.htm" name="Page2">
</FRAMESET>
```

In the page1.htm file (link section only):

```
<A HREF="page3.htm" target="Page2">
Link to Page 3</A>
<A HREF="page4.htm" target="Page2">
Link to Page 4</A>
<A HREF="page5.htm" target="Page2">
Link to Page 5</A>
```

For pages with many links to the same frame, an easier way to establish the target for all links is to set the *target* attribute for the BASE element in the head of the page containing the links. The following code shows an example of this type of targeting:

```
<HTML><HEAD><TITLE>Setting the Target using the
   BASE Element</TITLE>
<BASE HREF="http://www.e4free.com" target="Page2">
</HEAD>
```

In the remainder of the document all links will default to the target frame specified in the BASE element, and have no need of a target frame within themselves. However, if an individual link does have a target attribute specified, then that target supersedes the one set in the BASE element. By the way, if no target is set, the default behavior of a link is to open in the frame in which it resides.

6.14   The NOFRAMES Element

Frames were not a part of the orginal HTML recommendations, arriving rather late on the scene after the introduction of several versions of both Netscape Navigator and Internet Explorer. It is therefore not surprising that these early versions of the popular browsers did not support frames. Because there are many areas where Internet access is costly and spotty, some users prefer not to download a new version of their favorite browser every time one is available, and a significant portion of users are running browsers that do not support frames. This presents a problem to users of older browsers (of whom there are still many) when viewing framed Web pages.

To cope with older browsers, the NOFRAMES element is available. When used, it instructs frames-capable browsers to ignore its content. For older browsers, the default behavior is to ignore any tags not understood, while processing the rest of the elements in a normal manner. Older browsers ignore the FRAME-SET, FRAME, and NOFRAMES elements, processing what's left.

What's left inside the NOFRAMES element is a normal BODY element, containing whatever content the author has thoughtfully provided for older browsers. This handy capability means authors can easily insert some content for older browsers, although the technically superior method is to detect browser type and capabilities (using scripts) and provide Web pages accordingly.

Starting and ending tags are not noted in the recommendation, but should be used. The DTD of the NOFRAMES element is:

```
<![ %HTML.Frameset; [
<!ENTITY % noframes.content "(BODY) -(NOFRAMES)">
]]>
<!ENTITY % noframes.content "(%flow;)*">
<!ELEMENT NOFRAMES - - %noframes.content;
  -- alternate content container for non frame-based
    rendering -->
<!ATTLIST NOFRAMES
  %attrs;                    -- %coreattrs, %i18n, %events --
  >
```

The NOFRAMES element supports the usual core attributes and the intrinsic events, but it is primarily intended only to allow older browsers to display some content (or when newer browsers are set not to display frames, as users sometimes do). Microsoft's FrontPage automatically inserts the NOFRAMES element when a framed page is created, although the elements included are not really very helpful to a user whose browser doesn't support frames, as shown in the following code (notice that the names for each frame were automatically assigned as well):

```
<html><head><title>New Page 2</title>
<meta name="GENERATOR" content="Microsoft FrontPage 4.0">
<meta name="ProgId" content="FrontPage.Editor.Document">
</head>
```

```
<frameset rows="64,*">
 <frame name="banner" scrolling="no" noresize
   target="contents" src="new_page_3.htm">
 <frameset cols="150,*">
  <frame name="contents" target="main"
   src="new_page_4.htm">
  <frame name="main" src="new_page_5.htm">
 </frameset>
 <noframes>
 <body>
 <p>This page uses frames, but your browser doesn't support
   them.</p>
 </body>
 </noframes>
</frameset>
</html>
```

6.15 Inline Frames and the IFRAME Element

Sometimes dividing a page into frames in the traditional manner is not appropriate, but simply creating a frame inline is. The IFRAME element was created for just such usage, and simply makes a frame inside whatever page it occurs on. It actually inserts the frame inline, meaning it is an inline element and may be aligned with surrounding text.

The recommendation does not specify, but starting and ending tags should be used for the IFRAME element. The DTD for the IFRAME element is:

```
<!ELEMENT IFRAME - - (%flow;)*            -- inline subwindow -->
<!ATTLIST IFRAME
 %coreattrs;                               -- id, class, style,
                                              title --
 longdesc      %URI;      #IMPLIED -- link to long
                                       description
                                       (complements
                                       title) --
 name          CDATA      #IMPLIED -- name of frame for
                                       targeting --
 src           %URI;      #IMPLIED -- source of frame
                                       content --
 frameborder   (1|0)      1        -- request frame
                                       borders? --
 marginwidth   %Pixels;   #IMPLIED -- margin widths in
                                       pixels --
 marginheight  %Pixels;   #IMPLIED -- margin height in
                                       pixels --
```

```
scrolling       (yes|no|auto)  auto      -- scrollbar or none --
align           %IAlign;       #IMPLIED -- vertical or
                                            horizontal
                                            alignment --
height          %Length;       #IMPLIED -- frame height --
width           %Length;       #IMPLIED -- frame width --
>
```

The core attributes *id*, *class*, *title*, and *style* are supported, but no intrinsic events. A name may be given to the frame via the *name* attribute and the content to be retrieved by the frame is specified by the value of the *src* attribute, a URL. The *longdesc* attribute provides a means of offering a long description (from a separate file) for the frame.

Formatting of the appearance of the frame is handled in the usual manner by the *align*, *width*, and *height* attributes. Whether or not to display a border for the frame is determined by the value of the *frameborder* attribute, which may be a 1 or 0. The size of the horizontal and vertical margins is set using the *marginheight* and *marginwidth* attributes, in pixels. And finally, scrolling can be set for the frame with the scrolling attribute, which may take on the values "yes", "no", and "auto". Resizing is not permitted with inline frames, therefore no attribute related to resizing is available. The following code demonstrated the workings of the IFRAME element, and the result is shown in Fig. 6-6.

```
<html><head><title>Untitled Document</title>
<meta http-equiv="Content-Type" content="text/html;
    charset=iso-8859-1">
```

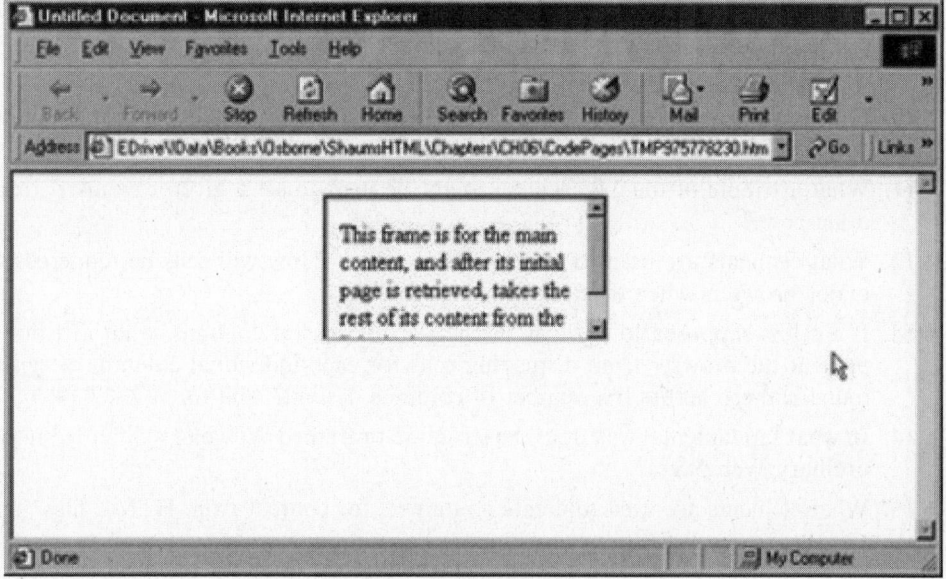

Fig. 6-6.   An IFRAME element in a Web page.

```
</head>
<body bgcolor="#FFFFFF">
<center>
<IFRAME src="Frame1.htm" width="200" height="100"
    scrolling="auto" frameborder="1">
</IFRAME>
</center>
</body></html>
```

Review Questions

6.1. How are tables more useful as layout mechanisms than plain HTML? Give an example that shows their usefulness in this regard.

6.2. What is the default placement of a table in a browser screen?

6.3. Are starting and ending tags required for tables? What happens in the major browsers if ending tags are left off?

6.4. If a table is started with the tag < TABLE >, and no attributes are set, how will the table appear when rendered?

6.5. How is the width of a table set? What types of values can the *width* attribute take? What effect do these values have?

6.6. What is the purpose of the THEAD, TFOOT, and TBODY elements? How do they work?

6.7. What is the purpose of the COLGROUP element? How is it related to the COL element?

6.8. If there are no COL or COLGROUP elements in a table, how many columns will be rendered?

6.9. Within a column in a table, what attribute can be used to line up the contents of each cell in the column by an individual character chosen by the author? Under what circumstances might this capability be useful?

6.10. How is a row created within a table? What limitations are placed on the number of rows that may be created in a single table?

6.11. What attribute of the TR element might be used to set a given row apart from all other rows?

6.12. What elements are used to create cells in tables? How will cells be rendered in the major browsers when they have no content?

6.13. If a cell is supposed to serve as the header for several columns, what attribute will prevent the browser from displaying cells for each individual column, merging the individual cell across the number of columns desired? And for rows?

6.14. In what fundamental way does the structure of framed Web pages differ from that of ordinary Web pages?

6.15. What elements are used to create containers for content from HTML files?

6.16. How may a FRAMESET element divide the screen? What measures may be used?

6.17. What are nested frames? How do these differ from other FRAMESET element configurations?

6.18. What is a common configuration for framed Web pages? What is the advantage of using this configuration?

6.19. How does the browser know what frame space a particular FRAME element goes with?

6.20. How does a FRAME element know where to get content? May the frame be resized by the user?

6.21. What determines the rendering of scroll bars in a frame? What choices does an author have concerning scroll bars?

6.22. What is the default behavior of a link clicked in a frame, in terms of where the resource opens?

6.23. How can links be set to open in a frame other than the one in which they reside?

6.24. What element can be used to create a frame as an inline object?

6.25. What element can be used to provide content to browsers that do not support frames?

Solved Problems

6.1. Show the code to build a table 75% of the width of the screen, with a border 2 pixels wide, with three columns and three rows, without using COL or COLGROUP elements.

```
<TABLE width="75%" border="2">
<TR><TD>Col1Row1</TD><TD>Col2Row1</TD><TD>Col3Row1
</TD></TR>
<TR><TD>Col1Row2</TD><TD>Col2Row2</TD><TD>Col3Row2
</TD></TR>
<TR><TD>Col1Row3</TD><TD>Col2Row3</TD><TD>Col3Row3
</TD></TR>
</TABLE>
```

6.2. Show the code for making a table with a width of 75% and a border of 2 pixels having two rows and two columns, with a table of the same width and border also having two rows and two columns, in row 2 column 1 of the first table.

```
<TABLE width="75%" border="2">
<TR><TD>Col1Row1</TD><TD>Col2Row1</TD></TR>
<TR><TD>

<TABLE width="75%" border="2">
<TR><TD>Col1Row1</TD><TD>Col2Row1</TD></TR>
<TR><TD>Col1Row2</TD><TD>Col2Row2</TD></TR>
</TABLE>

</TD><TD>Col2Row2</TD></TR>
</TABLE>
```

6.3. Show the code for making the second cell of the second row (in the example just given) span two columns.

Starting from the second row:

```
<TR><TD>Col1Row2</TD><TD colspan="2">Col2Row2</TD></TR>
```

6.4. Show the code for specifying three columns with a COLGROUP element, with each column 33% of the screen, and applying vertical alignment to the bottom in all columns (using the example started in Solved Problem 6).

```
<TABLE width="75%" border="2">
<COLGROUP span="3" width="33%" valign="bottom">
  <tr>
    <td>Column 1</td>
    <td>Column 2</td>
    <td>Column 3</td>
  </tr>
</table>
```

6.5. Show the code for producing a table in which the third column, a series of currency amounts, are aligned upon the period, with an offset of 10 pixels from the margin.

```
<table width="75%" border="1">
<COLGROUP><COL>
<COL align="char" char="." charoff="10">
</COLGROUP>
<tr><td width="15%">January</td><td width="11%">75.00
    </td></tr>
<tr><td width="15%">February</td><td width="11%">125.00
    </td></tr>
<tr><td width="15%">March</td><td width="11%">150.00
    </td></tr>
</table>
```

6.6. Show the code for specifying a table with three columns and three rows, but with the first cell spanning all three rows.

```
<table width="75%" border="1">
  <tr><td rowspan="3"> </td>
    <td> </td><td> </td></tr>
  <tr><td> </td><td> </td></tr>
<tr><td> </td><td> </td></tr>
</table>
```

6.7. Show the code for specifying a table with three columns and three rows, but with the first cell spanning all three columns.

```
<table width="75%" border="1">
  <tr><td colspan="3"> </td></tr>
  <tr><td> </td><td> </td><td> </td></tr>
<tr><td> </td><td> </td><td> </td></tr>
</table>
```

6.8. Show the code for building a framed Web page, with three rows and three columns, that will display an ordinary BODY element to browsers that do not support frames.

```
<html><head><title>Untitled Document</title>
<meta http-equiv="Content-Type" content="text/html;
charset=iso-8859-1">
</head>
<frameset cols="33%,33%,34%" rows="33%,33%,34%">
<frame src="Frame-1.htm"><frame src="Frame-2.htm">
<frame src="Frame-3.htm"> <frame src="Frame-4.htm">
<frame src="Frame-5.htm"><frame src="Frame-6.htm">
<frame src="Frame-7.htm"><frame src="Frame-8.htm">
<frame src="Frame-9.htm">
```

```
<noframes><body bgcolor="#FFFFFF">Here is the plain BODY
content
</body></noframes>
</frameset>
</html>
```

6.9. Show the code for making a framed Web page with two rows of 20% and 80%, then splitting the bottom row into two columns of 20% and 80%.

```
<html><head><title>Untitled Document</title>
<meta http-equiv="Content-Type" content="text/html;
charset=iso-8859-1">
</head>
<frameset rows="20%,80%">
<frame src="Frame-1.htm">
<frameset cols="20%,80%">
<frame src="Frame-3.htm">
<frame src="Frame-4.htm">
</frameset>
</frameset>
</html>
```

6.10. Show the code for inserting an IFRAME element with a width of 100 pixels and a height of 200 pixels in the right-hand side of an ordinary HTML page.

```
<html><head><title>Untitled Document</title>
<meta http-equiv="Content-Type" content="text/html;
charset=iso-8859-1">
</head>
<body bgcolor="#FFFFFF">
<P align="right">
<IFRAME src="Frame1.htm" width="100" height="200"
scrolling="auto" frameborder="1">
</IFRAME>
</P>
</body></html>
```

Answers to Review Questions

6.1. Plain HTML automatically forces text, graphics, and other elements to the left and top of a Web page. It is difficult to columnize text, for example, without resorting to preformatted text elements, unless tables or some other, more advanced structure is used. Tables allow easy columnization of text, and offer vertical alignment as well.

6.2. Tables, like other HMTL elements, naturally flow to the top left of the document.

6.3. According to the HTML 4.01 recommendation, starting and ending tags are required. However, Internet Explorer will still display the table if an ending table tag is not included, but Netscape Navigator will not.

6.4. The table will be invisible, unless formatting attributes are set for other elements, such as the background color for individual cells. Invisible tables are still often used to provide a high degree of control over the placement of elements on Web pages.

6.5. The *width* attribute can be set for a table to force a particular width parameter on it. Width can be set in terms of pixels or as a percentage of the screen. If table width is set in pixels, the table will appear a different size according to the screen resolution set. If table width is set as a percentage of the screen, the table will appear to be the same relative size for the screen, no matter what the screen size is. In any case, no table cell can be smaller than its content.

6.6. These elements provide a level of structure for tables, dividing them logically into groups of one or more rows in a head section, a foot section, and one or more body sections. They should be coded with the THEAD and TFOOT sections coming first and then the TBODY section(s). If no THEAD and TFOOT sections are present and only one TBODY section is present, these elements may be omitted.

6.7. The COLGROUP element allows the author to designate a specified number of columns as a group for the purpose of assigning those columns formatting properties. COL elements can be placed inside COLGROUP elements to specify properties of individual columns within a group.

6.8. The table will be rendered with as many columns as there are cells in the row with the highest number of cells. If other rows contain fewer cells, blank cells will be placed in them until the appropriate number has been attained.

6.9. The COLGROUP and COL elements support the *char* and *charoff* attributes. The *char* attribute signifies the character upon which to line up the contents of cells in the column. For example, if the author chooses to line up numbers by the decimal point, the *char* attribute's value would be the period or dot. The *charoff* attribute instructs the browser how far (in pixels or as a percentage) it is from the margin to the alignment character.

6.10. The TR element is used to create rows. There is no limitation on the number of rows that may be created in a single table.

6.11. The TR element supports use of the *bgcolor* attribute, and this attribute can be assigned a color value using either the hexadecimal color scheme or color name values that are recognized by browsers. Setting this attribute's value is a convenient way to distinguish some rows from others, and is often used when database results are rendered as rows in a table by server-side scripts.

6.12. The TH and TD elements create cells in tables. The TH element is very similar in appearance to the TD element, except that text inside it is rendered bold-faced in the popular browsers. In both cases, a cell without content is rendered as a raised area that appears flush with the rest of the table (no borders are rendered for that cell).

6.13. The *colspan* attribute can be assigned an integer value representing the number of columns the cell should span. The *rowspan* attribute performs essentially the same function across table rows.

6.14. Ordinary Web pages are rendered entirely from the contents of one HTML file (although this content may be supplemented or modified by using include files or external style sheet files). Framed Web pages consist of several HTML files, one of which creates containers for the content of the others.

6.15. The FRAMESET element replaces the BODY element for the Web page serving as the container of frames for content from other HTML files. The FRAMESET element builds the frame spaces, while individual FRAME elements within the FRAMESET element provide the reference to the files holding the content (via the *src* attribute). FRAME elements can also be assigned a name (via the *name* attribute) and basic formatting features, such as resizability and scrollability (via the *noresize* and *scrolling* attributes).

6.16. The *rows* and *cols* attributes may be used to divide the browser screen into frames, either independently or together. The values they take can be expressed as pixels, a percentage of the available screen, or relative values based on the proportions of relative integers.

6.17. Nested frames are FRAMESET elements inside FRAMESET elements. They allow the author to specify various configurations of frames that are not possible with only one frameset. For example, if one column of a FRAMESET is to be split into two, nested FRAMESETs make this work.

6.18. It is quite common to see Web pages split into two rows, and then the bottom row split into a right and left column. The top row is usually about 20% of the screen, and serves as an area for a company logo and other static information. The bottom left-hand column serves as a menu area with links to content throughout the site. Because the left-hand column never changes, navigation links are always available. The bottom right-hand column serves to display content pages across the site.

6.19. The browser reads the HTML from top to bottom and left to right (by default). The first allocated space encountered in the rows or cols attribute is assigned to the first FRAME element encountered, and so on.

6.20. The value of the *src* attribute of the FRAME element is a URL to the file holding the Web content. The default behavior for frames is that the user can resize them, but this can be canceled by including the *noresize* attribute.

6.21. The *scrolling* attribute determines whether scroll bars are rendered. By default, without the *scrolling* attribute, scroll bars will appear whenever content exceeds frame size. This is the same as setting the *scrolling* attribute to "auto". Setting the *scrolling* attribute to no prevents scroll bars from appearing under any circumstances, while setting the *scrolling* attribute to "yes" forces scroll bars to appear under all circumstances.

6.22. A link in a frame opens in that frame, by default.

6.23. First, the frames must be given names. Once this is done, links can reference those frames by their names, using the *target* attribute of the A element.

6.24. The IFRAME element can be used to specify a frame as a separate object within a page. Authors have the ability to determine the width and height of the IFRAME element, and as an inline element an IFRAME element will float to a relative position within a document just like text, images, or any other object.

6.25. The NOFRAMES element is recognized by browsers that support frames as an element whose content is to be ignored, providing a place to insert content for browsers that do not support frames. Accordingly, a normal BODY element and any other ordinary content may be inserted into this space and will be ignored by a frames-capable browser. Browsers unable to support frames will, in turn, ignore all FRAMESET and FRAME elements, and instead see only the ordinary content between the NOFRAMES element tags.

CHAPTER 7

Web Page Forms

7.1 Gathering Data with Forms

Forms have been included with HTML almost since the beginning, primarily because they offer such a fabulous capability to Web page authors: the potential for users to communicate directly back to the author. People generally have an intuitive understanding of how forms work, probably because of the thousands we all fill out as we proceed through our lives.

The purpose of forms, of course, is to collect individual pieces of information about one or more specific things. For example, if you are buying a product online, you will probably have to fill out a form collecting personal information about you, such as name, address, phone number, and so on. You will also have to specify what product you want to buy, and what features it should have. The data collected will most likely go into a database. Within the database will be tables for customers (where your personal information will go), orders (where your order will go), and order items (where the line items of your order will go).

Having an understanding of how databases work is helpful when building HTML forms, not because all form data ends up inside a database, but because the nature of data in forms and databases (and in other data structures, as we will see in Chapter 10, Introduction to XML and the Future) is so similar. Knowing a few of the guidelines of effective database design helps in the construction of effective HTML forms.

For example, in the same way that each field in a database table has a name, each form element in an HTML form also has a name. Note that the form element names are assigned in the code, and have nothing to do with the labels provided to the user (although it is very important to provide the user with clear, easy-to-understand labels so forms are likely to be filled with the correct data). By the way, it will save you quite a bit of time if you leave out all special characters and spaces when you are devising form control names. Although special characters and spaces might be permissible in HTML, many scripting languages that may need to use them stumble on unusual names.

7.2 Web Page Forms and the FORM Element

HTML forms all start with the starting form tag and end with the ending form tag. It is important to remember this point because it is possible (and in some instances common) to create FORM element controls outside of any starting and ending form tags. Controls outside the starting and ending form tags are useful for activating and controlling script functions, but their contents or values do not get submitted with any form on the page. Form submission, via the submit action, occurs when the user activates the submit action, usually by clicking a submit button (although there are numerous ways to make this action happen). When a form is submitted, the names and values of form controls are typically sent by the browser back to the server on which the Website resides, often for further processing.

FORM elements can contain all the ordinary HTML elements, such as text, images, tables, hypertext links, and so forth. These elements are useful for creating a pleasant layout and design for the form, as well as labeling each INPUT element for the user. Text boxes, radio buttons, submit buttons, and so forth are called *controls*, and their appearance is pretty well fixed, unless special controls (**OBJECT** and **BUTTON** elements, for example) are used. As mentioned, each control must be individually named (via the *name* attribute), so the author (and any scripts that might have an action required) can determine the control to which a particular value is associated.

The DTD for the FORM element is:

```
<!ELEMENT FORM - - (%block;|SCRIPT)+ -(FORM) -- interactive
                                            form -->
<!ATTLIST FORM
  %attrs;                      -- %coreattrs, %i18n, %events --
  action    %URI;              #REQUIRED -- server-side form
                                           handler --
  method    (GET|POST)         GET       -- HTTP method used to
                                           submit the form --
  enctype   %ContentType;      "application/x-www-form-
                               urlencoded"
  accept    %ContentTypes;     #IMPLIED  -- list of MIME types for
                                           file upload --
  name      CDATA              #IMPLIED  -- name of form for
                                           scripting --
  onsubmit  %Script;           #IMPLIED  -- the form was submitted
                                           --
  onreset   %Script;           #IMPLIED  -- the form was reset --
```

```
accept    %Charsets;        #IMPLIED -- list of supported
 -charset                            charsets --
>
```

The core attributes and intrinsic events are supported, and the FORM element has a number of other attributes supported, several of which are crucial to the correct operation of the form. For example, the *method* attribute specifies the HTTP method by which form contents are submitted, and the *action* attribute controls where the form's contents (the form's data set) are submitted to.

The *method* attribute can assume one of two values: "GET" (the default value) and "POST". The vast majority of forms use the "POST" method (by the way, both "GET" and "POST" are case-insensitive), but "GET" is also workable for some common situations. Using the "GET" method makes the browser attach the name-value pairs of the form to the URL request sent to the server, while using the "POST" method makes the browser send the name-value pairs in the body of the form. Either method will get the form contents to the server, but the "GET" method restricts characters in the contents to the ASCII character set.

The *action* attribute may be a relative or absolute URL pointing to the script or application responsible for processing submitted form contents. Web servers sometimes have default processing requiring no script for activation, but the processing is generally so limited as to be useless in most cases. We will discuss server-side script processing later in this chapter.

The *enctype* attribute can be assigned a content type value, such as text, images, and so forth. The default value is "application/x-www-form-urlencoded". The *accept-charset* attribute can be used to specify a particular character set that the server will interpret, such as ASCII, but the values must be those recognized by the recommendation (see www.w3.org for links to accepted charset values). The default value is the reserved word "UNKNOWN", and this value means that the character set used to transmit the document containing the form will be used.

The *name* attribute has the same functionality as the *id* attribute, giving a name to the form so that it can be referred to by scripts. Apart from the normal intrinsic events are the onsubmit and onreset events. These events are activated whenever the submit or reset methods are performed, usually by submit or reset INPUT elements (buttons).

The following example shows the construction (in Fig. 7-1) of a very simple form for entering and sending an email address back to the server:

```
<FORM METHOD="POST" ACTION="collectemailaddresses.asp">
Please enter your email address here:
<INPUT TYPE="text" SIZE="40" NAME="emailaddress"><BR>
<INPUT TYPE="submit" VALUE="Send">
</FORM>
```

In the example given, notice that the *action* attribute specifies an Active Server Page (ASP) that is in the same folder as the form. This means when the submit button is clicked, the browser will send the contents of the form back to the server, to that ASP for processing. The script may perform some processing on the value and return information to the user, it may place the email address in a text file for

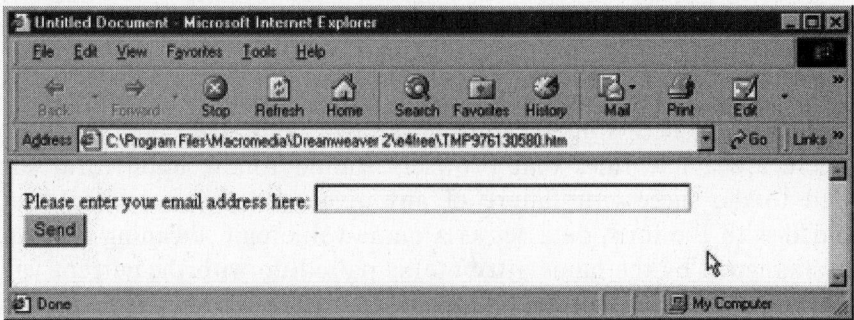

Fig. 7-1. A form for email addresses.

later retrieval by the author, or it may put the email address into a database for subsequent use. The point is, HTML allows data to be retrieved from the user via forms, but almost anything is possible once the data gets back to the server for processing by a script or program. Additional information on scripts and script processing is given later in this chapter.

7.3 Handling User Input with Form Controls

Obviously, one of the primary capabilities of forms is the collection of user input. Ordinary Web pages display information but do not accept input, so *form control elements* were introduced to provide users with a means of entering data. Like form controls in modern DBMS applications, HTML form controls come in a variety of useful types. For example, there is the plain text box, in which users can enter text such as a name or a phone number. There are also radio buttons and check boxes, equivalent to yes/no fields, SELECT elements that display as drop-down menus, and text areas, which form larger boxes for entering multi-line data. And of course there are submit and reset buttons, for submitting the contents of a form or resetting the form to its original configuration. In addition, authors may decide to include controls made from an OBJECT element. These may be anything the author desires, so they are not discussed in detail in this chapter (see Chapter 3 for a discussion of the OBJECT element).

Because the data sent back to the server consists of name-value pairs, it behooves the author of a form to give each control a unique name, making it possible to distinguish the value of one control from that of another. Note that HTML does not bar the author from giving multiple controls the same name (there are some situations in which this is desirable) and that the name is valid only for the form in which it exists.

Controls have an *initial value* and a *given value*, each character strings. When the form is first loaded the initial value (which may be nothing) is assigned, while the user or scripts may change this value to a given value. Whatever value is currently assigned to the control is called its *current value*, but if a form is reset it reverts to its initial value.

When a form is submitted, controls for which a value is assigned are combined into a name-value pair string and sent back to the server. However, while there may be many controls on a form, only those that have a properly assigned current value are included, and these controls are said to be "successful". For example, in the case of radio buttons, only a selected radio button is submitted. The other buttons are "unsuccessful".

There are a few rules that browsers should follow upon form submission, related to the success or failure of any given control. Successful controls are included with the form data set as a name-value pair, meaning that the control name (assigned by the name attribute) is paired up with the current value of the control (either the initial value, if any, or the value entered by the user, or a zero-length string). But controls that have the *disabled* attribute set cannot be successful. And since forms may contain more than one submit button, only the submit button that has been activated will be successful (other submit buttons, reset buttons, or objects whose *declare* attribute has been set will be ignored). If several checkboxes of the same group (having identical names) are checked, their values will be returned as a comma-separated list paired with the single name of the group.

7.4   The INPUT Element

The INPUT element offers authors the ability to create most HTML form controls, except the TEXTAREA element and the SELECT element. During the evolution of HTML these two control types were built with their own separate form elements, not using the INPUT element. The DTD of the INPUT element is:

```
<!ENTITY % InputType
  "(TEXT | PASSWORD | CHECKBOX |
    RADIO | SUBMIT | RESET |
    FILE | HIDDEN | IMAGE | BUTTON)"
  >
<!-- attribute name required for all but submit and reset -->
<!ELEMENT INPUT -- O EMPTY            -- form control -->
<!ATTLIST INPUT
  %attrs;                             -- %coreattrs, %i18n,
                                         %events --
  type      %InputType;   TEXT     -- what kind of widget is
                                       needed --
  name      CDATA         #IMPLIED -- submit as part of
                                       form --
  value     CDATA         #IMPLIED -- Specify for radio
                                       buttons   and   check-
                                       boxes --
  checked   (checked)     #IMPLIED -- for radio buttons and
                                       checkboxes --
  disabled  (disabled)    #IMPLIED -- unavailable in this
                                       context --
```

```
readonly   (readonly)     #IMPLIED -- for text and
                                      password --
size       CDATA          #IMPLIED -- specific to each
                                      of field --
maxlength  NUMBER         #IMPLIED -- max chars for text
                                      fields --
src        %URI;          #IMPLIED -- for fields with
                                      images --
alt        CDATA          #IMPLIED -- short description --
usemap     %URI;          #IMPLIED -- use client-side image
                                      map --
ismap      (ismap)        #IMPLIED -- use server-side image
                                      map --
tabindex   NUMBER         #IMPLIED -- position in tabbing
                                      order --
accesskey  %Character;    #IMPLIED -- accessibility key
                                      character --
onfocus    %Script;       #IMPLIED -- the element got the
                                      focus --
onblur     %Script;       #IMPLIED -- the element lost the
                                      focus --
onselect   %Script;       #IMPLIED -- some text was
                                      selected --
onchange   %Script;       #IMPLIED -- the element value was
                                      changed --
accept     %ContentTypes; #IMPLIED -- list of MIME types for
                                      file upload --
>
```

INPUT elements begin with the starting INPUT tag (required) and have no ending tag (forbidden). The core attributes and intrinsic events are supported, as well as a wealth of other attributes specifically designed to make HTML forms highly functional user input devices. They can be formatted, via the *type* attribute, as follows:

- Text – Creates a single line of text entry.
- Password – Creates a text box in which entered data is displayed as asterisks, therefore shielding the actual data entered from prying eyes. Submitted data is not affected, only displayed data.
- Hidden – Creates a control the user does not see, but whose value can be set by the author and then returned to the server upon submission.
- Radio – Creates a single radio button within a group, only one of which can be selected.
- Checkbox – Creates a single checkbox within a group, all of which can be selected.
- Submit – Creates a button which, when clicked, submits the form contents.

- Reset – Creates a button which, when clicked, resets the form controls to their initial values.

- File – Creates a text box and button that allows users to select files to submit (using the enctype attribute value "multipart/form-data").

- Button – Creates a push button that may be manipulated by scripts.

- Image – Uses an image as a submit button.

The default value for an INPUT element's *type* attribute is "text". The *name* attribute assigns a name to an INPUT element, and the *value* attribute, if assigned, gives the element its initial value. If radio buttons or checkboxes are assigned the same name, they become part of a group, in the case of radio buttons mutually exclusive (typically used for choosing among credit card types). Checkboxes, on the other hand, while not mutually exclusive, will return a comma-separated string of values, one for each checkbox chosen from the group.

For INPUT element text boxes and password controls, the *size* attribute specifies the size of the box displayed, while the *maxlength* attribute specifies the maximum length of data (in characters) that can be entered. The default for the *maxlength* attribute is no limit on the amount of data that can be entered. If the INPUT element is other than text or password, the *size* attribute sets the width of the control in pixels. For INPUT elements of type "image", the *src* attribute specifies the URL of the image used.

The *alt* attribute can be used to specify alternate text messages when using an image as a submit button for browsers that do not render images. The *readonly* and *disabled* attributes make form data available but not changeable. A control for which the *readonly* attribute is set can receive focus and can be tabbed to, but the opposite is true of disabled controls.

The *tabindex* attribute can be set with a numerical value (some integer) in order to specifically assign a tab order to a form. By default, when a form is loaded a tab order is assigned automatically, but it is often useful in the case of complex forms to assign a tab order explicitly. A sequence of integers forms the tab order, with no particular starting or ending number, and no particular amount between numbers. For example, 1, 2, 3, 4, 5, and 2, 5, 7, 10, 14 are both valid and have exactly the same effect on tab order.

If an author uses the *accesskey* attribute, a key can be assigned that brings focus to a form control. *Bringing focus* usually means the same thing as clicking on the control. For example, for a text box it means that the user will be able to enter text, but does not actually place any text in the control. For a radio button, on the other hand, bringing focus usually means that the button will be selected.

Focus is also involved in the onfocus, onblur, onselect, and onchange events. When a control receives focus, the onfocus event activates, and can be used to trigger scripted actions. Likewise, when a control loses focus the onblur event fires. In a similar manner, when text is selected in a control the onselect event is triggered, and when a change is made to the value of a control the onchange event fires. All of these events can be used to trigger processing by scripts, and therefore changes in the page being viewed by the user in real-time.

When an image is used as a submit button (by setting the type attribute of the INPUT element to "image") that image can also function as an image map. The *usemap* (client-side) and *ismap* (server-side) attributes are used to designate map coordinates. The image map is constructed in exactly the same way as ordinary image maps, the only differences being:

- When a region on the image is clicked the form is submitted in addition to the normal image map actions.

- The name of the INPUT element is attached to x and y coordinates and sent to the server as part of the collection of name-value pairs in the form.

For example, if an INPUT element named "imagebutton" is clicked, the form will be submitted, including two extra pairs named "imagebutton.x" and "image-button.y". The value of the first will be the pixel coordinate for X, and the value of the second will be the pixel coordinate for Y.

The following code sections provide examples of a workable form including many of the controls and attributes discussed so far, with a table arranging controls nicely on the page.

To start the form:

```
<html><head><title>Registration Form</title>
<meta http-equiv="Content-Type" content="text/html;
charset=iso-8859-1">
</head>
<body bgcolor="#FFFFFF" link="#663333">
<form method="POST" action="register.asp">
```

Notice the method attribute is set to "**POST**" and the action attribute is set to return the results to a file that is designated an ASP script by its extension.

To start the tables that hold the contents of the form together:

```
<table width="100%" border="0"><tr>
<td width="98%" valign="top" height="247">
<table width="100%" border="0"
bordercolordark="#CC9966" bordercolorlight="#CC9966">
<tr valign="top" bgcolor="#CC9966"><td>
<p align="center"><b><font face="Arial, Helvetica,
sans-serif" size="+1"
color="#FFFFFF">REGISTER HERE </font></b></p></td>
</tr><tr valign="top"><td><table border="0" width="100%">
<tr bordercolor="#CC9966" bgcolor="#FFCC99">
<td align="right" width="100%" colspan="2">
<div align="left"><b><font face="Arial, Helvetica,
sans-serif" color="#FFFFFF"><font
color="#663333" size="+1">PLEASE FILL IN CONTACT DATA
</font></font></b></div></td></tr>
```

The first table holds the entire form, while an inner table holds the contents of the first section of the form. As can be seen from the content (and from the name of the script file, for that matter) the purpose of this form is to take registration information from potential buyers and suppliers, such as name, address, city, state, zip, and so forth. The form also requests company information and asks the user to choose a user name and password.

The first INPUT element is a radio button rather than a text box, because for the purposes of processing the registration the script needs to identify the type of user registering, either Buyer or Supplier.

```
<tr bordercolor="#CC9966" bgcolor="#FFCC99">
<td align="right" width="39%">
<div align="center"><font color="#663333" size="-1"
face="Arial, Helvetica, sans-serif"><b>I am a Buyer<input
type="radio" name="BorS" value="Buyer" checked> Supplier
<input type="radio" name="BorS" value="Supplier">
</font></font></b></div></td><td align="right"
width="61%"><td></tr>
```

Notice there is no *tabindex* attribute set, but the *checked* attribute is present in the first of the radio buttons. The first radio button will be checked when the form is loaded, but clicking the other button will unclick the first. Even if the reset button is clicked, the form will always start with the first radio button checked, because of the *checked* attribute. Therefore, there is no way for a user not to submit themselves as either a Buyer or Supplier. Also, notice the names of both radio buttons are identical. No matter where on the form these two buttons are placed, they remain part of a group, connected by name, and only one will be successfully submitted.

To start the first fill-in section for ordinary contact information:

```
<tr><td width="39%" align="right"><font face="Arial,
Helvetica, sans-serif" color="#663333" size="-1"><b>First
and Last Name:</b></font></td>
<td width="61%"><input type="text" name="FirstName"
size="20" tabindex="1">
<input type="text" name="LastName" size="20" tabindex="2">
</td></tr><tr>
<td width="39%" align="right"><font face="Arial,
Helvetica, sans-serif" color="#663333" size="-1"><b>
Address:</b></font></td>
<td width="61%"><input type="text" name="Address" size="40"
tabindex="3"></td></tr><tr>
<td width="39%" align="right"><font face="Arial, Helvetica,
sans-serif" color="#663333" size="-1"><b>City, State,
Zip:</b></font></td>
<td width="61%"><input type="text" name="City" size="20"
maxlength="20">
<input type="text" name="State" size="2" tabindex="4">
<input type="text" name="ZipCode" size="10" tabindex="5">
</td></tr><tr>
<td width="39%" align="right"><font face="Arial, Helvetica,
sans-serif" color="#663333" size="-1"><b>Phone, Fax:</b>
```

```
</font></td>
<td width="61%"><input type="text" name="Phone" size="20"
tabindex="6"> <input type="text" name="Fax"
size="20" tabindex="7"></td></tr><tr>
<td width="39%" align="right"><font face="Arial, Helvetica,
sans-serif" color="#663333" size="-1"><b>Email:</b></font>
</td>
<td width="61%"><input type="text" name="Email" size=
"40"></td></tr>
```

Each field in this section is created with an INPUT element, and has a name, size, and tabindex. The label text is just ordinary text rather than a LABEL element, and is assigned font face, color, and size.

For the remaining section, there are fields for username and password, and then a drop-down menu created with a SELECT element, and finally the *submit* and *reset* buttons created with INPUT elements. Notice that the caption for the buttons comes from the setting for the value attribute. While the value of these buttons is not ordinarily useful as data because it is preset by the author and usually constitutes instructions to the user, the submit button can be useful to scripts because it indicates what button was pushed.

```
<tr><td width="100%" align="right" bgcolor="#FFCC99"
colspan="2">
<div align="left"><font face="Arial,
Helvetica, sans-serif" color="#663333" size="-1"><b><font
face="Arial, Helvetica, sans-serif" size="+1" color=
"#FFFFFF"><font color="#663333">CHOOSE USER NAME/ PASSWORD
</font></font> </b></font></div></td></tr><tr>
<td width="39%" align="right"><font face="Arial, Helvetica,
sans-serif" color="#663333" size="-1"><b>User Name,
Password:</b></font></td>
<td width="61%"><input type="text" name="UserName"
size="20" tabindex="15">
<input type="text" name="Password" size="20" tabindex="16">
</td></tr>
<tr bordercolor="#CC9966" bgcolor="#FFCC99">
<td width="39%" align="right"><font face="Arial, Helvetica,
sans-serif" color="#663333" size="-1"><b>How Did You Find
Us?</b></font></td>
<td width="61%"><select name="HowFound"> <option value=
"SearchEngine" selected>Search
Engine</option>
<option value="Newspaper">Newspaper</option>
<option value="Magazine">Magazine</option>
<option value="Radio">Radio</option> <option value="TV">
TV</option>
<option value="Other">Other</option> </select>
<input type="submit" value="Submit" name="B1">
```

Fig. 7-2.   The registration form.

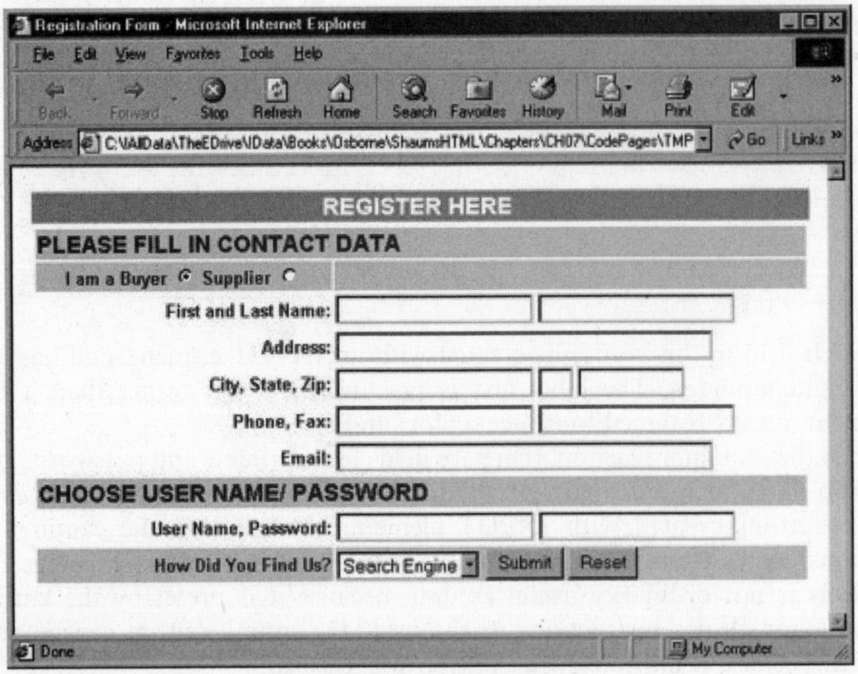

```
<input type="reset" value="Reset" name="B2">
</td></tr></table></table></td></tr></table>
</form></body></html>
```

The resulting form is shown in Fig. 7-2.

7.5   The BUTTON Element

While it is possible to create fine buttons with an INPUT element, there is the BUTTON element as well. The chief difference between the two is that the BUTTON element can hold content, such as text and images, while the INPUT element does not hold content (in the strict sense of the word). The button created with an INPUT element can hold simple text, but a button created with a BUTTON element has the ability to display images on its surface, or highly styled text of various colors, font faces, and sizes.

The starting and ending tags are required for the BUTTON element, and the DTD is:

```
<!ELEMENT BUTTON - -
    (%flow;)* -(A|%formctrl;|FORM|FIELDSET)
    -- push button -->
<!ATTLIST BUTTON
  %attrs;                                   -- %coreattrs, %i18n,
                                               %events --
```

```
name        CDATA               #IMPLIED
value       CDATA               #IMPLIED -- sent to server when
                                            submitted --
type        (button|submit|reset) submit -- for use as form
                                            button --
disabled    (disabled)          #IMPLIED -- unavailable in this
                                            context --
tabindex    NUMBER              #IMPLIED -- position in tabbing
                                            order --
accesskey   %Character;         #IMPLIED -- accessibility key
                                            character --
onfocus     %Script;            #IMPLIED -- the element got the
                                            focus --
onblur      %Script;            #IMPLIED -- the element lost the
                                            focus --
>
```

The core attributes are supported, as well as the intrinsic events. The *name* attribute can be used to assign a name to the control (always a good idea in a form) and the *value* attribute can be used to assign an initial value when the form opens. The type attribute can be set to one of three values: "submit", "reset", and "button", creating a submit button, a reset button, or just a plain button useful for activation by a script, respectively.

The *disabled, accesskey,* and *tabindex* attributes work the same way as for INPUT elements. Please note, the button element, if used with an image, may not have an image map assigned. Following is a short example (shown in Fig. 7-3) of code using the BUTTON element in a form:

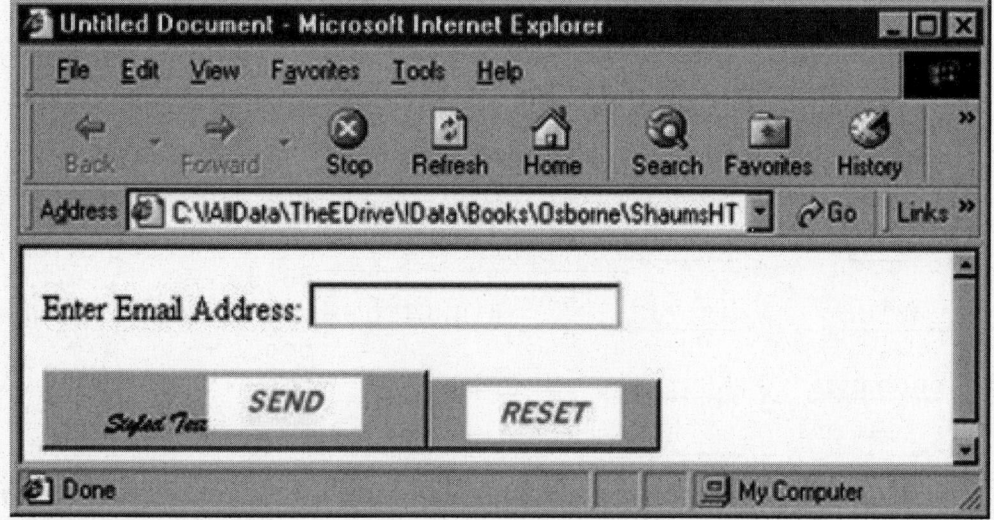

Fig. 7-3.   An example using the BUTTON element.

```
<form method="post" action="emaildbase.asp">
<p> Enter Email Address: <input type="text"
name="textfield"></p>
<BUTTON name="submit" value="submit" type="submit">
<Font face="Brush Script MT">Styled Text</font>
<IMG src="Send.jpg" alt="send" width="76" height="26">
</BUTTON>
<BUTTON name="reset" type="reset">
<IMG src="Reset.jpg" alt="reset" width="76" height="26">
</BUTTON>
</form>
```

7.6 Drop-down Menus and the SELECT, OPTGROUP, and OPTION Elements

In the registration form example earlier in this chapter, one of the last controls was a drop-down box or menu list created with the SELECT element. This control is very popular on and off the Web, allowing users to quickly view and find one or several choices from among many. While the SELECT element carries the name returned by the form at submission, individual OPTION elements make up each option in the list, and carry the content and values of each option.

Starting and ending tags are required for the SELECT element, and the DTD is:

```
<!ELEMENT SELECT - - (OPTGROUP|OPTION)+ -- option selector -->
<!ATTLIST SELECT
    %attrs;                          -- %coreattrs, %i18n,
                                        %events --
    name        CDATA       #IMPLIED -- field name --
    size        NUMBER      #IMPLIED -- rows visible --
    multiple    (multiple)  #IMPLIED -- default is single
                                        selection --
    disabled    (disabled)  #IMPLIED -- unavailable in this
                                        context --
    tabindex    NUMBER      #IMPLIED -- position in tabbing
                                        order --
    onfocus     %Script;    #IMPLIED -- the element got the
                                        focus --
    onblur      %Script;    #IMPLIED -- the element lost the
                                        focus --
    onchange    %Script;    #IMPLIED -- the element value was
                                        changed --
>
```

The core attributes and intrinsic events are supported, and as usual the *name* attribute gives the SELECT element its name. The onfocus, onblur, and onchange events function for the SELECT element in the same way they work for the

INPUT element. The *disabled* and *tabindex* attributes also operate in the standard way in browsers.

The *size* attribute determines the number of rows of options that are displayed in the drop-down box, and also whether it is displayed as a single drop-down box or a list of choices (at least in Internet Explorer). The *multiple* attribute, if included, requires no value but forces the returned data to include more than one value if more than one option is selected by the user. If multiple options are selected, the values appear in the name-value pair as a comma-separated list. This has interesting consequences when the data is inserted into a field in a table in a database, because that field will now hold multiple values. Entering multiple values in a single field is taboo from a database design standpoint, but in certain cases may not do much harm or cause much inefficiency.

Within the SELECT element each choice in the list is created by an OPTION element, and it is possible to group the options into an OPTGROUP element, although this capability does not seem to be supported in the major browsers. A valid SELECT element must contain at least one OPTION element.

The DTD for the OPTGROUP element and for the OPTION element are:

```
<!ELEMENT OPTGROUP - - (OPTION)+ - - option group -->
<!ATTLIST OPTGROUP
  %attrs;                           -- %coreattrs, %i18n,
                                       %events --
  disabled   (disabled)  #IMPLIED  -- unavailable in this
                                      context --
  label      %Text;      #REQUIRED -- for use in
                                      hierarchical menus --
  >
```

and

```
<!ELEMENT OPTION -- O (#PCDATA) -- selectable choice -->
<!ATTLIST OPTION
  %attrs;                           -- %coreattrs, %i18n,
                                       %events --
  selected   (selected)  #IMPLIED
  disabled   (disabled)  #IMPLIED -- unavailable in this
                                     context --
  label      %Text;      #IMPLIED -- for use in
                                     hierarchical
                                     menus --
  value      CDATA       #IMPLIED -- defaults to element
                                     content --
  >
```

Starting and ending tags are required for the OPTGROUP element, but the ending tag is optional for the OPTION element. While the core attributes and intrinsic events are supported for the OPTGROUP element, the *label* attribute is the only other attribute supported, so that an OPTGROUP element may present the user with a label for the group, next to which the individual options should appear in a list when the group label is selected. Contained within the OPTGROUP element are the individual OPTION elements.

The OPTION element, on the other hand, may contain data between the beginning and ending OPTION tags. If an OPTION element has a value specified (via the value attribute) then this is the value returned when the form is submitted (if that option is selected, of course). If not, the data between the beginning and ending tags is its value. Authors can specify the *selected* attribute for an option, in which case that option is preselected when the form is loaded. The OPTION element may also use the *label* attribute to provide a shorter label for an option than the contents of the element, but this does not seem to be supported in browsers either.

7.7   The TEXTAREA Element

In many database applications there is a "memo" data type, referring to a field that holds plain text, usually a rather large amount. The TEXTAREA element fills this role in HTML forms, allowing the author to specify a control capable of holding many lines of text. Often, this control is used as a comments field.

Like the SELECT element, the TEXTAREA element has its own set of HTML tags, and like an OPTION element the TEXTAREA element can contain content in the form of plain text between its beginning and ending tags. The DTD for the TEXTAREA element is:

```
<!ELEMENT TEXTAREA - - (#PCDATA)          -- multi-line text
                                             field -->

<!ATTLIST TEXTAREA
  %attrs;                                 -- %coreattrs, %i18n,
                                             %events --

  name         CDATA          #IMPLIED
  rows         NUMBER         #REQUIRED
  cols         NUMBER         #REQUIRED
  disabled     (disabled)     #IMPLIED -- unavailable in this
                                          context --
  readonly     (readonly)     #IMPLIED
  tabindex     NUMBER         #IMPLIED -- position in tabbing
                                          order --
  accesskey    %Character;    #IMPLIED -- accessibility key
                                          character --
  onfocus      %Script;       #IMPLIED -- the element got the
                                          focus --
  onblur       %Script;       #IMPLIED -- the element lost the
                                          focus --
  onselect     %Script;       #IMPLIED -- some text was
                                          selected --
  onchange     %Script;       #IMPLIED -- the element value was
                                          changed --
  >
```

Starting and ending tags are required for the TEXTAREA element, and the core attributes and intrinsic events are supported. The *name* attribute assigns a name to the control, and the *rows* and *cols* attributes specify the number of rows and number of columns available for the user to enter text into, columns being equivalent to characters. For example, a TEXTAREA element assigned 4 rows of 50 columns will produce a box on screen that has space for 4 rows of text with 50 characters in each row. Naturally, how this is rendered depends upon the default font for the browser, as the default font affects the space allotted to each character.

There is no attribute limiting the amount of text a user may enter, but browsers support the *wrap* attribute, controlling how text wraps in a TEXTAREA control. The *disabled*, *readonly*, *tabindex*, and *accesskey* attributes operate in the usual manner, and the onfocus, onblur, onselect, and onchange events also work the same way they do for INPUT elements.

7.8   The LABEL Element

While it is common to use plain text for labels in an HTML form, the LABEL element can also serve that purpose, associating a label with a specific control. The DTD for the LABEL element is:

```
<!ELEMENT LABEL - - (%inline;)* -(LABEL) -- form field label
                                        text -->
<!ATTLIST LABEL
  %attrs;                       -- %coreattrs, %i18n,
                                   %events --
  for          IDREF        #IMPLIED -- matches field ID
                                   value --
  accesskey    %Character;  #IMPLIED -- accessibility key
                                   character --
  onfocus      %Script;     #IMPLIED -- the element got the
                                   focus --
  onblur       %Script;     #IMPLIED -- the element lost the
                                   focus --
  >
```

The starting and ending tags are required for the LABEL element, and the core attributes and intrinsic events are supported, as well as the *accesskey* attribute. All work in the usual manner. The only addition is the *for* attribute, which can be assigned a value equivalent to the id value assigned to a particular control, thereby associating the LABEL element with the control.

7.9   The FIELDSET and LEGEND Elements

The purpose of the FIELDSET and LEGEND elements is to provide a visual grouping to controls, as well as a legend that indicates their meaning. For example, if an author has a form that is broken down into several sections of information to be provided (such as Contact Information, Credit Card Information, and Shipping Information) the FIELDSET element can group controls together while the LEGEND element places a legend into each group.

The DTDs of the FIELDSET and LEGEND elements are:

```
<!ELEMENT FIELDSET - - (#PCDATA,LEGEND,(%flow;)*) -- form
control group -->
<!ATTLIST FIELDSET
  %attrs;                                -- %coreattrs, %i18n,
                                            %events --
>
<!ELEMENT LEGEND - - (%inline;)*      -- fieldset legend -->
<!ATTLIST LEGEND
  %attrs;                                -- %coreattrs, %i18n,
                                            %events --
  accesskey    %Character;   #IMPLIED -- accessibility key
                                            character --
>
```

Starting and ending tags are required for these elements, and the FIELDSET element supports only the core attributes and the intrinsic events, while the LEGEND element supports the core attributes, intrinsic events, the *accesskey* attribute, and the *align* attribute. The *align* atribute may be set to "top", "bottom", "left", and "right", allowing the author to place the legend at any of these locations around the perimeter of the FIELDSET element, as rendered on screen.

7.10   Using Server-side and Client-side Scripting

HTML, although it serves its intended purposes fairly well for now, is not considered a programming language because it does not allow for processing information, only the display of information. It is primarily for the formatting and display of text, images, multimedia, hypertext links, and HTML forms, with tables and frames thrown in to provide added display capability.

In order to process information, either within the client (the browser) or back at the server, some programming language must be employed. To maintain broad platform compatibility, the language must run on most browsers. The language of choice is currently Javascript, an interpreted language with limited ability to perform standard programming language functions. The limitations are included so the possibility of loading a Web page and contracting a virus are minimized.

Javascript commands are inserted directly into the HTML, and are interpreted as the browser reads through the code, rather than being compiled as executable binary files. This means the source code is readily available to users (simply by clicking View|Source from the browser menu), and it also means the code runs slower than compiled programs, in most cases. However, because Javascript programs tend to be much smaller and narrowly focused than ordinary compiled applications, humans do not usually notice the speed difference.

Javascript can be used to perform functions in Web pages that ordinary HTML cannot, and when this is done they are referred to as *client-side scripts*. Javascripts may also be used to run programs back at the server, and these are referred to as *server-side scripts*. On the server, since the platform is known in advance and portability is not an issue (for the most part), many scripting languages, programming languages, and application-development technologies are in use. For example, VBScript (Microsoft's Visual Basic Scripting Edition) and Perl (Practical Extraction and Reporting Language) are common as back-end languages, as well as Visual Basic and Visual C++. New languages and technologies are being introduced rapidly, and the programming language landscape is in constant flux.

Microsoft's ASP is a technology highly favored in programming circles for the ease it brings to dealing with Website programming and database applications. Notice that ASP is called a technology, rather than a programming language. The reason for this designation is that ASP consists of a set of built-in objects and a processing engine, and these objects may be processed using any scripting language for which an engine is installed on the server.

One of the primary functions of these objects is to make communication to and from Web pages easier, hence the central importance of the Request and Response objects. Here is an example of server-side scripting, using ASP technology and VBScript, starting with an HTML form for submitting form contents, and a response processed and created by an ASP page (named "script10.asp", referenced in the *action* attribute of the FORM element):

```
<HTML><HEAD><TITLE>My New Form</TITLE></HEAD>
<BODY BGCOLOR="lightblue" TEXT="black">
<CENTER>
<FORM ACTION="script10.asp" METHOD="POST">
<TABLE BORDER=1><TR>
<TD>Name:</TD><TD><INPUT TYPE="text" SIZE=40
NAME="fullname"></TD>
</TR><TR>
<TD>Address:</TD><TD><INPUT TYPE="text" SIZE=60
NAME="address"></TD>
</TR><TR>
<TD>Phone:</TD><TD><INPUT TYPE="text" SIZE=20
NAME="phonenumber"></TD>
</TR><TR>
<TD COLSPAN=2><INPUT TYPE="submit" VALUE="Send Info"><INPUT
TYPE="reset" VALUE="Clear"></TD>
</TR>
</TABLE>
</FORM>
</BODY></HTML>
```

And for the processed script (embedded in HTML, residing on the server and processed there):

```
<HTML><HEAD><TITLE>My Form Results</TITLE></HEAD>
<BODY BGCOLOR="lightblue" TEXT="black">
<CENTER>
<H2><% Response.Write "Thank you for responding" %></H2>
Today's Date is:
<% tDate = Date()
Response.Write tDate %>
<P>Your personal data entries were:<BR>
<% Response.Write(Request.Form("fullname")) %><BR>
<% Response.Write(Request.Form("address")) %><BR>
<% Response.Write(Request.Form("phonenumber")) %><BR>
</CENTER>
</BODY></HTML>
```

As the server reads through this code (once activated by the submission of the form in the first example) it begins to process the HTML as an ordinary Web page. When it reaches the ASP code (delimited by % signs) it refers this code to the ASP and VBScript processing engines. The variable tDate and the Date( ) functions are processed by VBScript, while the Request and Response object methods and collections are processed by the ASP processing engine. Once processed, the results are returned as ordinary HTML to the server and included in sequence with the remaining plain HTML. The finished page is then sent to the user. Note that all the user ever sees are finished results in plain HTML, thereby preventing user access to scripting code.

7.11 Using Client-side Scripting with the DOM

The Document Object Model (DOM) for HTML allows all objects (windows, pages, forms, controls, text blocks, and so on) to be addressed and referred to by name or id in a hierarchy of objects. A FORM element is a child of a document, and a control is a child of a FORM element, and so on. Objects can be referenced by a script by their name, id, or within an indexed list based on the hierarchy of objects occurring in a page. For example, the window object is the highest level object and is always present, and referencing a form control (named formcontrol) may be done like this:

```
myVar = window.document.form.formcontrol
```

Once a reference to an object is established, the events affecting it may be detected and used to trigger processing. The properties of an object may also be read and in some cases changed (such as changing the background color of the BODY element from white to black). Finally, methods may be invoked, performing specific processing functions.

Events occur during a session with a Web page, such as the loading of the page the loading of the BODY element, the placing of a mouse over an image, the changing of some text in a control, and so forth. When events occur, scripts can be activated. Scripts written within the SCRIPT element are executed when the document is loaded, while scripts that are part of an element run when events supported by that element occur.

7.12 The SCRIPT Element

The SCRIPT element inserts a script within a document, and there may be multiple scripts within the HEAD and BODY elements of an HTML page. Although Javascript seems to be the language of choice, HTML itself does not specify a preference for one language over another. The browser loading a page must recognize and be capable of utilizing the scripting language specified. The DTD of the SCRIPT element is:

```
<!ELEMENT SCRIPT - - %Script; -- script statements -->
<!ATTLIST SCRIPT
   charset    %Charset;        #IMPLIED  -- char encoding of
                                            linked resource -
   type       %ContentType;    #REQUIRED -- content type of script
                                            language -
   src        %URI;            #IMPLIED  -- URI for an external
                                            script --
   defer      (defer)          #IMPLIED  -- UA may defer execution
                                            of script -
   >
```

Both the starting and ending tags are required for the SCRIPT element, and the *src* attribute may specify an external file (via URL) containing the contents of the script. The *type* attribute specifies the scripting language for the script, as does the deprecated *language* attribute, the difference being that the *type* attribute specifies the language as a content type (text/Javascript) while the *language* attribute specifies the language as a string (Javascript). The *type* attribute must be specified.

The *defer* attribute, when included, takes no value but tells the browser the script returns no content, so the browser can continue rendering the page without interruption. The *charset* attribute specifies the character encoding of the script designated by the *src* attribute, but not the content of the SCRIPT element.

7.13 Intrinsic Events

Many of the elements covered so far support intrinsic events, and some support additional events. Each event occurs when a specific thing happens, and sometimes events occur sequentially, one right after another. Associating scripts with events provides a means of controlling program flow based on user interaction with Web pages and their elements. The intrinsic events are:

Table 7-1 Intrinsic events.

Name	Occurs when	Used with
Onload	The browser completes loading a window or all frames of a page	BODY, FRAMESET
Onunload	The document is removed from the window or frame	BODY, FRAMESET
Onclick	The mouse arrow is over an element and the button is clicked.	Most elements
Ondblclick	The mouse arrow is over an element and the button is clicked twice.	Most elements
Onmousedown	The mouse arrow is over an element and the button is held down.	Most elements
Onmouseup	The mouse arrow is over an element and the button is released.	Most elements
Onmouseover	The mouse arrow is over an element.	Most elements
Onmousemove	The mouse arrow is over an element and is moved.	Most elements
Onmouseout	The mouse arrow is over an element and is moved out of the element.	Most elements
Onfocus	The element receives focus.	A, AREA, LABEL, INPUT, SELECT, TEXTAREA, BUTTON
Onblur	The element loses focus.	A, AREA, LABEL, INPUT, SELECT, TEXTAREA, BUTTON
Onkeypress	A key is pressed and released while over an element.	Most elements
Onkeydown	A key is pressed down and held while over an element.	Most elements
Onkeyup	A key is released while over an element.	Most elements
Onsubmit	A form is submitted	FORM
Onreset	A form is reset	FORM
Onselect	A user selects text in a text control	INPUT, TEXTAREA
Onchange	The value of a control has been changed and then it loses focus	INPUT, SELECT, TEXTAREA

7.14 The NOSCRIPT Element

Like the NOFRAMES element, the NOSCRIPT element serves the purpose of shielding non-script supporting browsers from a total lack of content. If the NOSCRIPT element is present, authors can use it to provide content and HTML tags that will display content only if the browser doesn't support scripting, or if the browser doesn't recognize the language specified. The DTD of the NOSCRIPT element is:

```
<!ELEMENT NOSCRIPT - - (%block;)+
  -- alternate content container for non script-based
     rendering -->
```

```
<!ATTLIST NOSCRIPT
  %attrs;                        -- %coreattrs, %i18n, %events --
  >
```

Both the starting and ending tags are required, and as the DTD indicates the core attributes and intrinsic events are supported. By the same token, when browsers do not recognize the SCRIPT element, unless the contents of the SCRIPT element are in an external file they may be inclined to print the contents of the SCRIPT element as plain text, not a good result at all. Therefore, scripting language developers have made provisions in their processing engines to read scripting commands embedded in HTML comment tags between the starting and ending SCRIPT tags. For example, the following code shows Javascript commands in a SCRIPT element, within HTML comment tags:

```
<SCRIPT type="text/javascript">
<!-- scripting commands hidden in here
  function pressbutton() {
    alert("Hello")
  }
-->
</SCRIPT>
```

Review Questions

7.1. What is the relationship of HTML forms to paper forms?

7.2. What element is the container for an HTML form? What attributes cause it to work?

7.3. Where are the contents of a form submitted to? What action causes submission?

7.4. What events are triggered when a form is submitted or reset? What common script processing is used with these events?

7.5. In what format are the contents of a form returned to the server? What attribute affects the format?

7.6. May two form controls have the same name? Give an example of a situation in which this might be desirable. When might it not be desirable?

7.7. What is the initial value of a control? What is the initial value of a control for which no value is set? When does the value change?

7.8. What types of controls can be created with the INPUT element? What syntax is used for INPUT element controls?

7.9. What is the meaning of the *checked* attribute. To what controls does it apply?

7.10. What is the *tabindex* attribute, and how does it work?

7.11. For an INPUT element of type text, what function do the *size* and *maxlength* attributes perform?

7.12. What is focus, and how is it related to form controls?

7.13. How do the onselect and onchange events work?

7.14. What do the *disabled* and *readonly* attributes do? How are they different?

7.15. The INPUT element can be used to create what kind of buttons? How are these buttons different from buttons created with the BUTTON element?

7.16. How are menu choices added to a SELECT element form control? How many may be added? What control can be exercised over the number of choices displayed?

7.17. What is the function of the *multiple* attribute for SELECT elements?

7.18. If a user selects more than one choice from a drop-down list, what effect does this have on the data being returned to the server when the form is submitted?

7.19. How does the OPTION element determine a value?

7.20. What kind of data entry is the TEXTAREA element commonly used for? What attributes control its appearance?

7.21. What kinds of script processing can be performed with Web pages? How are scripts typically written?

7.22. Javascript is a popular Web page scripting language. Why is this so? How do Javascripts interact with the Web pages within which they run?

7.23. How do events work?

7.24. How are server-side scripts activated and processed?

7.25. What types of functions can server-side scripts perform?

Solved Problems

7.1. What code would create a form with a single text box for entering an email address, pointing to a script named "emailfile.asp"?

```
<FORM Method="POST" Action="emailfile.asp">
Please enter your email address:<INPUT Type="text" size="20"
name="emailaddress">
<INPUT Type="submit" value="Send"></FORM>
```

7.2. In the example above, where on the server is the script file located? What are the consequences of not including a reset button? And what will the caption of the submit button read?

Because the URL specified in the *action* attribute is relative, the browser can expect to find the script file in the same folder as the current HTML page of which the form is a part. The only consequence of not including a reset button on this form is that the user must manually erase any data they have entered. When radio buttons are involved however, not including a reset button can be a serious deficiency, as the user has no way of changing the value of the button once selected.

7.3. Using the example in the first question, show the code for adding a control that includes a drop-down menu in which multiple choices may be selected, the second choice is selected when the form opens, and the values are:

Displayed	Internal
Green	1
Red	2
Blue	3

```
<SELECT multiple name="color">
<OPTION value="1">Green</OPTION>
<OPTION value="2" selected>Red</OPTION>
<OPTION value="3">Blue</OPTION>
</SELECT>
```

7.4. Show the code for adding to the example in the first question radio buttons representing a choice of credit card types for Mastercard, Visa, and American Express. Why would radio buttons be useful for this purpose? What makes them a group rather than individuals?

```
Credit Card Type Used:
MC<INPUT Type="radio" name="CCType" value="MC">
Visa<INPUT Type="radio" name="CCType" value="Visa">
American Express<INPUT Type="radio" name="CCType"
value="Amex">
```

Radio buttons are useful whenever a small series of choices is allowed and only one may be chosen to the exclusion of the other choices. Radio buttons are often most convenient in these situations because all choices are visible and the user may quickly click on the appropriate choice. The fact that they have the same name makes them a group, and of the buttons in the group only the value of the selected button will be returned.

7.5. Show the code for adding to the example in the first question a textarea control rendered with 2 rows, 40 characters across, reading "This is the first row of 40 characters, and following this is the second row." Make it so the contents of the control cannot be changed.

```
<TEXTAREA rows="2" cols="40" readonly>This is the first row
of 40 characters and following this is the second row
</TEXTAREA>
```

7.6. Show the code for adding to the example in the first question an image serving as a submit button. What additional data is returned to the server when an image is used as a submit button, and what might this data be used for?

```
<INPUT Type="image" name="mybutton" src="mybuttonimage.
gif">
```

When an image is used as a submit button, the x and y coordinates of the spot on the image that was clicked are also passed to the server, and are named (in this case) mybutton.x and mybutton.y. This data can be used for any purpose, such as for an image map, or for conditional processing by the server-side script.

7.7. Show the code for placing a Javascript in the HEAD element of an HTML page. Make the script hidden from browsers that do not undersatand Javascript, and make the script create a function, named "sayhi", put an alert box on screen telling the user "Hi".

```
<HEAD>
<SCRIPT language="Javascript">
<!--
function sayhi() {
alert("Hi")
}
-->
</SCRIPT>
</HEAD>
```

7.8. Show the code for activating the "sayhi" function when a text box loses focus.

```
<INPUT Type="text" size="20" name="mytextbox"
Onblur="sayhi()">
```

7.9. Show the code for activating the "sayhi" function when the mouse moves over an image.

```
<IMG src="myimage.gif" Onmouseover="sayhi()">
```

7.10. Show the code for building a form with a place to enter first name, last name, and birth date, that automatically sends back to the server the value "JX1" (not visible to the user) with the name "formserialnumber", to the server-side script "basicinfo. asp".

```
<FORM Method="POST" Action="basicinfo.asp">
First Name:<INPUT Type="text" size="20"
name="firstname"><BR>
Last Name:<INPUT Type="text" size="20"
name="lastname"><BR>
Birth Date:<INPUT Type="text" size="20" name="birthdate">
<INPUT Type="hidden" size="20" value="JX1"
name="formserialnumber">
<INPUT Type="submit" value="Send"><INPUT Type="reset"
value="Clear">
</FORM>
```

7.11. Show how the form data set from the form in the previous example would appear when received raw by the server, if the value submitted were "John", "Doe", "February 1, 1975".

```
firstname=John&lastname=Doe&birthdate=February+1,+1975
&formserialnumber=JX1
```

Answers to Review Questions

7.1. Paper forms capture written data in hard copy form, allowing it to be manually processed and stored. Each field or element on a paper form typically has a name, and the named fields on a paper form usually represent an attribute associated with one thing being tracked (a person, an order, a building, a car, and so forth). HTML forms work in a similar manner, except that the displayed form is the user interface, and the field naming and data capture mechanisms are coded, on the browser and on the server. HTML forms capture data electronically, allowing for electronic processing and storage.

7.2. The FORM element is the container for HTML forms. The starting FORM tag begins the form, and the ending FORM tag ends the form. Form controls can be created either inside or outside these tags, but controls outside the tags are not submitted with the form.

7.3. The *action* attribute of the FORM element specifies the URL to which form contents are submitted. Often, this URL points to a script on the Webserver where the Website resides. The scripts may be ASP, CGI scripts (perhaps written in Perl), executable applications, and so forth. The submit action causes form submission, an automatic function occurring when a "submit" button is clicked.

7.4. The onsubmit event is triggered when a form is submitted, and the onreset event is triggered when a form is reset. The submit() and reset() functions are built into the actions of submit and reset buttons, some of the only real programmatic processing

HTML objects can perform. Authors commonly use the onsubmit event to trigger Javascript processing that checks the contents of form controls to make sure that if they are required fields they contain new values. Using the same process authors often validate the values entered (making sure email addresses contain the @ sign, for example).

7.5. The *enctype* attribute affects the way form data is encoded, while the *method* attribute affects the way it is composed for sending. The default *enctype* attribute value is "application/x-www-form-urlencoded". When the "GET" method is used, a question mark (?) is appended to the URL specified in the *action* attribute, followed by the form data. The form data itself is encoded by replacing spaces with the plus sign (+) and separating name-value pairs.

7.6. Authors may give form controls the same name, but ordinarily this is not desirable because it might cause confusion if both controls return name-value pairs to the server. However, there is a case in which both controls will not be successful (returned to the server). For example, if there are two submit buttons, only the one clicked on will be successful, and the name of the button and its value (the value of a submit button is the same as its caption) will return to the server with the rest of the form's successful controls.

  This is useful when the action attribute points to a script, for the script can detect the value of the button and conditionally process the returned data based on that value. So if one button has the value "Order Now", while the other button of the same name has the value "Empty My Shopping Cart", appropriate processing will occur based on the detected value of the caption.

7.7. The initial value of a control may be set by the author in the case of many HTML form controls. For example, the initial value of a text box can be set (using the *value* attribute) to a string. This value will appear inside the text box when the form is first loaded. If no value is explicitly set, the default value (and the one that is returned to the server when the submit button is clicked if no new value has been entered) is a zero-length string. The value can be changed by the user, and if this is done the new value is referred to as the current value. When the submit button is clicked and the form is submitted, the current value is returned to the server.

7.8. INPUT element controls are written as a single, empty element having no content, and therefore requiring no ending element. They may form text boxes, radio buttons, check boxes, submit and reset buttons, hidden fields, plain buttons, password fields, file fields, and even image controls. Using a text box for a phone number as an example, they are written:

```
<INPUT Type="text" size="20" maxlength="50" name=
"PhoneNumber">
```

7.9. The *checked* attribute has no value, but if included it makes the radio button or checkbox control selected as an initial value.

7.10. Users are familiar with the method of using the tab key to move from control to control as they enter data. HTML includes the *tabindex* attribute in form controls so authors may define a tab order other than the default one created when a form is loaded. *Tabindex* attributes take integer values in sequential order, the order of the numbers reflecting what order controls will be tabbed to. The numbers may start and end at any number, and the interval between numbers may be anything, so long as the numbers are sequential. The reason any numbers and any interval is allowed is so that authors may add or remove controls from the form as necessary, without having to renumber every control. For example, suppose a form is created with 5 controls, and the tabindex attributes for those controls have the numbers 10, 20, 30, 40, and 50 applied. If a control is added between the third and fourth, the new control's *tabindex* attribute may be set to 31, preserving tab order without renumbering the other controls.

7.11. For a text box control, the *size* attribute specifies the size, in characters, that the control will appear to have on screen, based on the size of the default font. The *maxlength* attribute specifies the total number of characters that may be entered. If no *maxlength* attribute value is specified, the default is an unlimited number of characters.

7.12. When a form is used, before a control's value can be changed that control must receive focus. A control can receive focus by being clicked, tabbed to, or through script processing. HTML form controls respond to events related to form controls, such as onfocus and onblur. The onfocus event is triggered when a control receives focus and is ready to be used, and the onblur event is triggered when a form control loses focus and changes no longer affect it.

7.13. Text can be selected in a number of ways, for example, by clicking and dragging across the text. When text is selected in a form control (such as a text box or TEXTAREA element) the onselect event fires. Likewise, when the value of a form control changes (such as when a radio button is clicked or text is entered in a text box) the onchange event fires.

7.14. Including the *disabled* attribute makes the control grayed-out and unusable. This is convenient when, through processing, a particular choice or control shouldn't be available to the user. The *readonly* attribute, on the other hand, doesn't change the appearance of the control or its contents, it just prevents changes from being made to the value. Note that savvy users would find it easy to save the HTML file, change these attributes, and then use the form as they please.

7.15. The INPUT element can be set to types submit, reset, and button. Using types submit and reset creates submit or reset buttons, having a built-in action that either submits or resets the form. Using "type = button" with the INPUT element simply creates a button, but the BUTTON element, having starting and ending tags, may hold content such as text or images. These text or images are inserted on top of the button as a caption. Button captions for buttons created with the INPUT element can only be text inserted as the *value* attribute inside the INPUT element.

7.16. To create a drop-down menu the SELECT element is used, and choices are added by inserting OPTION elements between the starting and ending SELECT tags. There is no limit to the number of OPTION elements that may be added, but the *size* attribute (for the SELECT element) specifies the number of choices that appear on screen.

7.17. Including the *multiple* attribute causes the element to allow more than one choice to be selected.

7.18. Typically, form controls have only one value, and only one value is returned when the form is submitted, as a name-value pair, where the name is the name of the control, and the value is the current value of the control when the form is submitted. However, some controls may take multiple values (SELECT elements and checkbox groups), and it is also possible for multiple controls with the same name to be submitted. If this occurs, the values will be submitted (associated with the name) as a string of comma-separated values.

7.19. The value of the OPTION element is either the value set with the *value* attribute, or the content the author places between the starting and ending OPTION tags. If *value* attributes are set for OPTION elements but no content is placed between the starting and ending tags, the list will still work but no choices will appear (although the value will still be there, and will be returned when the form is submitted). If no *value* attributes are set for the OPTION elements but content is included between the starting and ending tags, the OPTION elements will assume the values of the content, and those values will be returned when the form is submitted.

7.20. The TEXTAREA element has its own tags, rather than being created with an INPUT element, and it appears as a large box for entering multiple lines of text. It is commonly used as a comments or memo field, and its size is dictated by the *rows* and *cols* attributes. These attributes specify the number of rows and columns rendered on screen.

7.21. Client-side and server-side scripts can be processed with Web pages, the client-side scripts incorporated into the HTML as part of the page and processed on the client within or from the browser, and the server-side scripts processed on the server. Server-side scripts may be written as standalone applications or incorporated into HTML as well.

7.22. One of the reasons Javascript is so popular is that the majority of the browsers in use can process it, although not all. Netscape Navigator and Internet Explorer both process Javascript, and together these two browsers make up a large percentage of the market share of browsers in use.

Javascripts interact with the Web pages they run inside by referencing objects on the page, such as the BODY, FORMs, and FORM controls. Javascripts can be written within SCRIPT elements and refer to objects using the DOM and dot notation, or they can be written inside the element they interact with and activated by events supported by that element.

7.23. Objects in a Web page, such as a form control or image, support events, and when these events are triggered, Javascript processing can be initiated. For example, the IMAGE element supports the onmouseover event. Therefore, when the page is displayed on screen and the user places the mouse over the image, the event is triggered. Using Javascript code the event can be set to initiate processing when it is triggered, like this:

```
<IMG src="myimage.gif" Onmouseover="doprocessing()">
```

In the example above, the event onmouseover is set equal to the name of a Javascript function authored elsewhere on the page. The author can make up any name desired for the function ("doprocessing" in this example) but must write the function using valid Javascript commands, like this:

```
<SCRIPT type="text/javascript">
<!-- scripting commands hidden in here
  function doprocessing() {
    alert("The alert command makes a box pop up onscreen with
    these words inside")
  }
  -->
</SCRIPT>
```

7.24. One of the most common ways to activate a server-side script is upon form submission. The *action* attribute of the FORM element can be set to point to a server-side script. When this script is activated it receives the contents of the form data set, the name-value pairs of all successful controls submitted with the form. It can then examine these pairs (or not, depending on the processing instructions in the script) and perform processing conditionally based on these values if desired.

Another way to activate server-side scripts is via the A element. Simply referencing the script as a URL will activate it, although no values are delivered for processing (other than the standard HTTP headers, which can be still be processed).

7.25. Server-side scripts can do simple things such as return a static message without any reference to submitted values, more complex things such as conditional processing of values submitted, up to highly complex functions, such as database searches and complex processing of values submitted.

CHAPTER 8

Cascading Style Sheets and Dynamic HTML

In many of the chapters so far the HTML elements covered, while still supported in the popular browsers, have been deprecated in favor of style sheets. Style sheets offer more flexibility, a greater range of control, and simply a neater and more well-defined mechanism for applying and controlling stylistic presentation than the multitude of other methods used in the Web development community. *Cascading style sheets* refers to a special processing method by which multiple style sheets may be applied to a single Web page, but is not supported by all style sheet languages. The World Wide Web Consortium has developed the Cascading Style Sheets, Level 2 (CSS2) Specification, which does support this type of merging of style sheets.

Using style sheets to apply stylistic formatting to Web page elements has a number of advantages over the traditional method of using individual element attributes to modify style. For example, as mentioned above, style sheets can be separate documents available to many pages in a Website, enabling the author to apply identical styles across many documents, while only having to modify styles in one file. A change to styles in that one file will automatically modify styles in whatever Web pages are linked to it.

And since there can be many style sheet languages, the ability to specify what language is being used makes it possible to use the author's language of choice. Coupled with the ability of some style sheet languages to "cascade" their style instructions, this means that authors have a wealth of options for implementing styles.

Additional capabilities offered by the style sheet mechanism include specifying the media with which styles should be displayed, specifying an alternate style sheet to be used in certain circumstances, and placing rendering instructions in the affected elements themselves to improve rendering performance.

8.1 Style in HTML Pages and Style Sheets

Style sheets refer to code written in a special syntax/language that can be used to apply stylistic formatting to a single element, an entire document, or multiple documents from a separate file. A style sheet command consists of the *selector*, which matches one or more elements, and the *declaration*, which declares the property affected and the value that property should take for the elements selected. The following code gives a simple example of using an external file for retrieving style information:

```
<HTML><HEAD><TITLE>Style Sheet Demo 1</TITLE>
<LINK href="externalstyle1.css" rel="stylesheet"
   type="text/css">
</HEAD>
<BODY bgcolor="#FFFFFF">
<P class="parastyle">This paragraph has brown text.
<P>This paragraph does not.
</BODY></HTML>
```

The code in the example above links the current HTML page to the external style sheet file named "externalstyle1.css". Setting the *rel* attribute to "stylesheet" makes this a persistent style sheet, and setting the *type* attribute to "text/css" tells the browser what style sheet language is being used. The contents of the style sheet file are:

```
P.parastyle {
color : brown;
}
```

In the style sheet file the capital P is the selector, and immediately following it (after the dot) is the name of the class this selector is associated with. This name is created by the author of the document, and applied to any P elements desired (notice that in the HTML file the *class* attribute of the first paragraph is assigned a value of "parastyle").

The color attribute of P elements (in the P selector) is set in the external style sheet file to "brown" via the declaration (the property in this declaration is "color" and the value for that property is set to "brown"), and this color is then applied to any P elements in the HTML file whose class attribute is set to "parastyle". If a P element has no class attribute value, or a different one, then the external style sheet has no effect. However, if no class is referenced in the external style sheet, the style given to that selector will be applied to all P elements by default.

8.2 CSS2 Selectors and Syntax

Selectors are used to identify the elements a particular style will apply to, and in their most basic form are simply the same as element names. For example, the P selector above refers to the P element. However, CSS2 is termed a style sheet language, and its developers included methods for identifying more than one element in a document to make using the language convenient. Upon consideration, it is apparent that an author may want to identify all elements, a single element occurring many times, an element of a given class, or an individual element among many occurrences of that element. Because there are many ways authors might want to identify elements, there are many ways CSS2 can target elements.

For example, the asterisk can be used as a *universal* selector, matching all elements in a document. A *type* selector is equivalent to the element name it is intended to match. A *type* selector could be any element followed by the appropriate properties (such as color) and their values (such as brown). There are also *descendant* selectors, which occur within the context of another element (italicized text within an H element, for instance), *child* selectors, which are elements that are children of other elements (an LI element that is a child of an OL element, for instance), selectors which match when a particular attribute (even down to the value an attribute takes) is present in an element, and selectors matching on *class* or *id* attributes, as shown in our example code above.

Generally, the syntax of CSS2 resembles the example already given, where the selector is followed by one or more statements or rules associating properties and their values with an element or a set of elements. For example, the following code makes all H2 elements appear green and italicized:

```
H2 { color : green; font-style : italic;}
```

Notice that the properties and their values appear within curly braces, properties and values separated by colons, and property-value pairs ending with semicolons. Each property-value pair is called a *declaration* or *rule*, and they can be on separate lines or on the same line.

8.3   Setting the Style Sheet Language for HTML Documents

Because there are many style sheet languages that may be applied to a document, it is important to set the language an author wishes to use. This can be done by inserting the identifier for the language into a META element, as shown here:

```
<META http-equiv="Content-Style-Type" content="text/css2">
```

If the style sheet language is specified in a META element, that takes precedence. If the author has control over the server, it is possible to set the style sheet language using an HTTP header, where the header is identified as "Content-Style-Type" of "text/css2". An HTTP header style sheet language setting has a lower precedence than a setting in a META element. If no settings are present, the default setting is "text/css".

8.4 Creating Style References in Inline Elements

One of the core attributes applicable to just about every HTML element is the *style* attribute, for the good reason that most HTML elements should be capable of having formatting styles associated with them. This attribute can be set for any appropriate property-value pair, thereby modifying the style of that element alone. For example, the following code changes the style for a single paragraph within an HTML document, without using the STYLE element or external style sheets:

```
<ul>
  <li>Option 1</li>
  <li>Option 2</li>
  <li style="font-weight : bold;">Option 3 Bold</li>
  <li>Option 4</li>
</ul>
```

Notice the selector is not necessary, because the style information appears within the element itself. Also, it only applies to that single LI element and no other. Remember, the syntax for the property-value pair depends on the style sheet language used.

8.5 The STYLE Element

The STYLE element should be used to create style sheet settings in a group, inside an HTML document. Style sheet settings can be made for all elements, a single element, elements of a class, or individual elements identified with an id attribute. Typically these settings are found in the HEAD element of a document. Multiple STYLE elements can be present in the HEAD element, as well as multiple rules within a single STYLE element, like this:

```
<HEAD>
  <STYLE type="text/css2">
    <!--
      H2 {text-align : center}
      P { color : brown}
    -->
  </STYLE>
</HEAD>
```

Notice that there is no need for the ending semicolon when only one property-value pair is present for a selector. By the way, notice that there are HTML comment delimiters in the style sheet example. CSS2 allows for "commenting out" style sheet commands, so they won't appear as plain text in older browsers.

Both the starting and ending tags are required for the style element, and the DTD is:

```
<!ELEMENT STYLE - - %StyleSheet          -- style info -->
<!ATTLIST STYLE
  %i18n;                                  -- lang, dir, for use
                                             with title --
  type      %ContentType;   #REQUIRED -- content type of style
                                          language --
  media     %MediaDesc;     #IMPLIED  -- designed for use with
                                          these media --
  title     %Text;          #IMPLIED  -- advisory title --
  >
```

The *lang*, *dir*, and *title* attributes are supported by the STYLE element as well as the *type* and *media* attributes. The *type* attribute can be used to specify the content type for the style language (such as text/css2) and the *media* attribute can be used to specify the media to which the style applies (the default is "screen", meaning the style will be implemented on a screen).

To set styles for HTML elements of a class, the class name is first applied to the elements using their *class* attributes, like this:

```
<P class="style1">Any paragraph of this class has this style</P>
```

Next, the STYLE element is added to the HEAD of the document, with the class following the selector using dot notation (a period after the selector and then the class name), like so:

```
<HEAD>
  <STYLE type="text/css2">
   P.style1 { color : brown}
  </STYLE>
</HEAD>
```

Finally, to differentiate id from class (identifying elements not by selector, but by the *id* attribute), the pound sign is used, as in:

```
<HEAD>
  <STYLE type="text/css2">
   #astyle { color : brown}
  </STYLE>
</HEAD>
<P id="astyle">Any paragraph of this id has this style</P>
```

8.5.1   USING THE DIV AND SPAN ELEMENTS WITH THE STYLE ELEMENT

The DIV element is useful for containing and identifying blocks of elements, while the SPAN element serves essentially the same purpose for inline elements. Setting the *class* or *id* attribute to a particular value for either of these elements (and setting a style associated by the name of the *class* or *id* attribute with the STYLE element) is a convenient way to apply style across an entire block or within a paragraph. Here is an example of using the SPAN element and an associated class name:

```
<html><head><title>New Page 1</title>
<style>
<!--
span.thespan { color: #00FF00; font-size: 18pt; font-variant:
small-caps }
-->
</style>
</head><body>
<p>The text within the <span class="thespan">SPAN element
</span> is green, 18 points, and small caps</p>
</body></html>
```

Using the **DIV** element works in much the same way, as shown here:

```
<html><head><title>New Page 1</title>
<style>
<!--
div.thediv { color: #00FF00; font-size: 18pt; font-variant:
small-caps }
-->
</style>
</head><body>
<div class="thediv">
<p>Paragraphs within the DIV element have text that is green,
18 points, and small caps</p>
<p>Paragraphs within the DIV element have text that is green,
18 points, and small caps</p>
</div>
</body></html>
```

8.6   Conditional Use of Style Properties with Media Types

The *media* attribute of the STYLE element allows authors to choose style settings based on the media in which the content will be rendered. When a *media* attribute value is specified, the browser only loads style sheet information for the rendering media, thereby saving time as well.

Approved values for the *media* attribute are called *media descriptors*. The list is not yet a recommedation, and so may change, but the list of descriptors includes many common rendering media types. There are:

- All – Can be rendered on all devices.
- Aural – Can be rendered on speech synthesizers.
- Braille – Can be rendered on braille tactile feedback devices.
- Embossed – Can be rendered on paged braille printers.
- Handheld – Can be rendered on handheld devices.
- Print – Can be rendered on paper and is also useful for documents viewed in print preview mode.
- Projection – Can be rendered on projectors.
- Screen – Can be rendered on color computer screens.
- Tty – Can be rendered on media using a fixed-pitch character grid.
- Tv – Can be rendered on television-type devices.

An example of code setting various media types for the STYLE element is:

```
<HEAD>
  <STYLE type="text/css2" media="tv">
    P { font-size: 24pt}
  </STYLE>
  <STYLE type="text/css2" media="handheld">
   P { font-size: 8pt}
  </STYLE>
</HEAD>
```

8.7   Style Sheet Files and External Style Sheets

As the first style sheet example in this chapter indicated, style sheets may also be referenced from an external file. Using style sheets in this manner has a number of advantages, primarily ease of use and modification. Generating and modifying a style sheet once for thousands of pages is preferable to pasting the style sheet commands thousands of times, and making the same modification thousands of times.

Using the LINK element, an external style sheet can be referenced with a URL pointing to the style sheet, written in plain text. The *href* attribute of the LINK element is used for this purpose. The LINK element must be placed in the HEAD element of the Web page, and any number of external style sheet references may be included in the HEAD element. The *type* attribute of the LINK element is used to specify the language type for the style sheet (text/css2, for example). The *rel* and *title* attributes are used to determine whether the style sheet is persistent, preferred, or alternate. The meaning of these is:

- Persistent – The style sheet contains formatting that must be applied regardless of whatever other styles are applied. A style sheet is persistent when the *rel* attribute is set to "stylesheet" and no title attribute is present.

- Alternate – Users should be able to choose from among a number of style sheets. A style sheet is alternate when the *rel* attribute is set to "alternate stylesheet" and the *title* attribute is provided with a name for the alternate style sheet.

- Preferred – The author has specified a preferred style and the browser should use that style unless the user deliberately picks another style. A style sheet is preferred when the *rel* attribute is set to "stylesheet" and the *title* attribute is provided with a name for the preferred style sheet.

The *media* attribute of the LINK element can also be used with external style sheets, with the same results as the same attribute of the STYLE element. External style sheet files will only be loaded for the media in use, avoiding downloading style sheets inappropriate for the current media.

8.8   Cascading Style Sheets

Some style sheet languages (such as CSS2) have the ability to incorporate elements from several style sheets into one document, according to a set of rules. This ability is called the ability to *cascade*, the idea being that one set of formatting characteristics is "poured" in, and then another set "cascades" in, and so forth, until all the formatting characteristics are applied. Technically, the styles are applied for the style sheet encountered first, but succeeding styles are applied preferentially, the last style encountered having the final say.

In the following example, the user is presented with several alternate style sheets to choose from: alt for "first.css" and alt1 for "second.css". If the user chooses "alt", styles from both style sheets (the one named first.css and the one named second.css) are mixed together and applied. The persistent style sheet named basic.css is applied in all cases.

```
<LINK rel="alternate stylesheet" title="alt"
href="first.css" type="text/css2">
<LINK rel="alternate stylesheet" title="alt"
href="second.css" type="text/css2">
<LINK rel="alternate stylesheet" title="alt2"
href="third.css" type="text/css2">
<LINK rel="stylesheet" href="basic.css" type="text/css2">
```

8.9   The Visual Formatting Model in CSS2

One of the features of CSS2 is the ability to specify, exactly to the pixel, positions of HTML elements on screen. Not only does this offer a level of two-dimensional positioning accuracy difficult or impossible to achieve with ordinary HTML, it also allows positioning in three dimensions. As an added bonus, scripting languages provide the capability to dynamically reposition objects on screen. Coupled with timer mechanisms in the popular scripting languages, the effect is animated motion of HTML elements, making for very lively pages.

Within the CSS Level 2 specification there is a discussion of the Visual Formatting Model. Within this model, each element in the DOM document tree (the hierarchy of elements of the DOM) generates zero or more boxes. Boxes, in turn, are described by a model of their own, called the Box Model. The Box Model should be thought of as a box surrounding the content within an element, with space around the box divided into (from the outside of the box) a margin, a border, padding, and finally the content of the element. Each section surrounding the box has a top, bottom, left, and right and dimensions for width and height that can be set in pixels.

The height and width of the content box are determined by the rendered size of the content (be it text, an image, an object, and so forth). Setting the border, height, and width attributes for an element affects the content box. The margin, border, and padding of a box, being divided into top, bottom, right, and left, can be addressed by abbreviations, such as LM for left margin, LP for left padding, and TB for top border. Each of these spacing constructs around a box can be sized in pixels, and the total size of a box depends upon the content size, the padding size, the border size, and the margin size. Note that margins are always transparent, while borders can assume a color value.

8.10   Positioning HTML Elements with CSS2

Once the sizing of a box is set, the box can be positioned in several ways with CSS2. They are called:

- Normal Flow – Includes block formatting of block boxes, inline formatting of inline boxes, as well as the positioning of compact and run-in boxes.

- Floating Boxes – Like images and tables, boxes can float to the right or left, and other content, such as text, can wrap around a box.

- Absolute Positioning – A box is arbitrarily assigned an exact position and is undisturbed by the position of other elements or boxes on the page, whether or not it intrudes upon their space.

Positions for content boxes are set in relationship to the *containing box*. This is either the screen itself (for high-level objects) or a box which contains the box in question. It may help to think of a Web page as being a box in itself (the screen in which the content is displayed) containing many smaller boxes which themselves can contain boxes, all the way down to the smallest elements.

To set the position of a box, the *position* and *float* properties can be set. The *position* property can take the values static (normal flow), relative (offset from the normal flow position), absolute (positioned absolutely from the top, bottom, left, and right edges), and fixed (absolute positioning that remains in the same spot on the screen even when scrolled). The *float* property can be set to left or right, as usual. Here is an example of code in which some of these properties are set:

```
<HTML><HEAD><TITLE>CSS2 Positioning Properties</TITLE>
<STYLE type="text/css">
  BODY { height: 14in }
  #head {
   position: fixed;
   width: 100%;
   height: 10%;
   top: 0;
   right: 0;
   bottom: auto;
   left: 0;
  }
  #menu {
   position: fixed;
   width: 10em;
   height: auto;
   top: 10%;
   right: auto;
   bottom: 100px;
   left: 0;
  }
  #content {
   position: fixed;
   width: auto;
   height: auto;
   top: 10%;
   right: 0;
   bottom: 100px;
   left: 10em;
  }
  #foot {
   position: fixed;
   width: 100%;
   height: 100px;
   top: auto;
   right: 0;
   bottom: 0;
   left: 0;
  }
</STYLE>
</HEAD>
<BODY>
<DIV id="head">This text goes in the head of the document</DIV>
```

```
<DIV id="menu">This text goes in the menu of the document</DIV>
<DIV id="content">This text goes in the content area of the
document</DIV>
<DIV id="foot">This text goes in the foot of the document</DIV>
</BODY></HTML>
```

8.11   Absolute Positioning in the Third Dimension: The Z Index

While Virtual Reality Modeling Language (VRML) Websites can be rendered in three dimensions, ordinary HTML Web pages do not have this capacity. However, objects on screen can be "layered" in three dimensions, using the CSS2 z-index property. Using this property does not produce a three-dimensional effect, but will cause objects to appear on top of or below one another. For example, in Fig. 8-1 two flags are shown, one on top of the other. This is actually two image files, one absolutely positioned so that it falls on top of the other. Since the first flag is not positioned and the second one is, it automatically falls on top of the first image. However, if the z-index property is explicitly set, objects with a lower z-index value will be rendered "below" any objects with a higher z-index value. There is no starting value, no ending value, and no specified interval for z-index values; the only thing that counts is the sequential order of the integers.

8.12   Dynamic HTML

Dynamic HTML (DHTML) is an odd step-child of ordinary HTML, and in fact it has no formal mention anywhere in the HTML 4.01 recommendation. Instead, the recommendation refers to an author's ability, with scripts, to dynamically reassign the attribute values and content of coded HTML elements. Essentially, DHTML is the name given to this ability, but it means different things within the various browsers.

Within Internet Explorer the SPAN element is used to apply dynamically changing styles and positioning for a particular element or set of elements, while Netscape extends HTML with the LAYER tag, which performs essentially the same function (except that Navigator 4 and below do not allow dynamic changes to properties). In both cases, the bulk of the documentation refers to how to define a section, define styles, and change them (and content) with scripting languages.

8.13 Using Scripts to Dynamically Modify Attributes and Content

As we've mentioned previously, there are many events supported by HTML elements (as objects), and within scripting languages additional objects may be referenced, including the entire window displaying the contents of a Web page.

When a document is loaded the page load event may fire, and scripts can detect and use this as a trigger for executing script commands, including the modification of content values (such as text or an image) or attribute values (such as what color the background is or the location on screen of an element).

The HTML recommendation offers a few rules for processing dynamic modifications. For example, SCRIPT elements are evaluated and processed in the order in which they occur in the document, and any commands that produce SGML CDATA are processed and then inserted into the document in place of the SCRIPT element, after which the document is re-evaluated. In practice these rules mean that the browser reads through the document, processes each SCRIPT element in order, replaces the elements with the results of its processing, and then rebuilds the page accordingly.

Microsoft and Netscape have differing interpretations and implementations of DHTML, but many of the principles used are the same. In the following sections both will be discussed.

8.14 Using Dynamic HTML with Internet Explorer

Microsoft's Internet Explorer versions 4.0 and above support DHTML with the DOM and intrinsic events. All Web page elements are considered objects that can be manipulated, having their attributes changed or methods applied to them anytime during use. For example, a script function could be written to change the background color of the BODY element (an attribute of the BODY element) or write text upon the page (the application of the *write* method to the document) in response to any event, such as clicking on a button. Microsoft calls the ability to dynamically change content Dynamic Content, the ability to dynamically change attributes (or element styles) Dynamic Styles, and the ability to dynamically position elements within a Web page Dynamic Positioning.

Internet Explorer versions 5.0 and above are also capable of Data-Binding. This term refers to the ability to connect data displayed in a Web page directly to a back-end database, and to modify the display of the data (showing more or less data, filtering data, and so forth) without having to reconnect and re-retrieve data from the database each time.

Microsoft's FrontPage contains features that automate the process of generating code (scripting, HTML, and CSS2 code) to create animations, page transitions, outlining, and enhancements to forms. Some of these features rely on prewritten Javascript that comes with FrontPage while other features rely on built-in capabilities of Internet Explorer. Some of the built-in capabilities do not exist in other browsers, making it inadvisable to use them except in restricted environments where users have only Internet Explorer (such as in certain Intranets). Here is an example of code that works for Internet Explorer, created in FrontPage 2000:

```
<html><head>
<meta http-equiv="Content-Language" content="en-us">
<meta http-equiv="Content-Type" content="text/html;
charset=windows-1252">
<meta name="GENERATOR" content="Microsoft FrontPage 4.0">
<meta name="ProgId" content="FrontPage.Editor.Document">
<title>Here is some ordinary text</title>
<script language="JavaScript" fptype="dynamicanimation">
<!--
function dynAnimation() {}
function clickSwapImg() {}
//-->
</script>
<script language="JavaScript1.2" fptype="dynamicanimation"
src="animate.js">
</script>
</head>
<body onload="dynAnimation()" language="Javascript1.2">
<p>Here is some ordinary text.</p>
<p><font face="Arial Black" color="#800000">Here is text with
a style applied using the FONT element.</font></p>
<p dynamicanimation="fpAnimformatRolloverFP1"
fprolloverstyle="font-size: 24pt; color: #FF00FF;
font-style: italic" onclick="clickSwapStyle(this)"
language="Javascript1.2">Here is text with a dynamic style
applied.</p>
<p dynamicanimation="fpAnimdropWordFP1"
id="fpAnimdropWordFP1" style="position: relative
!important; visibility: hidden"
language="Javascript1.2">Here is text that is animated, the
animation running when the page load event occurs.</p>
<p>Here are two flags, positioned absolutely, one on top of the
other:</p>
<p><img border="0" src="BrazilFlag.gif" width="104"
height="62"><span style="position: absolute; left: 56; top:
236"><img border="0" src="SpainFlag.gif" width="102"
height="60"></span></p>
</body></html>
```

Notice that the animate.js script was referenced rather than completely written into the page. Fig. 8-1 shows how this looks in the browser, with the third line

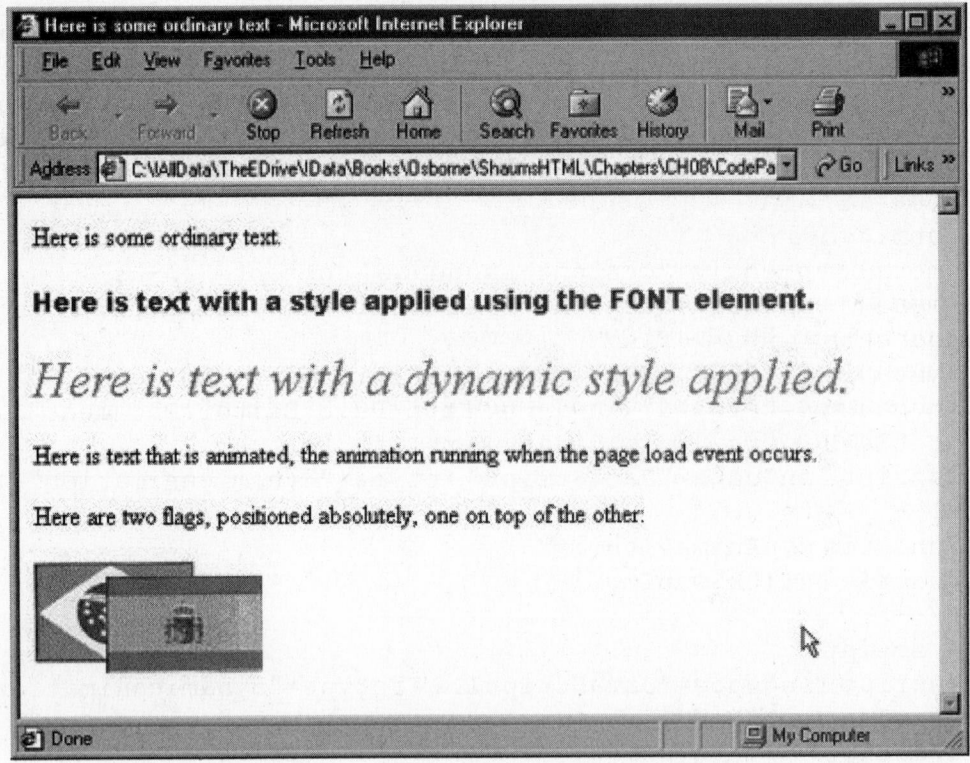

Fig. 8-1.   DHTML effects in Internet Explorer.

clicked on to activate the dynamic style (the fourth line dropped in when the page was loaded).

8.15   Using Dynamic HTML with Netscape Navigator

Netscape Navigator version 4.0 also incorporated DHTML capabilities into its list of features, but used a somewhat different approach. All the same DHTML capabilities are present in Netscape Navigator, but they are applied using either a *style* attribute with a defined position or the LAYER element, which is Netscape specific. Here is an example of code created with Macromedia's Dreamweaver, using both the DIV element and the LAYER element. The second box, created with the LAYER element, has also been animated.

```
<!-- Please note that the scripting in this code was created
with Macromedia's Dreamweaver 2.0, and is subject to copyright
by Macromedia -->
<html><head><title>Untitled Document</title>
<meta http-equiv="Content-Type" content="text/html;
charset=iso-8859-1">
```

```javascript
<script language="JavaScript">
<!--
function MM_initTimelines() {
   //MM_initTimelines() Copyright 1997 Macromedia, Inc. All
     rights reserved.
   var ns = navigator.appName == "Netscape";
   document.MM_Time = new Array(1);
   document.MM_Time[0] = new Array(2);
   document.MM_Time["Timeline1"] = document.MM_Time[0];
   document.MM_Time[0].MM_Name = "Timeline1";
   document.MM_Time[0].fps = 15;
   document.MM_Time[0][0] = new String("sprite");
   document.MM_Time[0][0].slot = 1;
   if (ns)
      document.MM_Time[0][0].obj = document["Layer2"];
   else
      document.MM_Time[0][0].obj = document.all ?
        document.all["Layer2"] : null;
   document.MM_Time[0][0].keyFrames = new Array(1, 15);
   document.MM_Time[0][0].values = new Array(2);
   document.MM_Time[0][0].values[0] = new
Array(463,463,463,463,463,463,463,463,463,463,463,463,
        463,463,463);
   document.MM_Time[0][0].values[0].prop = "left";
   document.MM_Time[0][0].values[1] = new
Array(55,55,55,55,55,55,55,55,55,55,55,55,55,55,55);
   document.MM_Time[0][0].values[1].prop = "top";
   if (!ns) {
      document.MM_Time[0][0].values[0].prop2 = "style";
      document.MM_Time[0][0].values[1].prop2 = "style";
   }
   document.MM_Time[0][1] = new String("sprite");
   document.MM_Time[0][1].slot = 1;
   if (ns)
      document.MM_Time[0][1].obj = document["Layer2"];
   else
      document.MM_Time[0][1].obj = document.all ?
        document.all["Layer2"] : null;
   document.MM_Time[0][1].keyFrames = new Array(16, 31, 35,
        36, 37, 38, 39, 40, 58, 65);
   document.MM_Time[0][1].values = new Array(2);
   document.MM_Time[0][1].values[0] = new
Array(25,35,44,54,63,73,82,92,101,109,118,125,133,140,
147,153,168,177,185,191,199,205,207,207,207,215,223,
231,240,250,260,271,283,295,308,320,332,343,354,365,
374,384,393,407,419,428,437,446,454,463);
   document.MM_Time[0][1].values[0].prop = "left";
```

```
   document.MM_Time[0][1].values[1] = new
Array(163,159,154,150,145,141,136,132,127,123,120,116,
113,110,107,104,99,97,97,97,91,85,84,83,82,81,80,78,77,
76,74,73,71,69,67,65,64,62,61,59,58,57,56,55,54,54,54,
54,55,55);
   document.MM_Time[0][1].values[1].prop = "top";
   if (!ns) {
      document.MM_Time[0][1].values[0].prop2 = "style";
      document.MM_Time[0][1].values[1].prop2 = "style";
   }
   document.MM_Time[0].lastFrame = 65;
   for (i=0; i<document.MM_Time.length; i++) {
      document.MM_Time[i].ID = null;
      document.MM_Time[i].curFrame = 0;
      document.MM_Time[i].delay = 1000/document.MM_Time
        [i].fps;
   }
}
//-->
</script>
</head>
<body bgcolor="#FFFFFF">
<div id="Layer1" style="position:absolute; width:200px;
height:115px; z-index:1; background-color: #CCFFFF; layer-
background-color: #CCFFFF; border: 1px none #000000">This box
contains the first Layer, and has a background color different
from the page </div>
<p> </p>
<p> </p>
<p> </p>
<layer id="Layer2" width="200" height="115" z-index="2"
bgcolor="#FFCCCC" left="463" top="55"> <p>This box contains
the second Layer, which also has a different background color
as well as an image<img src="BrazilFlag.gif" width="104"
height="62"> This box is created with the LAYER tag, and
therefore is not accessible with Internet Explorer.</p>
<p> </p>
</layer>
<p> </p>
</body></html>
```

Review Questions

8.1. What issues does the word "style" address, in the context of HTML style sheets?

8.2. What is a style sheet selector?

8.3. What is the relationship between style sheets and HTML?

8.4. How may styles be referenced in an HTML page?

8.5. What property can be set in order to change the color of paragraph text to red (from the default black)?

8.6. Besides a direct reference to an HTML element via a style sheet selector, in what other ways can CSS2 selectors be set to reference HTML elements?

8.7. What is the purpose of identifying a style sheet language in a META tag? Give an example.

8.8. Why would it be convenient to use a STYLE element or an external style sheet file rather than putting the style directly into the element whose style is to be modified?

8.9. What method can be used to make style property values apply to an HTML element, but only specific elements found within a document?

8.10. What does the term "cascading" mean with reference to style sheets?

8.11. How might using the DIV and SPAN elements make the application of styles to particular elements easier?

8.12. There are many platforms upon which Web pages may be displayed. What provisions exist within CSS2 to cope with the possibility that a single Web page may be displayed on a variety of platforms?

8.13. What HTML is used to set styles in inline elements? How might it be written?

8.14. What provisions does CSS2 have for avoiding the possibility that older browsers might mistakenly render style selectors and settings as plain text?

8.15. What are the main components of the Visual Formatting model in CSS2? How do they work?

8.16. What positioning methods may be used with object boxes in CSS2?

8.17. What properties affect the position of an object when absolute positioning is used? How do these properties work?

8.18. What is Dynamic HTML, and how is it discussed in the HTML recommendation?

8.19. What benefit is there in scripting changes to a Web page?

8.20. How would processing by scripting be initiated when a form is submitted?

Solved Problems

8.1. Show the inline element CSS2 code to make a heading of size 2 (H2) rendered in green.

```
<H2 style="color:green">The Green Heading</H2>
```

8.2. Show the STYLE element CSS2 code to make all H2 elements on a page render as green.

```
<STYLE>
<!--
H2 {color:green}
-->
</STYLE>
```

8.3. Show the code for referencing a persistent external style sheet in a file named "mystyle.css", in which all elements on a page are rendered green. What makes the style sheet persistent?

Within the page itself the reference is made:

```
<HTML><HEAD><TITLE> Green Style Sheet Demo</TITLE>
<LINK href="mystyle.css" rel="stylesheet" type="text/css">
</HEAD>
<BODY bgcolor="#FFFFFF">
<P>This paragraph has green text.</P>
<P>So does this paragraph.</P>
</BODY></HTML>
```

Within the style sheet file the following code, using the wildcard element selector *, sets all elements to be rendered green:

```
* {color:green}
```

The style sheet is considered persistent because the *rel* attribute is set to "stylesheet" and there is no *title* attribute.

8.4. Using a STYLE element, show the HTML and CSS2 code that would be appropriate for making a block of several paragraphs, images, and a form all have a background color of turquoise.

For the STYLE element, the code might look like this:

```
<STYLE>
<!--
DIV.myblock {background-color: #00FFFF}
-->
</STYLE>
```

For the block of paragraphs, images, and the form, the code might look like this:

```
<DIV class="myblock">
<P>First paragraph</P>
<P>Second paragraph</P>
<IMG src="myimage.gif">
<FORM METHOD="POST" ACTION="myasppage.asp">form contents
</FORM>
</DIV>
```

8.5. Show the HTML and CSS2 code that could be used to generate a series of images on top of one another, using the same image five times, each time getting a bit smaller, making an effect similar to that shown in Fig. 8-2.

```
<html><head>
<meta http-equiv="Content-Type" content="text/html;
charset=windows-1252">
<title>New Page 1</title></head>
<body>
<p align="center">
<img border="0" src="FranceFlag.gif" width="412"
height="282">
<span style="position: absolute; left: 178; top: 47">
<img border="0" src="FranceFlag.gif" width="351"
height="228"></span>
<span style="position: absolute; left: 211; top: 86"> <img
border="0" src="FranceFlag.gif" width="285"
height="158"></span>
<span style="position: absolute; left: 247; top: 115">
```

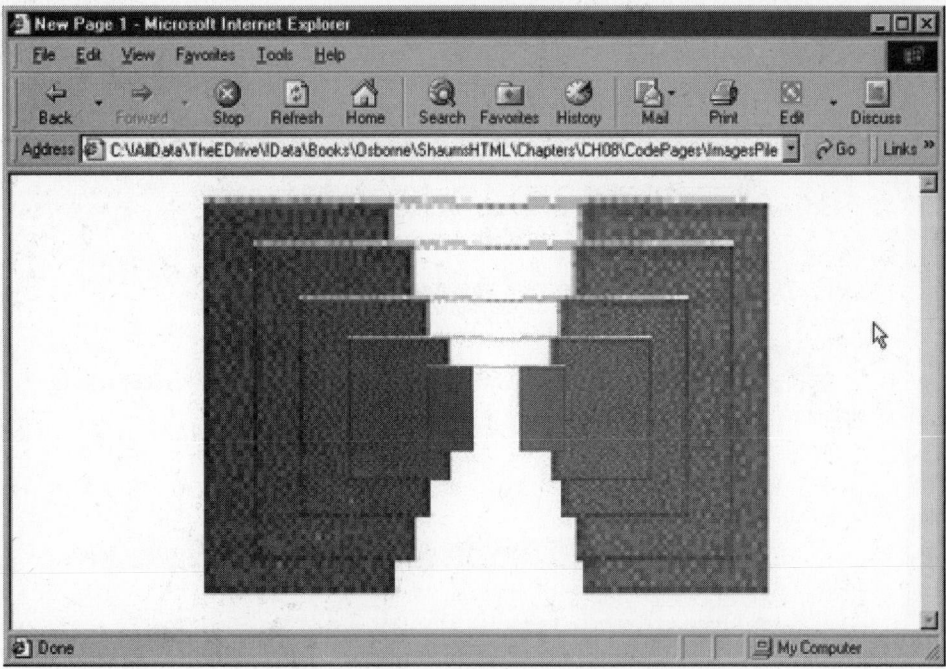

Fig. 8-2.   An image piled on top of itself.

```
<img border="0" src="FranceFlag.gif" width="222"
height="103"></span>
<span style="position: absolute; left: 305; top: 136">
<img border="0" src="FranceFlag.gif" width="101"
height="61"></span></p>
</body></html>
```

8.6. Show the HTML, Javascript, and CSS2 code which would create three buttons, with two of the buttons in the same space on screen, overlapping but not completely covering one another. Include a Javascript that references the second button and changes its z-index so that it changes from being under the first button to being over the first button, and make the Javascript active when the Onclick event occurs for the third button. In appearance it should resemble Fig. 8-3.

```
<html><head><title>Buttons Swapping Places</title>
<script language="JavaScript">
function swapplaces() {
document.all.button2.style.zIndex=99
}
</script>
</head>
<body>
<p>
<input id="button1" name="button1" style="LEFT: 75px;
POSITION: absolute; TOP: 135px; Z-INDEX: 100" type="button"
value="Button Number 1">
<input id="button2" name="button2" style="LEFT: 99px;
POSITION: absolute; TOP: 149px; Z-INDEX: 101" type="button"
value="Button Number 2">
<input id="button3" name="button3" style="LEFT: 130px;
```

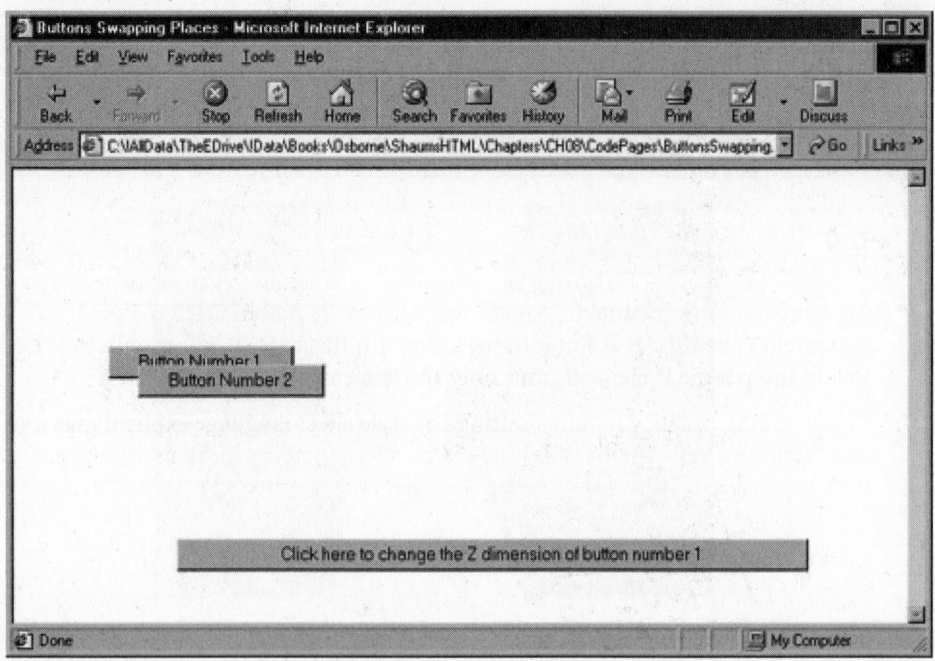

Fig. 8-3.   Three buttons; two swapping places.

```
POSITION: absolute; TOP: 281px; Z-INDEX: 102" type="button"
value="Click here to change the Z dimension of button number 1"
onclick="swapplaces();">
</p>
</body></html>
```

 # Answers to Review Questions

8.1. Style refers to the visual presentation of information on a Web page. Plain text documents do little to enhance the presentation of information, although it can certainly be said that a well-written text document is more valuable than a poorly written or flawed but very nicely styled document. HTML style sheets offer the author control over such things as font face, color, font size, and other individually selectable elements on a Web page.

8.2. A style sheet selector is a reference to an HTML element. For example, the P element is one of the elements in HTML, and the style sheet selector P refers to the P element in HTML. Styles applied to the P selector may affect P elements in a Web page.

8.3. The Cascading Style Sheets Level 2 (CSS2) specification is a current version of one style sheet language that may be applied to Web pages, but it is not the only one. However, CSS2 is not the only style sheet language that may be applied, but it is important because the major browsers happen to support it. CSS2 is not a part of the HTML recommendation, but is easily referenced from Web pages.

8.4. Styles can be referenced within a single element using the *style* attribute, from a STYLE element, or from an external style sheet file. When referenced from a STYLE element or from an external style sheet file, more than one style may be set.

8.5. The color property can be set to red for the P selector, thereby changing paragraphs in a Web page from the default black to red.

8.6. Selectors can be direct references, such as the P selector referencing the P element. But selectors can also use wildcard characters to refer to individual elements or groups of elements. For example, the asterisk is a universal selector and refers to all elements in a document. And if one selector is placed after the other in a CSS2 statement (like this: P B { color:red}), then (in this case) it refers only to B elements inside the parent P element, and only those elements will be red.

8.7. Good coding practice requires setting the style sheet language explicitly via a META tag. Doing so tells the browser the style sheet language to be used, like so:

```
<META http-equiv="Content-Style-Type"
content="text/css2">
```

8.8. Setting several style property values in a STYLE element or an external style sheet is easier to do initially from a STYLE element or an external style sheet because all style information is contained in one area and is therefore easier to read. Using this method also makes maintenance easier, especially with external style sheets when a Website has many pages to which the same or similar styles must be applied.

8.9. The author may use dot notation to indicate the class of object within a set of HTML elements to which the style properties apply. Within the STYLE element or external style sheet the name of the class follows the selector, like this:

```
P.theclass {color:brown}
```

Within the HTML document, P elements to be styled with a brown color should have the value of their class attribute set to the name of the class, like this:

```
<P class="theclass">This will be brown</P>
```

8.10. Some style sheet languages support a cascading mechanism by which multiple style sheets can be applied to a single document. The term cascading refers to the process by which style sheet properties are applied to HTML elements from several style sheets in a preferential order.

8.11. The DIV and SPAN elements are convenient containers of text and other HTML elements, and making them part of a class of elements or giving them a particular *id* attribute value allows styles to be applied to these elements, and thereby to the elements they contain.

8.12. CSS2 uses media descriptors to identify, in a general way, some of the platforms upon which Web pages may be displayed or rendered. Including a media descriptor via the *media* attribute of the STYLE element, for example, provides information to the browser that can be used to distinguish between styles that are appropriate for a given platform and those that aren't, thereby avoiding downloading style information that cannot be used.

8.13. For inline elements, the style attribute is used to designate a particular style for a given element. Because the style information is already inside the element, no selector is needed to "find" the element in the code. The value of the style attribute is the name of the property (and this property must be appropriate for the element it affects) followed by a colon, followed by the property setting.

8.14. With CSS2 the *style* attribute in an inline element will be ignored by older browsers, but selectors and settings inside STYLE elements may be interpreted as text by older browsers. Therefore, authors may enclose style settings inside the STYLE element within HTML comment delimiters, like so:

```
<STYLE>
<!--
P.thepara{ color: green; font-size: 10pt }
-->
</STYLE>
```

8.15. The Visual Formatting Model in CSS2 refers to the methodology used to identify objects on screen and provide them with rendering information. Each object is part of the DOM, and has a place in the document tree, or hierarchy. For example, a form is an object in a Web page, and the form's parent object is the document, while child objects of the form may be form controls. The form is inside the document, and form controls are inside the form. A form named "myform" can be referenced by its name using dot notation, like so: Document.myform. If there is a control on the form named "phonenumber" it can also be referenced in the same manner, like this: Document.myform.phonenumber.

Each object on the screen generates a box in which it "lives" and this box has several definable edges, representing margins, borders, padding, and so on. This is called the Box Model. Object boxes are contained within boxes generated by parent objects, in the same way boxed gifts may be packed inside a larger mailing box for shipment. Each box has its own properties, but may be impacted by its parent boxes depending upon the positioning method used. The size and type of content of each object affects the boxes generated for each object, and the structure of these boxes and the positioning method used ultimately defines the layout on screen of all objects in a page.

8.16. The normal flow method positions objects according to how they would ordinarily fall in an HTML page. For example, text and images normally flow to the left and to the top of a page, until they "bump into" another element. In the Box Model the edges of each element or object is defined in pixels, and two objects will not intrude upon each other when the normal flow method is used.

The float method can be used with CSS2 so that objects may be floated to the right or left, in the same way images and tables can be floated to the right or left. When an object is floated, text will wrap around it, similar to the way text wraps around an image that has its *align* attribute set to "left" or "right".

The absolute position method can be used to set a place on the page for an object regardless of the positions of other objects on the page, meaning that objects can intrude upon each other, and overlap on screen. This makes it possible to place one image on top of another, or even one block of text on top of another.

8.17. An object absolutely positioned has an x-index property, a y-index property, and a z-index property. The x and y indexes are set from the top (for the y-index) and from the left (for the x-index) in pixels. The z-index is simply a sequence of integers, starting with any number, ending with any number, and with any amount (in integers) used as any interval. Browsers automatically place objects with higher numbers "on top of" objects with lower z-index numbers on screen.

8.18. Dynamic HTML has a number of interpretations, depending upon the browser maker in whose browser it is supported, but basically refers to the ability to change properties of elements after a page is initially rendered. There is no specific reference in the HTML recommendation to DHTML, but there is mention of the ability to dynamically change object attributes using scripting. Because objects can be identified using dot notation, their attributes can be changed when a scripted function occurs.

8.19. A good example is the ability to detect the current value of a form control when the form is submitted. If a field designated by the author as required has not been filled in by the user, this can be detected and a warning message immediately supplied to the user, asking that the field be filled in before the form is submitted. This is called form validation, and it is a very common addition to HTML forms on Web pages.

While the primary benefit of form validation is an increased likelihood that valid data will be submitted with a given form, a more subtle benefit is that the processing occurs on the user's machine, relieving the server of a task, and also saving a round-trip to the server, thereby making the process work more quickly.

8.20. Each object on a Web page has events it supports, and scripting can detect these events occurring. For example, when a submit button is pushed, the onsubmit event occurs. Prior to the submit action being completed, scripted functions defined as being activated by the onsubmit event must be completed.

CHAPTER 9

The XHTML Specification

9.1   What is XHTML 1.0?

XHTML 1.0 is actually the World Wide Web Consortium's (W3C) next iteration of the HTML standard. XHTML itself is a series of document types that conform to the XML standard. According to the documentation it is HTML 4.01 reformulated to include the strengths of HTML (including, no doubt, the fact that HTML is very widely accepted and used) and the power of XML. XHTML is now the current recommendation for HTML. XHTML is also an XML application, and we discuss XML in greater detail in Chapter 10.

XHTML is closely related to HTML. In fact, it relies upon the HTML 4.01 meaning for each element, making the XHTML specification itself much smaller. However, it is more rigid in its standards for syntax and coding than HTML 4.01. The purpose of this chapter is to illustrate the differences between HTML and XHTML, and offer examples of how to code documents properly with XHTML, as opposed to HTML. Therefore, HTML elements and attributes may be discussed.

XHTML has some advantages over ordinary HTML. For example, XHTML is XML *conforming*, meaning it can be viewed and edited with XML tools. XHTML also can utilize scripts or applications that conform to the DOM. Essentially, XHTML is the next step in the evolution of HTML.

XHTML is a logical next step for HTML because of HTML's inherent limitations, and the major browsers seem to respond fine to XHTML's version of HTML's syntax. HTML cannot be individualized or extended in a very practical way (as is evident from the browser wars in which both the major browser manufacturers introduce their own HTML extensions, which the other rarely supports), while XHTML extensions are relatively easy to support. As an added benefit, if the author follows a few guidelines XHTML documents can still be understood by older browsers, and so the transition can begin now, rather than waiting for browsers supporting XHTML to appear.

9.2   Transitional, Strict, and Frameset XHTML

As for HTML, there are three DTDs for XHTML: *transitional*, *strict*, and *frameset*. The frameset version supports everything in the transitional version plus framesets, while the strict version is useful for highly conforming code that doesn't include deprecated (old) elements and attributes. To specify one of these versions you must include the DTD line at the beginning of your document. See section 9.5.1, "All Documents Must Have a DOCTYPE Declaration", for more details.

9.3   Converting HTML Documents to XHTML

Web authors are sure to ask what tools are available for converting standard HTML documents to XHTML documents, as it seems likely that the translation can be accomplished by following fairly well-defined procedures, and performing the translation by hand would be tedious and prone to error. The World Wide Web consortium (www.w3.org) maintains a tool named "HTML Tidy" at its Website. HTML Tidy is a free download, and it cleans up regular HTML code. This is the first step in conversion. You can then use the tool to convert HTML code into a format compatible with XHTML. One of the benefits of converting HTML documents to XHTML is they can be processed by XML-capable browsers, a likely requirement in the future, in view of XML's increasing popularity.

9.4   The Modularization of XHTML

The authors of XHTML 1.0 have broken the language into a number of modules defined using the XML DTD language, and expect to redefine these modules using XML Schemas when this standard is ready. The purpose for modularization is to create separate, intact subsets of XHTML functionality, so that the modules may be combined together to form a coherent, complete language and also so the modules may be used with other, yet-to-be-defined modules created by anyone with an interest in using XHTML as a content language, no matter what platform the content is to be rendered on.

Essentially, XHTML modules are language building blocks oriented towards user interface and display, while XML languages (of which XHTML is one) are general purpose languages suitable not only for user interface and display, but for machine interface and communication as well. The beauty of modularized XHTML is that it lends itself to building new user interface and display (or rendering) easily, using modules of the language appropriate for a particular platform. One of the goals of modularization is to help browser makers avoid the "extension" syndrome, whereby each new version of a browser supports some but not all of the core HTML elements and only certain proprietary "extensions" to HTML.

9.4.1 ABSTRACT MODULES

Each XHTML document consists of a set of modules, and abstract modules give meaning to the data. In a given module the data is semantically different from any other module, and the abstract module helps people understand what that data means by explaining the contents in terms people can understand, rather than simply being machine-readable. The modules can then be combined to make coherent documents without the author necessarily understanding every aspect of the underlying structure of the data in the modules.

The DTD for an XHTML module is referred to as an *implementation*, and there is work underway in XML to use XML schemas to define modules. XML schemas are discussed in further detail in Chapter 10. As with HTML DTDs, an XHTML DTD defines elements, attributes, and the types of content that may be contained in them. Attributes and content defined in one module may affect elements defined in another module.

9.4.2 BUILDING ABSTRACT MODULES

Certain conventions are followed when authoring XHTML modules, to make them understandable and coherent. For example, if an element is to be included in a module, its name must be listed. If sets of element names are defined (called *content sets*) the names of these sets will be listed. If expressions are allowed, the frequency with which they are allowed can be set with *wildcards*, such as the question mark ? (meaning zero or one instance of an expression is allowed), the asterisk * (zero or more instances allowed), the plus sign + (one or more), and so forth.

XHTML module elements have content types that are allowed, just like HTML. For example, an element may be "EMPTY" (having no content) or "PCDATA" (parsed character data or text) and so forth. XHTML element attributes also have allowable types, such as "CDATA" (character data), "ID" (document-unique identifiers), and so forth. In addition to the ordinary HTML attribute value types, XHTML adds a few new ones, such as "DATETIME", making XHTML more like traditional languages.

9.5 Differences Between HTML and XHTML

Making the conversion to XHTML is not very difficult for HTML authors, and in many cases simply tightens up coding practices. As mentioned, there are tools available to convert existing HTML pages to XHTML pages, but many authors find it necessary to understand hand-coding XHTML in the same way they understand hand-coding HTML. Hand-coding HTML (and XHTML) is often necessary when writing front-end or back-end scripting code such as Javascript, Perl, or Active Server Pages, whose output may include plain HTML or XHTML.

In this section the differences between HTML and XHTML are summarized, and in subsequent sections illustrations and examples are given, to assist HTML authors in making the transition. One of the primary requirements is that XHTML documents must be well-formed, or adhere to the rules of XML. For example, the HEAD and BODY elements are required, and the TITLE elements must be in the HEAD element. More of the XML rules, as well as the primary differences between HTML and XHTML, are listed here and then explained in more detail:

- All documents must have a DOCTYPE declaration.
- The root element of the document must be < HTML >.
- Elements and attributes must be lowercase.
- Attribute values must be encased in quotes, and not minimized.
- Leading and trailing spaces in attribute values will be stripped.
- Only the *id* attribute can be used to identify an element uniquely.
- Non-empty elements must be terminated, or have an ending tag.
- Elements must be nested, not overlapping.
- SCRIPT and STYLE elements must be marked as CDATA areas.

9.5.1   ALL DOCUMENTS MUST HAVE A DOCTYPE DECLARATION

The DOCTYPE declaration for HTML was discussed in Chapter 2, and it is optional for HTML documents, as the browsers automatically recognize HTML documents and support HTML elements. The DOCTYPE declarations for XHTML are based on those for HTML, and may change somewhat before being finalized as a recommendation. Essentially, they serve to inform programs what legal syntax is within an XHTML document, just as they would for an XML document of any type.

In XHTML all documents are required to have a DOCTYPE declaration and it must occur before the root element in the document, such as (for the Frameset DTD):

```
<!DOCTYPE html PUBLIC "-//W3C//DTD XHTML 1.0 Frameset//EN"
"http://www.w3.org/TR/xhtml1/DTD/frameset.dtd">
```

One of the three DTDs (Strict, Transitional, and Frameset) may be used. Note that if an HTML document contains style information within FONT or TABLE tags the Transitional DTD should be used for the XHTML document it is converted to, otherwise older browsers that don't support style sheets may not render elements as intended. The Strict DTD is used when style sheets provide for all style information, the Transitional DTD is used when deprecated HTML elements and attributes are used, and the Frameset DTD is used when the document has frames.

The Transitional DTD DOCTYPE declaration is:

```
<!DOCTYPE html PUBLIC "-//W3C//DTD XHTML 1.0
Transitional//EN"
"http://www.w3.org/TR/xhtml1/DTD/transitional.dtd">
```

The Strict DTD DOCTYPE declaration is:

```
<!DOCTYPE html PUBLIC "-//W3C//DTD XHTML 1.0 Strict//EN"
"http://www.w3.org/TR/xhtml1/DTD/strict.dtd">
```

9.5.2 THE ROOT ELEMENT OF THE DOCUMENT MUST BE <HTML>

Except for the DOCTYPE declaration, no other elements may come before the starting <html> tag, and no other elements may come after the ending </html> tag. Therefore, XHTML documents must begin with a DOCTYPE declaration immediately followed by the starting tag for the HTML element. The starting tag must also contain a reference to the XML namespace the document uses.

A *namespace* is a closed set of names that identify tags from a particular DTD. Because XHTML and XML are modularized, there is the possibility that two different DTDs (for two different modules) will have tags with the same names but meaning two different things according to their own DTD definition. Therefore, unique names must apply, and these names precede the tags when they are used, providing the browser with a way to properly render these tags. XML namespaces are discussed in greater detail in Chapter 10, in section 10.5, "XML Namespaces".

Here is an example of the coding for the HTML element in XHTML:

```
<html xmlns="http://www.w3.org/1999/xhtml">
```

9.5.3 ELEMENTS AND ATTRIBUTES MUST BE LOWERCASE

Unlike HTML, *XML is case-sensitive*, so all elements and attributes are written lowercase. Macromedia's Dreamweaver and other popular HTML editors allow authors to set the case for HTML produced, so it's often fairly easy to change or convert case. For example, the following code shows a typical HTML document and the HTML transformed to XHTML, with the appropriate case:

```
<HTML>
<HEAD>
<TITLE>This is the title</TITLE>
</HEAD>
<BODY bgcolor="#FFFFFF">
This is the body
</BODY>
</HTML>
```

For the transformed document:

```
<!DOCTYPE html PUBLIC "-//W3C//DTD XHTML 1.0 Transitional//EN"
"http://www.w3.org/TR/xhtml1/DTD/transitional.dtd">
<html xmlns="http://www.w3.org/1999/xhtml">
<head>
```

```
<title>This is the title</title>
</head> <body bgcolor="#FFFFFF">
This is the body
</body>
</html>
```

Note that attribute values are excluded from the case rule. This makes sense, because things like file name in URLs may be upper or lower case, and so cannot be restricted to lowercase.

9.5.4   ATTRIBUTE VALUES MUST BE IN QUOTES AND MUST NOT BE MINIMIZED

Another way XHTML differs from HTML, and is more strict, is that all attribute values must be in quotes, and minimized attributes are not allowed. This simply means that all attribute values are clearly indicated by quotation marks, and is an easy habit to pick up. Browsers currently allow nonquoted attribute values in some cases, but not others, so as a rule it is easy (and good coding practice) to use quoted attribute values anyway.

Somewhat harder to get used to is the lack of support for minimized attribute values. Minimized attribute values are those where simply entering the name of the attribute causes its function to occur. For example, in HTML, in an OPTION element within a SELECT element, including the *selected* attribute without a value makes that option selected when the form is rendered. In XHTML, the attribute must include a specific assignment of the value, in this case "selected", so the element would be coded:

```
<option selected="selected" value="thevalue">
The Value</option>
```

9.5.5   LEADING AND TRAILING SPACES IN ATTRIBUTE VALUES WILL BE STRIPPED

If an author includes leading or trailing white spaces in an attribute value, they will be stripped out. If there are white spaces within an attribute value, they will be mapped to a single space between words. For western scripts this is an ASCII space character.

9.5.6   ELEMENTS CAN ONLY USE THE *ID* ATTRIBUTE

Although the *name* attribute was heavily used in HTML to uniquely identify elements, in XHTML only the *id* attribute can be used. This conforms to XML but may pose some problems for converted HTML documents, especially where these documents are built on-the-fly by scripts. Technically, the name attribute is only deprecated in XHTML 1.0, but it will be eliminated in future versions, so it is best not to use it at all. Another thing to watch out for is that the range of values that may be applied to the *id* attribute is very restricted compared to the old *name* attribute. During the conversion process it is important to keep track of the values assigned to *id* attributes that were assigned to *name* attributes. Finally, the *id* attribute value for an element can only be used once within a document, and must be unique, unlike the same *name* attribute values which could be used many times in the same document.

9.5.7   NON-EMPTY ELEMENTS MUST BE TERMINATED

Any elements that have both a starting and ending tag must use both in XHTML. For example, whereas in HTML a paragraph could be delimited by only the starting <P> tag (placed at the end of every paragraph, if desired) in XHTML both the starting and ending tags must be in place.

For empty elements, an ending symbol with a space and a slash must be used, as shown here for the line break tag (<BR>):

```
<br />
```

The exception is when a non-empty element is used but has no content (so that it appears empty). In this case the author must not use the syntax above, but instead rely on the syntax using both the starting and ending tags, like this (for a paragraph with no content in it):

```
<p></p>
```

9.5.8   ELEMENTS MUST BE PROPERLY NESTED, NOT OVERLAPPING

In HTML, if an H element (a heading) of size 2 is to be italicized, the author can write:

```
<H2><I>Here is the italicized heading</H2></I>
```

In this example the H element starts before the I element and ends before the I element, overlapping it. This is supported in HTML, but not XHTML. In XHTML these elements would have to be properly nested, as shown here:

```
<h2><i>Here is the italicized heading</i></h2>
```

There is no provision in XML to exclude nesting certain elements within one another (as long as it is properly coded) but there are some that should never be nested. They are:

- The a (hyperlink or anchor) element should not contain other a elements.
- The pre element should not contain the img, object, big, small, sub, or sup elements.
- The button element should not contain the input, select, textarea, label, button, form, fieldset, iframe, or isindex elements.

- The label element should not contain label elements.
- The form element should not contain form elements.

9.5.9 SCRIPT AND STYLE ELEMENTS MUST BE DELIMITED BY CDATA SYMBOLS

Elements such as script and style make use of languages other than HTML (such as CSS2 and Javascript) to perform specialized functions that sometimes include a bit of HTML here and there. Without some way to tell the browser specifically to exclude that HTML (and not to render other parts of a script or style sheet as plain text) browser rendering may be unpredictable. The method for doing this in HTML often means enclosing script or style sheet code in HTML comment tags; effective but inelegant. In XHTML the method for excluding script and style sheet code is to mark the code in these elements as a "CDATA" section. In the following example the "CDATA" section delimiters take the place of HTML comment markers, and are boldfaced so they stand out:

```
<script language="Javascript">
<![CDATA[
function clickme() {
alert("Hello")
}
  ]]>
</script>
```

If an author is using external style sheets or references to external scripts, a "CDATA" section does not need to be used (and shouldn't be).

9.6 XHTML and Cascading Style Sheets

Like HTML, XHTML can make use of style sheets for presentational requirements and, as a matter of fact, this method is specifically recommended. There are a few guidelines for correct presentation of XHTML documents with CSS2. For example, when using CSS2, lower-case element and attribute names should be used, and within a table the tbody element should be explicitly written. It is not implied in XML as it is in HTML.

9.7 XHTML Events Module and Basic Events Module

Again like HTML, XHTML supports events within the DOM, although it is now still considered a working draft and not yet a recommendation. The system for initiating and handling events is generic, meaning it can be used with extended elements (created within new XHTML modules). Event listeners can be registered, thereby giving events the capability to detect occurrences as they happen. And the context in which an event occurs is available for each event.

The DOM provides what is called "an *event flow architecture*". Basically, this means that events do not happen only to a single element; rather, events occur at some point in the hierarchy of elements and then flow down (in a capturing phase) and up (in a bubbling phase) the document tree. During this process, events may be captured, bubbled, and canceled. This is useful because there may be some situations in which an author does not wish every occurrence of an event to fulfill actions assigned to a given event of an element. Sometimes, depending upon the context in which an event occurs or other conditions arising in a session, the author may wish the event to be canceled.

The working draft provides for two event processing modules: the XHTML Basic Events Module and the XHTML Events Module. The Basic Events Module provides only lower level support while the Events Module provides complete DOM Level 2 support. In both modules there is an onevent element that is used to represent the DOM event listener. The primary difference between the two modules is the lack of support in the Basic module for some of the onevent element's attributes.

9.7.1   THE ONEVENT ELEMENT

The onevent element allows authors the ability to set an event listener for any element within an XHTML document. For example, an IMG element may have a *child* element (an element contained inside it) that is set to listen for onclick events. This expanded event model lets elements respond in many ways to events occurring throughout a document.

In DOM Level 2, events are initiated (no matter where they appear to start) from the top of the document tree hierarchy, go straight down the tree to the target element, and from there straight back up to the top of the tree. This process is broken into phases, the capture phase (down) and the bubbling phase (up). Events may be seen as they pass from parent element to child element and back through the tree.

The DTD for the onevent element is:

```
<!ENTITY % Boolean "(true | false )" >
<!ENTITY % onevent-content
((action,stopevent?)|(script,stopevent?)|stopevent)" >
<!ELEMENT onevent %onevent-content;>
<!ATTLIST onevent
  id              ID           #IMPLIED
  type            NMTOKEN      #REQUIRED
  eventsource     IDREF        #REQUIRED
  registerwith    IDREF        #IMPLIED
  onphase         (capturing|bubbling|target)    #IMPLIED
  capture         %Boolean;    #IMPLIED
>
```

Note that the XHTML Basic Events Module does not support the *eventsource* or *registerwith* attributes. The *id* attribute performs the usual function, uniquely identifying the element from other elements in the document. The purpose of the *type* attribute is to set the type of event for which the onevent element is targeted. The values of the type attribute are names of XHTML events, and should be chosen from the following list:

- Html-load
- Html-unload
- Html-abort
- Html-error
- Html-select
- Html-change
- Html-submit
- Html-reset
- Html-focus
- Html-blur
- Html-resize
- Html-scroll
- Dom-click
- Html-dblclick
- Dom-mousedown
- Dom-mouseup
- Dom-mouseover
- Dom-mousemove
- Dom-mouseout
- Html-keypress
- Html-keydown
- Html-keyup

The *eventsource* attribute specifies the source of the event (the node in the document tree) the onevent element is to look for, and if used the element will only respond to events from an element matching the values specified for the *type* and *eventsource* attributes.

The *registerwith* attribute specifies which element to register the onevent element with. This is important because it determines the element for which event detection takes place, the default being the parent element of the onevent element. If an author desires to register an onevent element with an element other than the onevent's parent element, the *registerwith* attribute is set to the same value as the *id* attribute of the other element.

The *onphase* attribute specifies the phase (capturing or bubbling) during which the onevent element may see an event occurring. For example, if the *onphase* attribute is set to the value "oncapture", then the onevent element will see events as they occur during the capture phase. If the value is set to "bubbling" the onevent element will see events as they occur during the bubbling phase. Finally, if the value is set to "target" the onevent element will see events when they reach the target element (the element to which the onevent element is registered via the *registerwith* attribute). The purpose of this capability is to allow elements to detect events even when they are happening to some other element entirely.

9.7.2 THE ACTION ELEMENT

XHTML onevent elements may contain an action element or a script element to handle events once they have occurred. The action element specifies for processing a script kept in an external file, while the script element contains the script to be processed within itself.

The DTD for the action element is:

```
<!ENTITY % action-content EMPTY>
<!ELEMENT action %action-content;>
<!ATTLIST action
  id        ID                #IMPLIED
  href      %URI              #REQUIRED
  type      %ContentType      #IMPLIED
>
```

The *id* attribute performs the usual functions for the action element, and the *href* attribute indicates where the script to be processed is located. The *type* attribute gives an indication what type of content the script contains (Javascript, and so forth). Action elements are always child elements of the onevent element, and serve to bind an onevent element with the event handler (the script to be processed).

9.7.3 THE STOPEVENT ELEMENT

In order to allow for stopping events once they have been handled (and thereby prevent further propagation along the bubbling or capturing phases) the stopevent element is provided. Inserting this element stops an event from continuing. The DTD for the stopevent element is:

```
<!ELEMENT stopevent %stopevent-content;>
<!ATTLIST stopevent
  id    ID    #IMPLIED
>
```

9.8 Using Events in XHTML

The first step in using events within XHTML is to register onevent elements as event listeners with other elements in the document. For example, suppose there is a requirement to make a button respond to being clicked in a document. The onevent element could be registered to the button element simply by making it a child of the button element, like this:

```
<button id="mybutton" value="click me">
  <onevent id="event1" type="dom-click">
   <script>script goes here</script>
  </onevent>
</button>
```

The onevent element could also be explicitly registered with the button element by using the onevent element's *registerwith* attribute, like this:

```
<onevent id="event1" type="dom-click" registerwith=
"mybutton">
    <script>script goes here</script>
</onevent>
<button id="mybutton" value="click me">
</button>
```

Notice the button element may occur in another location in the document.

The second step is to write the script that should be processed when the event is detected (called the *event handler*). Any script may be used, the same as it is used in HTML, but should be contained within a script element or referenced externally by an action element.

The third step is to decide when the event should be detected: during the capturing phase, the bubbling phase, or when the event reaches its target element. The default (which does not require setting the *onphase* attribute) is to detect the event when it reaches the target element. To detect an event during the bubbling phase, code like the following might be written:

```
<p id="para1">
  <onevent id="event1" type="dom-click" onphase="bubbling">
   <script>script goes here</script>
  </onevent>
  <button id="b1"></button>
  <button id="b2"></button>
</p>
```

In this example the onevent element will detect any clicks to either of the two buttons, because it is a parent of both, while at the same time being a child of the p element (both buttons are also children of the p element). Because it is set to bubbling it will detect clicks to the buttons only after they reach the button elements and begin to propagate back up to the root element of the entire document, not on the way down.

If an author wishes to prevent the onevent element in this example from detecting events occurring to the second button as they "bubble up", the stopevent element could be employed, like this:

```
<p id="para1">
  <onevent id="event1" type="dom-click" onphase="bubbling">
   <script>script goes here</script>
  </onevent>
  <button id="b1"></button>
  <button id="b2"><stopevent/></button>
</p>
```

Review Questions

9.1. What is XHTML, and in what primary aspects does it differ from HTML?

9.2. What is an XHTML module?

9.3. What standard DTDs does XHTML use?

9.4. Considering the number of Web pages written as HTML, it should be easier to convert existing pages to XHTML than to rewrite all pages from scratch. What tools are available for this job from the W3C, and what is the process for performing such a conversion?

9.5. What are XHTML modules? Why has XHTML been made into modules?

9.6. What are abstract modules? What purpose do they serve?

9.7. With tools like HTML Tidy available to convert documents for HTML to XHTML, why is it useful to know the differences between HTML and XHTML?

9.8. What difference is there in the way XHTML documents begin?

9.9. What element must be included in an XHTML document immediately following the DOCTYPE declaration?

9.10. Is XHTML case-sensitive? What impact does this have on XHTML code?

9.11. What symbols delimit attribute values? What does it mean when an attribute is minimized, and how does this affect XHTML code?

9.12. What happens to white spaces included in attribute values in XHTML code?

9.13. What happens to HTML elements identified by the *name* attribute, when documents are converted to XHTML?

9.14. In what way are starting and ending tags coded differently in XHTML?

9.15. What does it mean when a document is called "well-formed" in relation to XML standards?

9.16. Name three elements that should never contain elements of the same kind.

9.17. What new requirements exist in XHTML where scripts are concerned?

9.18. Is there much difference between the way style sheets are handled in XHTML and HTML? What is one of the differences for CSS2?

9.19. What is the model for handling events in XHTML?

9.20. How are events detected in XHTML?

9.21. What value should the *registerwith* attribute be set to, to register it with a particular element?

9.22. What value should the *onphase* attribute be set to, to detect events as they travel up the DOM hierarchy?

9.23. What is the purpose of the *eventsource* attribute?

9.24. Name a few of the event names appropriate for use with XHTML. How are these names different from event names in the DOM?

9.25. What is the purpose of the action element?

Solved Problems

9.1. Give an example of the code used to indicate that an XHTML document uses the strict DTD.

```
<!DOCTYPE html PUBLIC "-//W3C//DTD XHTML 1.0 Strict//EN"
"http://www.w3.org/TR/xhtml1/DTD/strict.dtd">
```

9.2. Give an example of an XHTML document with the minimum sections required to form a Web page.

```
<!DOCTYPE html PUBLIC "-//W3C//DTD XHTML 1.0 Transitional//EN"
"http://www.w3.org/TR/xhtml1/DTD/transitional.dtd">
<html xmlns="http://www.w3.org/1999/xhtml">
<head>
<title>The Title</title>
</head>
</html>
```

9.3. In the example code just given, what is the root element? What child elements does it contain?

The html element is the root element, and it contains the child elements head and title.

9.4. Convert the following code from HTML to XHTML:

```
<HTML>
<HEAD>
<TITLE>My Title</TITLE>
</HEAD>
<BODY BGCOLOR=white TEXT=black>
The body of the page
```

This code contains several things that are not tolerated by XHTML. All element and attributes must be lowercase, all attribute values must be enclosed by quotes, and all elements must include ending tags. Converted, it would look like this (following the DOCTYPE declaration):

```
<html xmlns="http://www.w3.org/1999/xhtml">
<head>
<title>My Title</title>
</head>
<body bgcolor="white" text="black">
The body of the page
</body>
</html>
```

The next five questions all pertain to a variation of the Registration form used in a previous chapter.

9.5. Convert the following code to XHTML, using the transitional DTD.

```
<HTML><HEAD><TITLE>Registration Form</TITLE>
<META HTTP-EQUIV="Content-Type" CONTENT="text/html;
CHARSET=iso-8859-1">
</HEAD>
<BODY BGCOLOR="#FFFFFF" LINK="#663333">
<FORM METHOD="POST" ACTION="register.asp">
```

In this code there is no DOCTYPE declaration, no *xmlns* attribute in the html element, and the elements and attributes are upper case.

```
<!DOCTYPE html PUBLIC "-//W3C//DTD XHTML 1.0 Transitional//
EN"
"http://www.w3.org/TR/xhtml1/DTD/transitional.dtd">
<html xmlns="http://www.w3.org/1999/xhtml"><head><title>
Registration Form</title>
<meta http-equiv="Content-Type" content="text/html;
charset=iso-8859-1">
</head>
<body bgcolor="#FFFFFF" link="#663333">
<form method="POST" action="register.asp" name="">
```

9.6. Convert the following code to XHTML.

```
<div align="center">
<table width=52% border=1 bordercolorlight="#CCCCFF"
bordercolordark="#CCCCFF">
<tr><td width=98% valign=top height=247>
<table width=100% border=0 bordercolordark="#CC9966"
bordercolorlight="#CC9966">
<tr valign=top bgcolor="#9999FF">
<td><p align="center"><b><I><font face="Arial, Helvetica,
sans-serif" size=+1 color="#FFFFFF">REGISTER HERE </font>
</b></I></p></td>
</tr><tr valign=top><td>
```

In this code several attribute values are not surrounded by quotes, some elements overlap, and one of them is in upper case.

```
<div align="center">
<table width="52%" border="1" bordercolorlight="#CCCCFF"
bordercolordark="#CCCCFF">
<tr><td width="98%" valign="top" height="247">
<table width="100%" border="0" bordercolordark="#CC9966"
bordercolorlight="#CC9966">
<tr valign="top" bgcolor="#9999FF">
<td><p align="center"><b><i><font face="Arial, Helvetica,
sans-serif" size="+1" color="#FFFFFF">REGISTER HERE
</font></i></b></p></td>
</tr><tr valign="top"><td>
```

9.7. Convert the following code to XHTML.

```
<table border="0" width="100%"><tr bordercolor="#CC9966"
bgcolor="#CCCCFF">
<td align="right" colspan="2"><div align="left"><b><font
face="Arial, Helvetica, sans-serif" color="#FFFFFF"><font
color="#663333" size="+1">PLEASE FILL IN CONTACT
DATA</font></font></b></div>
</td></tr><tr bordercolor="#CC9966" bgcolor="#FFCC99">
```

```
<td align="right" width="24%" bgcolor="#CCCCFF">
<div align="center"><b><font face="Arial, Helvetica,
sans-serif" size="+1" color="#FFFFFF"><font face="Arial,
Helvetica, sans-serif" color="#663333" size="-1"><b><font
face="Arial, Helvetica, sans-serif" size="+1" color=
"#FFFFFF"><font color="#663333"><font size="-1">
</font></font></font></b></font></font></b></div>
</td><td align="right" width="76%" bgcolor="#CCCCFF">
<div align="center"><b><font face="Arial, Helvetica,
sans-serif" size="+1" color="#FFFFFF"><font
color="#663333"><font color="#663333" size="-1" face="
Arial, Helvetica, sans-serif"><b>I am a Buyer</b></font>
<b><font face="Arial, Helvetica, sans-serif" size="+1"
color="#FFFFFF"><font color="#663333" size="-1">
<input type="radio" name="BorS" value="Buyer" checked>
</font><font face="Arial, Helvetica, sans-serif"
color="#663333" size="-1"><b>Supplier<font face="Arial,
Helvetica, sans-serif" size="+1" color="#FFFFFF"><font
color="#663333"><font size="-1">
<input type="radio" name="BorS" value="Supplier">
</font></font></font></b></font></font></b><font
size="-1"><i>
</i></font></font></font></b></div></td></tr><tr>
<td width="24%" align="right"><font face="Arial,
Helvetica, sans-serif" color="#663333" size="-1"><b>First
Name<br>Last Name</b></font></td> <td width="76%"> <font
face="Arial, Helvetica, sans-serif" color="#663333"
size="-1"><input type="text" name="FirstName" size="20"
tabindex="1"><br>
<input type="text" name="LastName" size="20"
tabindex="2"></font></td></tr>
<tr><td width="24%" align="right"><font face="Arial,
Helvetica, sans-serif" color="#663333" size="-1"><b>
Phone<br><br>Fax</b></font></td>
<td width="76%"> <font face="Arial, Helvetica, sans-serif"
color="#663333" size="-1"><input type="text" name="Phone"
size="20" tabindex="6"><br>
<input type="text" name="Fax" size="20" tabindex="7">
</font></td></tr>
<tr><td width="24%" align="right"><font face="Arial,
Helvetica, sans-serif" color="#663333" size="-1"><b>
Email:</b></font></td><td width="76%"> <font face="Arial,
Helvetica, sans-serif" color="#663333" size="-1">
<input type="text" name="Email" size="40"></font></td>
</tr>
<tr bgcolor="#CCCCFF"><td align="right" colspan="2">
```

In this code attribute values are minimized, empty elements are not terminated properly, and input elements use the *name* attribute rather than the *id* attribute.

```
<table border="0" width="100%"><tr bordercolor="#CC9966"
bgcolor="#CCCCFF">
<td align="right" colspan="2"><div align="left"><b><font
face="Arial, Helvetica, sans-serif" color="#FFFFFF"><font
color="#663333" size="+1">PLEASE FILL IN CONTACT
DATA</font></font></b></div>
```

```
</td></tr><tr bordercolor="#CC9966" bgcolor="#FFCC99">
<td align="right" width="24%" bgcolor="#CCCCFF">
<div align="center"><b><font face="Arial, Helvetica,
sans-serif" size="+1" color="#FFFFFF"><font face="Arial,
Helvetica, sans-serif" color="#663333" size="-1"><b><font
face="Arial, Helvetica, sans-serif" size="+1"
color="#FFFFFF"><font color="#663333"><font size="-1">
</font></font></font></b></font></font></b></div>
</td><td align="right" width="76%" bgcolor="#CCCCFF">
<div align="center"><b><font face="Arial, Helvetica,
sans-serif" size="+1" color="#FFFFFF"><font
color="#663333"><font color="#663333" size="-1"
face="Arial, Helvetica, sans-serif"><b>I am a Buyer</b>
</font>
<b><font face="Arial, Helvetica, sans-serif" size="+1"
color="#FFFFFF"><font color="#663333" size="-1">
<input type="radio" id="BorS" value="Buyer" checked=
"checked"></input>
</font><font face="Arial, Helvetica, sans-serif"
color="#663333" size="-1"><b>Supplier<font face="Arial,
Helvetica, sans-serif" size="+1" color="#FFFFFF"><font
color="#663333"><font size="-1">
<input type="radio" id="BorS" value="Supplier"></input>
</font></font></font></b></font></font></b><font
size="-1"><i>
</i></font></font></font></b></div></td></tr><tr>
<td width="24%" align="right"><font face="Arial,
Helvetica, sans-serif" color="#663333" size="-1"><b>First
Name<br />Last Name</b></font></td>
<td width="76%"> <font face="Arial, Helvetica, sans-serif"
color="#663333" size="-1"><input type="text"
id="FirstName" size="20" tabindex="1"></input><br />
<input type="text" id="LastName" size="20" tabindex="2">
</input>
</font></td></tr><tr><td width="24%" align="right"><font
face="Arial, Helvetica, sans-serif" color="#663333"
size="-1"><b>Phone
<br />Fax</b></font></td>
<td width="76%"> <font face="Arial, Helvetica, sans-serif"
color="#663333" size="-1"><input type="text" id="Phone"
size="20" tabindex="6"></imput> <br /><input type="text"
id="Fax" size="20" tabindex="7"></font></td></tr>
<tr><td width="24%" align="right"><font face="Arial,
Helvetica, sans-serif" color="#663333" size="-1">
<b>Email:</b></font></td><td width="76%"> <font face=
"Arial, Helvetica, sans-serif" color="#663333" size="-1">
<input type="text" id="Email" size="40"></input></font>
</td></tr>
<tr bgcolor="#CCCCFF"><td align="right" colspan="2">
```

9.8. Convert the following code to XHTML:

```
<div align="left"><font face="Arial, Helvetica,
sans-serif" color="#663333" size="-1"><b><font
face="Arial, Helvetica, sans-serif" size="+1"
color="#FFFFFF"><font color="#663333">CHOOSE USER
```

```
NAME/ PASSWORD </font></font> </b></font></div></td></tr>
<tr><td width="24%" align="right"><font face="Arial,
Helvetica, sans-serif" color="#663333" size="-1"><b>User
Name<br><br>Password:</b></font></td>
<td width="76%"><input type="text" name="UserName"
size="20" tabindex="15">
<br><input type="text" name="Password" size="20" tabindex=
"16"></td></tr>
<tr bordercolor="#CC9966" bgcolor="#FFCC99"><td
width="24%" align="right" bgcolor="#CCCCFF"
valign="bottom" height="22"><font face="Arial, Helvetica,
sans-serif" color="#663333" size="-1"><b>I Saw You In</b>
</font></td>
```

In this code several input elements use the *name* attribute instead of the *id* attribute, are not terminated properly, and an empty element (the line break) is not properly terminated.

```
<div align="left"><font face="Arial, Helvetica,
sans-serif" color="#663333" size="-1"><b><font
face="Arial, Helvetica, sans-serif" size="+1"
color="#FFFFFF"><font color="#663333">CHOOSE USER
NAME/ PASSWORD </font></font> </b></font></div></td></tr>
<tr><td width="24%" align="right"><font face="Arial,
Helvetica, sans-serif" color="#663333" size="-1"><b>User
Name<br />Password:</b></font></td>
<td width="76%"><input type="text" id="UserName" size="20"
tabindex="15"></input><br><input type="text"
id="Password" size="20" tabindex="16"></input></td></tr>
<tr bordercolor="#CC9966" bgcolor="#FFCC99"><td
width="24%" align="right" bgcolor="#CCCCFF"
valign="bottom" height="22"><font face="Arial, Helvetica,
sans-serif" color="#663333" size="-1"><b>I Saw You In</b>
</font></td>
```

9.9. Convert the following code to XHTML:

```
<td width="76%" bgcolor="#CCCCFF" valign="top"
height="22">
<select name="HowFound">
<option value="SearchEngine" selected>Search Engine
</option>
<option value="Newspaper">Newspaper</option>
<option value="Magazine">Magazine</option>
<option value="Radio">Radio</option>
<option value="TV">TV</option>
<option value="Other">Other</option>
</select>
<input type="submit" value="Register" name="B1">
<input type="reset" value="Clear" name="B1"
Onclick="sure()">
</td></tr></table></table></td></tr></table></div>
</form>
</body></html>
```

This code also uses a short Javascript function that is activated when the reset button is pushed, shown in the following code:

```
<script language="Javascript">
<!--
```

```
function sure() {
alert("Sure you want to clear the form?")
}
-->
</script>
```

In this code input elements are not properly terminated, one of the option elements uses a minimized attribute, the select element uses the *name* attribute instead of the *id* attribute, and both buttons use the same name value.

Assuming the same name is used for purposes of server-side scripts, changing the name of the second button may require changes to the operation of the server-side script as well. And the short Javascript in the page would also have to be inserted between the onevent element tags and modified a bit.

```
<td width="76%" bgcolor="#CCCCFF" valign="top"
height="22">
<select id="HowFound">
<option value="SearchEngine" selected="selected">Search
Engine</option>
<option value="Newspaper">Newspaper</option>
<option value="Magazine">Magazine</option>
<option value="Radio">Radio</option>
<option value="TV">TV</option>
<option value="Other">Other</option>
</select>
<input type="submit" value="Register" id="B1"></input>
<input type="reset" value="Clear" id="B2">
<onevent id="event1" type="dom-click">
<script language="Javascript">
<![CDATA[
function sure() {
alert("Sure you want to clear the form?")
}
]]>
</script>
</onevent>
</input>
</td></tr></table></table></td></tr></table></div>
</form>
</body></html>
```

Answers to Review Questions

9.1. XHTML is primarily HTML with an XML twist. XHTML documents are written with structures very similar to HTML, but following the rules of XML concerning well-formedness, and so on.

9.2. XHTML is modularized, meaning that there are a number of modules from which XHTML documents can be made. Anyone can write additional XHTML modules and incorporate them into XHTML documents, as long as they follow the standard rules, and thereby extend XHTML to whatever degree they wish, while maintaining the ability of a browser or other user agent to read them.

9.3.   XHTML uses the Strict, Transitional, and Frameset DTDs. These DTDs have been written for XHTML, but are similar to the HTML DTDs of the same designation.

9.4.   The first step in performing a conversion from HTML to XHTML is to clean up the code. HTML Web pages that work in the popular browsers often contain coding errors that are simply forgiven or overlooked by the browsers. For example, many versions of the major browsers don't require attribute values (such as file names) to be in quotes. This must be corrected before the pages can be converted.

The second step is to perform the actual conversion. This involves taking correctly written HTML code and converting it into correctly written XHTML code. The W3C provides a tool called HTML Tidy that performs both of these functions.

9.5.   XHTML modules are discrete sets of XHTML elements and attributes that perform specific, well-defined functions. Unlike HTML, in which all functions are massed into one application, XHTML functions are broken down into modules, so that authors may combine these modules into smaller or larger units. Then, if an author extends XHTML with a new module, that module can be used in conjunction with other existing modules to create a new version of XHTML for a specific purpose, while at the same time having no negative effect on other XHTML documents or browsers.

9.6.   It can be difficult to understand the contents of a module, and a clear understanding is required in order to successfully use a module when constructing XHTML documents from several XHTML modules. Therefore, abstract modules were created with a clearly defined set of rules for their construction, in order to provide XHTML authors an easy to understand definition of the contents of an XHTML module. Abstract modules make it easier for authors to use XHTML modules, without necessarily understanding every minute detail of the module itself.

9.7.   Even though there are many good HTML editors, and it is likely that these will be rebuilt to produce good XHTML code in the near future, authors often find it necessary to code HTML by hand, and the same is likely to be true of XHTML. One particularly important instance of the need to write code by hand is when documents are constructed on-the-fly by scripts, especially on the back-end. Knowing the code is extremely useful in these situations.

9.8.   XHTML documents must have the DOCTYPE declaration as the first line of the document, like this:

```
<!DOCTYPE html PUBLIC "-//W3C//DTD XHTML 1.0 Transitional//
EN"
"http://www.w3.org/TR/xhtml1/DTD/transitional.dtd">
```

The DOCTYPE declaration tells the browser what kind of document is to be produced, what DTD is to be used (in this case the Transitional DTD), and where the DTD is to be found (in this case at http://www.w3.org/TR/xhtml1/DTD/transitional.dtd).

9.9.   The html element is the root element, the parent of all other elements included in an XHTML document, and it must follow the DOCTYPE declaration. Within it must also be the namespace to be used, like this:

```
<html xmlns="http://www.w3.org/1999/xhtml">
```

A namespace is a closed set of tag names that can be used with a document. Closed sets of names are required so that tags with identical names from different DTDs can be used in the same document without causing confusion. The tag name prefix or namespace designation prevents applications such as browsers from confusing a tag from one DTD with a tag from another DTD when both have the same tag name.

9.10. Yes, XHTML is case-sensitive, whereas HTML is not. Therefore, all XHTML tags and attribute names must be written lowercase, like XML documents. However, attribute values must be written in the correct case, especially file names, since file names have a definite case on some operating systems.

9.11. Quotes must surround attribute values in XHTML, even numerical values. In HTML, there are some attributes that, when the name appears by itself, the effect of the attribute is made on the element. An attribute that appears without a value attached, and yet still has an effect, is said to be minimized. For example, the *noresize* attribute for the FRAME element in HTML prevents the frame from being resized when it is present, even though there is no value attached. In XHTML, all attributes must have values attached, so the *noresize* attribute would be written noresize="noresize".

9.12. If the white spaces come before or after (inside the quotation marks) the value of an attribute, the spaces will be stripped out. If they occur within an attribute value (between words, for example) only one space will be left and the rest will be stripped out.

9.13. In XHTML elements must not be identified with the *name* attribute, even though it still exists, because this attribute has been deprecated and will be removed in future versions. Instead, elements may be identified by the *id* attribute. The primary difference is that while several elements may share the same name in an HTML document (and this comes in handy in some scripting situations) each *id* attribute value in a document (and therefore each element identified by an *id* attribute) must be unique across the entire document.

9.14. In XHTML, the less-than and greater-than symbols still enclose element tags, but none of the ending tags are optional. All elements must have a starting and ending tag written the same way as in HTML, if they are non-empty. Non-empty means that they may contain content. For example, the TEXTAREA element may contain text content between its starting and ending tags. Empty elements, such as the BR (line break) element, use a different coding method to signify that they are closed. Rather than use a starting and ending tag, a slash is placed inside them preceded by a space and followed by the greater-than sign, like this:

```
<br />
```

9.15. Well-formedness is a new concept in XML, and it means that elements must all have an ending (using ending tags or, for empty element, an ending symbol in the tag itself) and that elements must be properly nested. Nested means that if an element starts inside another element, it must end inside that element as well, not overlapping. Thinking about this from the standpoint of the DOM, it is important because it unambiguously establishes the parentage of each element. There is no confusion as to what element is the parent and what element is the child.

9.16. Although XML does not prevent the nesting of any particular kind of element, there are some elements that should never be nested in XHTML. For example, the a element (for hypertext links) should never contain other a elements. The form and label elements are also in this category.

9.17. In HTML, SCRIPT and STYLE elements often contain code that may be rendered as plain text or as HTML tags by the browser, so script and style sections are usually commented out (using HMTL comment tags). Javascipt and CSS2 support this practice, but for XHTML, script and style elements should be delimited by the CDATA symbols, as shown here:

```
<![CDATA[ script or style code here ]]>
```

9.18. One of the primary differences is that lowercase elements and attribute names should be used, and expected. Therefore, while the selector for paragraphs in an HTML document is a capital P, the selector for paragraphs in an XHTML document must be a lowercase p.

9.19. Event handling in XHTML is based on the DOM Level 2, and works much the same way. Events propagate from the top of the document tree hierarchy and then travel through parent and child elements until they reach the element (object) in which they have occurred. For example, when a button in a form on a Web page is clicked, the event starts at the document, passes to the form containing the button, and finally to the button itself. When the event reaches the button it can activate any event handler (script) set for that event within the button.

Next, the event travels back up the hierarchy of elements in the document. Traveling down the hierarchy is known as the capture phase, reaching the element affected is known as reaching the target element, and traveling back up the hierarchy is known as the bubbling phase.

9.20. The onevent element is included in XHTML documents to detect events. The onevent element can be linked to (registered with) any element on a page, and can detect events when they arrive at the target or when they are traversing the DOM element hierarchy up or down.

9.21. The *registerwith* attribute should be set to the same value as the value of the *id* attribute of the element to which it is to be registered.

9.22. The *onphase* attribute should be set to "bubbling" in order for an onevent element to detect an event as it travels back up the hierarchy.

9.23. The *eventsource* attribute specifies the node of the hierarchy where the event originated. This is convenient for detecting events not directly associated with an onevent element.

9.24. In XHTML, event names are constructed using the context of the event (for example, html or dom) followed by a hyphen, and then followed by the type of event (such as load, unload, click, dblclick, and so forth). Examples are html-load, html-unload, and so forth. In the DOM, these event names consist only of the type of event (such as load, unload, and so forth).

9.25. The action element serves to reference scripts external to an XHTML document (stored as separate files). The action element is always a child of an onevent element, and it associates an event handler (a script) with the event detected. The *href* attribute of the action element points to the URL of the external file.

CHAPTER 10

Introduction to XML 1.0 and the Future

10.1 What is eXtensible Markup Language (XML)?

Since XML is not a markup language per se, the question "what is XML?" is not necessarily easy to answer. Perhaps the best concise explanation is that it is a means of creating markup languages conforming to a common standard. Just as HTML is a subset or application of SGML, XML is a subset of the SGML capabilities that allow the creation of applications or markup languages. XML is technically an application profile written with and conforming to SGML, and XML documents conform with SGML.

Originally, XML was developed by the World Wide Web consortium (the version we refer to here is XML 1.0) and the design goals included: usable on the Internet, support for many applications, compatibility with SGML, easy to use, no optional features, human-readable, and concise.

Because XML can be used so easily to make data available in a consistent way not just to people but to applications (think servers) many industry groups are now in the process of developing their own XML applications suitable for the special terms and definitions that are used within their industries, and in some cases competing XML applications are struggling for supremacy.

Think of XML entities as XML "pages", like HTML Web pages. XML documents are made up of one or more entities (the recommendation refers to entities as storage units) containing parsed or unparsed data. The parsed data includes text and markup. The markup (like tags in HTML) describes the layout and structure of the document. An XML processor reads XML documents, and typically provides the results to an application. Microsoft's Internet Explorer 5.0 supports XML 1.0 processing, as well as Namespaces, the DOM, and includes an engine for processing eXtensible Style Sheets (XSL, an XML version of CSS).

10.2   The XML Document Structure

XML documents can be considered to have two structures, one logical and the other physical. This is not unusual in the computer world; hard drive storage space may be physically separated among several drives, but may appear to the user to be on one "logical" drive. All the files or entities, taken together, comprise the physical components of the XML document. Logically, the document consists of elements, attributes, etc., much like an HTML document, although XML documents can contain declarations, processing instructions, and so forth, more like a traditional executable application. Well-formed XML documents (*well-formed* is a term used often in XML, meaning primarily that all XML structures conform to the basic structural rules of XML) are created from well-formed subunits, including entities, elements, and so forth.

An XML document may have three parts: a *prolog*, a *body*, and an *epilog*. The prolog and epilog are optional. The prolog may contain comments, version information, processing instructions, and a reference to a specific XML DTD, while the epilog may contain comments and processing instructions. The body consists of one or more elements (defined by the DTD), forming a hierarchical tree structure, and possibly containing character data. In the body, elements are very similar in structure, appearance and function to HTML pages, except that the elements are quite varied and their meaning may be arbitrarily assigned by the author of the DTD, hence the extensible nature of XML.

The following example shows how some elements may be constructed and arranged in the body of an XML document:

```
<nail_products>
  <nail_polish brand="Contours">
   <color>Light Red</color>
   <price>7.95</price>
   <polish_name>Sizzling Red</polish_name>
  </nail_polish>
</nail_products>
```

Notice the hierarchical structure. For example, within the overall category "nail products", there is the possibility of many such products, only one of which is named here, nail polish. And within the category of nail polish, obviously there may be many formulations and several brands.

In XML elements may contain other elements (just as the HTML BODY element contains other HTML elements such as the P and BR elements), character data, character references, entity references, processing instructions, comments, and CDATA (character data) sections. Elements are defined with angle brackets (< >) and both the starting and ending tags are required, unless the element is an empty element, in which case it has no content and must still have either a starting/ending tag combination or contain the slash (representing the ending tag) inside itself. A starting tag might be < nail_products >, an ending tag might be < /nail_products >, and an empty-element tag might be < nail_products > < /nail_products > or < nail_products/ > (with the slash marking the end inside the same tag).

10.3 Writing XML DTDs

The main focus of XML is the creation of languages (applications) that support unique and interesting elements and attributes, and this can be done by creating DTDs that conform to XML standards. As with HTML and XHTML, for XML the DTD language uses a number of common characters, such as the exclamation point, parentheses, asterisks, angle brackets, and so forth to define elements for an XML application that are required, optional, limited, have certain attributes, and other specific properties. Another method to define rules for XML documents is to create an XML schema, which will be discussed in greater detail in section 10.4, "XML Schemas".

Well-formedness is a concept often used in relation to XML documents, and it means that the document contains only one root element and that none of the document's elements overlap. Just being well-formed is not enough, though. A document can be well-formed and yet still be meaningless within the concepts the data it contains imply. Therefore, DTDs and schemas are used to supply the rules by which a document should live. An XML document is considered *valid* if it has a DTD or schema and if it complies with the rules (constraints) expressed in the DTD. The DTD must appear before the first element in the document.

In order to write conforming XML DTDs, there are some rules to be followed about the construction of elements, their attribute lists, and the way they are interpreted. For example, there can only be one document element, called the *root element*, and all other elements in the document are contained inside the root element. As discussed in Chapter 9, for XHTML the root element is the html element (lowercase, because XML elements are case sensitive). In addition, there can be no overlapping elements, meaning all elements in an XML document must be properly nested. Where an element is nested inside another element, the nested element is called the *child element*, and the element in which the other is nested is called the *parent element*.

10.3.1 XML DTD COMPONENTS

An XML DTD consists of a number of valid components which, using the correct syntax, forms the DTD. Table 10-1 contains the allowable components of an XML DTD, along with a short description of each.

Table 10-1. Allowable components of an XML document

Component	Description
Characters	A character is a single unit of text. Legal characters are tab, carriage return, line feed, and the legal characters of Unicode and ISO/IEC 10646.
White Space	One or more space characters, carriage returns, line feeds, or tabs.
Name (Nmtoken)	A token beginning with a letter or one of several punctuation characters, continuing on with letters, digits, hyphens, underscores, colons, or full stops.
Literals	Any quoted string not containing the quotation mark used as a delimiter for that string.
Markup	Start-tags, end-tags, empty-element tags, entity references, character references, comments, CDATA section delimiters, document type declarations, processing instructions, XML declarations, text declarations, and any white space that is outside the document element and not inside other markup.
Comments	A comment syntax identical to HTML comments, `<!– the comment –>`.
Processing Instructions	Processing commands that pass through to an application.
CDATA Sections	Used to delimit style and script sections, and other areas where the data is not part of the markup.
Prolog and Document Type Declarations	Declarations that the document is an XML document, and what DTDs it uses.

Note that DTDs may contain sections which do not necessarily appear in every version of an XML document. These sections are called *conditional sections*. The following code is a portion of an XML DTD:

```
<!DOCTYPE book [
 <!ELEMENT book (chapter*)>
 <!ELEMENT chapter (chapter.title, chapter.content)>
 <!ELEMENT chapter.title (#PCDATA )>
 <!ELEMENT chapter.content (#PCDATA | discussion | example
                            | figure | code | illustration )*>
 <!ELEMENT discussion (#PCDATA)>
 <!ELEMENT example ( (#PCDATA | code)* )>
 <!ELEMENT figure ( (#PCDATA | language | colororbw)* )>
 <!ELEMENT code ( (#PCDATA | language )* )>
 <!ELEMENT illustration (#PCDATA)>
 <!ELEMENT language (#PCDATA)>
 <!ELEMENT colororbw (#PCDATA)>
]>
```

This code sets the DOCTYPE as a book, and then lists the elements available in the book: chapters, chapter titles, discussion, figures, illustrations, code examples, and so forth. Note that some of the elements appear twice, and it is apparent what elements are child elements of others.

10.4 XML Schemas

Another method, more recently developed and rapidly gaining ground, for creating a set of rules by which to validate well-formed XML documents is called XML schemas. In fact, there are two XML schema-related documents under development at the W3C: *XML Schema Part 1: Structures* and *XML Schema Part 2: Data Types*.

Together, these documents form the basis of the standard syntax and constructs that should be used to build XML Schemas. *Schema* is a term well known in database circles, because a database schema identifies relationships between tables, what fields are in a table, what data types fields may assume, and what value ranges are permissible in those fields. An XML schema performs essentially the same function, and also provides for constraints to the sequence in which elements may appear, whether or not elements are empty, and what default values attributes have (as a DTD can).

XML DTDs offer a means of constructing XML document elements and attributes and constraining their roles, and XML schemas provide similar but more extensive and database-like capabilities. An XML document that conforms to an XML Schema is called an *instance document*, and it may or may not have a direct reference to the schema it conforms to. In many cases there will be a reference in the instance document, but sometimes the application processing the document will "already know" where to find the appropriate schema.

Instance documents are normal XML documents, with elements, attributes, and so forth. Instead of a DTD dictating their structure, the schema sets the rules. XML schemas lay out the allowable elements and their attributes and also dictate element data types, as can be done for fields in a table in a database. Simple data types resemble ordinary database or programming language data types, such as text, integers, dates, and so forth, while complex data types are assembled from one or more simple data types. For example, a complex data type may contain a component that is text, two components that are numbers, and a date, all in one.

XML schemas also allow the sequence in which elements are found to be set, as well as the number of occurrences, minimum and maximum values, and so on, just like contraints in a database. The following code shows an element in an instance document, and the next example shows the schema to which it conforms:

```
<?xml version="1.0"?>
<nail_polish releaseDate="2000-9-19">
  <marketingManager division="Marketing">
    <name>Dani Johnson</name>
    <title>VP US Marketing</title>
    <building>Main Headquarters</building>
    <phone>858-785-1212</phone>
    <ext>123</ext>
  </marketingManager>
</nail_polish>
```

This code refers to an element of type nail_polish, having an attribute called releaseDate. The releaseDate attribute is set to data type "xsd:date" in the schema. The element nail_polish has a subelement named marketingManager, which is a complex data type consisting of the name, title, building, phone number, and extension of the marketing manager for this particular product. The complex type is defined in the schema. The namespace for the schema is set in the first line of the schema, and all elements in the schema use the prefix "xsd" to associate themselves with this namespace.

```
  <xsd:schema
        xmlns:xsd="http://www.w3.org/2000/08/XMLSchema">
 <xsd:element name="nail_polish" type="nail_polishType"/>
 <xsd:attribute name="releaseDate" type="xsd:date"/>
 </xsd:complexType>
 <xsd:complexType name="marketingManager">
 <xsd:sequence>
 <xsd:element name="name" type="xsd:string"/>
 <xsd:element name="title" type="xsd:string"/>
 <xsd:element name="building" type="xsd:string"/>
 <xsd:element name="phone" type="xsd:string"/>
 <xsd:element name="ext" type="xsd:string"/>
 </xsd:sequence> </xsd:complexType>
</xsd:schema>
```

10.5   XML Namespaces

Anyone can create an XML application (language), and XML documents can be composed of a mixture of elements from multiple languages. This is the fundamental capability that makes XML so powerful, but it also leads directly to a problem: how to ensure that elements from different XML languages, which happen to have the same names are not confused when processed.

Naturally, the W3C has a recommendation addressing this issue, called "Namespaces in XML". A *namespace* is the set of names used for elements and so forth, and this recommendation sets in place standard rules for building and referring to XML namespaces, so as to eliminate confusion about the source and meaning of a particular element name.

To make each namespace truly unique (even when the names for two different namespaces may be identical) a URL must be supplied to point to the namespace applied to a particular element. The following code shows an example of a namespace declaration, and why it is unique:

```
<nail_polish xmlns:nail='http://beauty.org/schema'>
</nail_polish>
```

In this code, the nail_polish element is defined in the schema located at http://beauty.org/schema. The namespace declaration starts with xmlns, followed by a colon and then the name of the namespace (nail) and then the URL for that namespace.

Multiple namespaces can be used with a single XML document, as shown in the following code:

```
<?xml version="1.0"?>
<nail_products xmlns:developmentdate=
"http://beauty.org/date"
xmlns:releasedate="http://beautycompany.com/date">
<nail_polish name="Hot Pink">
<developmentdate:date>Jan 1, 2000</date>
<releasedate:date>Mar 1, 2000</date>
</nail_polish>
</nail_products>
```

Finally, a single element can also have multiple namespaces applied within it, to use for child elements from a number of namespaces, as shown in the following code:

```
<?xml version="1.0"?>
<nail:nail_polish xmlns:nail='urn:beauty.products:nails'
xmlns:sku='urn:sku.numbers'>
  <nail:brand>Hot Pink</nail:brand>
  <sku:code>1568491379</sku:code>
</nail:nail_polish>
```

Because the colon is used to separate parts of an XML namespace declaration, authors should not use the colon in XML element names.

10.6   XML Elements and Attributes – Logical Structure

Like HTML, XML documents contain elements and attributes. Elements are delimited by starting and ending tags, and they may be empty (containing no content) or non-empty (containing content). All elements have names, and the term for element names is Generic Identifier (GI). Elements may (but are not required to) have one or more attributes, and each attribute has a name and a value.

The order of attributes in a tag is not significant, and no attribute may appear in a tag twice. Possible attribute values may be arbitrarily restricted, and the values given must conform to the possible value types listed in the DTD. Also, no less-than (<) signs may appear in attribute values. Element and attributes names may not include some reserved characters (X, x, M, m, L, l). Element names in starting and ending tags must match for any given element.

When converting Word documents to HTML documents, Microsoft Word 2000 now converts the Word document into an XML document that can be read using Internet Explorer, as shown in this example:

```
<html xmlns:o="urn:schemas-microsoft-com:office:office"
xmlns:w="urn:schemas-microsoft-com:office:word"
xmlns="http://www.w3.org/TR/REC-html40">
<head>
<meta http-equiv=Content-Type content="text/html;
charset=windows-1252">
<meta name=ProgId content=Word.Document>
<meta name=Generator content="Microsoft Word 9">
<meta name=Originator content="Microsoft Word 9">
<link rel=File-List href="./XMLdocumentsDemo_files/
filelist.xml">
<title>XML documents</title>
<!--[if gte mso 9]><xml>
  <o:DocumentProperties>
    <o:Author>Dave Mercer</o:Author>
    <o:LastAuthor>Dave Mercer</o:LastAuthor>
    <o:Revision>2</o:Revision>
    <o:TotalTime>2</o:TotalTime>
    <o:Created>2000-11-25T23:07:00Z</o:Created>
    <o:LastSaved>2000-11-25T23:07:00Z</o:LastSaved>
    <o:Pages>1</o:Pages>
    <o:Company>AFC Computer Services</o:Company>
    <o:Lines>1</o:Lines>
    <o:Paragraphs>1</o:Paragraphs>
    <o:Version>9.2720</o:Version>
  </o:DocumentProperties>
</xml><![endif]-->
<style>
<!--
 /* Style Definitions */
p.MsoNormal, li.MsoNormal, div.MsoNormal
   {mso-style-parent:"";
   margin:0in;
   margin-bottom:.0001pt;
   mso-pagination:widow-orphan;
   font-size:12.0pt;
   font-family:"Times New Roman";
   mso-fareast-font-family:"Times New Roman";}
@page Section1
   {size:8.5in 11.0in;
   margin:1.0in 1.25in 1.0in 1.25in;
   mso-header-margin:.5in;
```

```
   mso-footer-margin:.5in;
   mso-paper-source:0;}
div.Section1
   {page:Section1;}
-->
</style>
</head>
<body lang=EN-US style='tab-interval:.5in'>
<div class=Section1>
<p class=MsoNormal><b>XML documents<o:p></o:p></b></p>
<p class=MsoNormal><![if !supportEmptyParas]> 
<![endif]><o:p></o:p></p>
<p class=MsoNormal>How XML can be constructed using Microsoft
Word 2000.</p>
<p class=MsoNormal><![if !supportEmptyParas]> 
<![endif]><o:p></o:p></p>
</div>
</body>
</html>
```

10.7　XML Processors

At this point, it should be clear that XML documents are made up of DTDs, schemas, and the markup and content files. The rendered document is created by processing the markup and content against the DTDs and schemas, followed by a transformation for the platform on which the finished document is to be displayed.

To process XML documents an XML processor is required. A number of XML processors are available, including the Microsoft XML processor and the Simple API for XML (SAX). XML processors perform functions akin to browsers (albeit with a great deal more precision and flexibility), and Microsoft's XML processor is shipped with Internet Explorer. As already mentioned, Microsoft Word 2000, when saving Word documents as HTML, actually saves them in XML format, which can then be interpreted by Internet Explorer. Note that often XML processors work in the background for an application such as Internet Explorer or Microsoft Word, and can perform their functions for any application (such as a Web server or a database), not just one in which the final output is human-readable.

XML processors fit into two categories: validating and non-validating. *Validating* processors detect any well-formedness errors, and deviations from the rules and constraints built into the DTD or schema for an XML document. *Non-validating* processors check only for well-formedness. In general, the specification that provides for the capability of reviewing and validating XML documents, and providing programmatic access to the structure, markup, and content within them, is called an Application Programming Interface or API. There are several specifications providing access to XML documents: the DOM that we're already familiar with, and the Simple XML API (SAX).

The DOM establishes a hierarchy of objects within an XML document, and provides methods that can be used within an application to navigate through the objects in a document and read or modify their properties. The main drawback to using the DOM is that it reads the entire document into memory, placing a large load on resources when overall file size is large. The main advantage over SAX is that documents can be processed and modified in real-time.

SAX, on the other hand, while not able to modify documents in real-time, can *parse* (provide access to) XML documents as they are read in, element by element. SAX uses what's called an *event-based interface*. This means that, as the document is read, events are triggered every time an element is started, when element content is read, and when the element ends. Each time an event is activated, a SAX processor informs the author's application, thereby providing the application with the data it needs to formulate an appropriate response to the event. As mentioned, SAX is read-only, and another drawback is that it is not well supported by browsers.

10.8   XML Transformations

Many people used to HTML assume that XML is similar, and as a matter of fact XML documents displayed in a browser come out looking as though they were written in HTML. The crucial difference is that XML documents must be transformed before they are displayed in a browser like an HTML document. In fact, much of the power of XML derives from the fact that XML documents can be transformed from XML into whatever other format is required, making XML the ideal standard from which to provide data to humans and machines. So, a single XML document may be transformed to HTML for display in a browser, to a compressed or clipped version of HTML for display on a cellphone or in a PDA, or to some database format or proprietary format for use by a machine-driven application where there is no human interaction at all.

Transforming XML documents into an appropriate format for use with a particular application can be done by writing a document-specific transformation routine into the application, but there is a better way. The W3C has developed what's called *eXtensible Stylesheet Language* (XSL) to provide a standard way of performing transformations. The most recent version is XSL 1.0, currently a candidate recommendation from the W3C.

As with XML, XSL requires a processor to perform transformations. The processor takes an XML document and its accompanying XSL style sheet and builds the finished product from them. The finished product, of course, is the Web page, PDA display, speech, paginated document, and so forth that the style sheet maker desired. Because the platform on which the XML document is to be displayed or rendered can be detected by the server providing the document, it is relatively easy to ensure that any given platform receives the appropriate XML document and an XSL style sheet.

Formally, the XML document provides the *source tree* of objects (from the DOM). The XSL processor first performs *tree transformation*, transforming the source tree into a *result tree*. The result tree may have objects from the source tree, as well as additional objects suitable for the specific platform on which the results are to be displayed. Within the result tree are formatting objects (these could be pages and paragraphs, for example) and formatting properties (these could be font face and background color, for example). Formatting of the content, using the result tree, formatting objects and formatting properties, may take place on the platform rendering the output.

10.9   XML Links (XLink, XML Base, XPointer)

Although XML documents can be transformed into HTML output, and HTML documents may contain A elements capable of creating simple hyperlinks, the authors of XML considered it a good idea to provide more power for creating a variety of linking structures in XML documents. There are several candidate recommendations undergoing the review process at the W3C: XLink, XML Base, and XPointer.

XML Linking Language (XLink) allows elements that create and describe links between resources to be inserted into XML documents. Resources are defined in this recommendation as "any addressable unit of information or service". Basically, this means any file that can be found, any information retrieved from an information source, or any service that can be performed, with a URL. Links created with XLink are explicitly defined as XLink elements, and six types are included in the recommendation: simple, extended, locator, arc, resource, title. Two of these (simple and extended) are considered linking elements, while the rest just offer information describing the characteristics of the link.

XLinks can build links between whole resources or just parts of them, and they can link to other XML documents or any other resource. When a link is created between resources, the resources *participate* in the link. The resource at the beginning of a link is called the *starting resource*, the resource at the end is called the *ending resource*, and the act of following the link from beginning to end is called *traversal*. The information required to follow a link (starting and ending resource URLs and the direction in which the link proceeds) is called the *arc*. If the links on either end point to each other, so that clicking on the starting link takes you to the ending link, and upon arrival the ending link becomes a starting link pointing back to the original starting link (which now becomes the ending link) the link is said top be multidirectional.

To write a link conforming to XLink, the XLink namespace must be declared, like this:

```
<somexmlelement xmlns:xlink="http://www.w3.org/1999/xlink">
</somexmlelement>
```

XLink's namespace provides for attributes that are global and serve to identify an element as a link. They are: *type, href, role, arcrole, title, show, actuate, label, from*, and *to*. Authors may use these global attributes, along with a reference to the XLink namespace, to include link data in any XML element from any namespace. Non-XLink attributes may also be used, creating a very rich link-producing capability.

Simple XLink links (type = simple) are very similar in structure and capability to standard HTML links (the A element and the IMG element). All they really require is a reference to a resource. Extended XLink links, on the other hand, can be associated with any number of resources, including special links inside themselves, and offer a much richer set of linking and information display possibilities. For example, if an author wants to include within a link a pop-up menu offering a choice of destinations (resources) to click on, XLink extended links can do it.

XML Base is a proposed recommendation that outlines a specification for an XML attribute that performs functions similar to the HTML BASE element, namely, to explicitly set a base URL for a document. To use the *xml:base* attribute it may be inserted into a document as follows:

```
<xml:base="http://thebase.com/" xmlns:
xlink="http://www.w3.org/1999/xlink">
```

XPointer is a language that supports addressing into the internal structure of an XML document, and not just to a resource or portion of a resource. What this means is that the document's hierarchical structure may be examined and analyzed, and that "locations" within the document can be identified by element type, attribute values, character content, and so forth. It provides a very rich mechanism for navigating and using XML documents, whether they are meant for human or machine consumption. In addition, the results can be used not only as targets for links but for any other application purpose desired.

10.10   XML Query

XML Schema gives XML documents a database-like structure, and like Structured Query Language (SQL) for ordinary databases, XML Query provides a query language capable of extracting data (formed as elements and attributes rather than fields from tables) from XML documents, and creating new documents based on what has been extracted.

Review Questions

10.1.   Is XML a markup language, like HTML? If not, what is it?

10.2.   Define the basic parts of XML that give XML authors the ability to create markup languages.

10.3.   Is there a standard XML language for ecommerce?

10.4. What platforms does XML work with?

10.5. What does it mean when an XML document is said to be well-formed?

10.6. What does it mean to validate an XML document?

10.7. What role does XML Schema play?

10.8. What are XML namespaces and why are they necessary?

10.9. How are XML elements and attributes similar to HTML elements and attributes, and how are they different?

10.10. How are XML elements represented in memory when processed by an XML processor?

10.11. What methods are available for working with XML documents from a programmatic standpoint?

10.12. How are XML documents transformed? What process is used and what does the output look like?

10.13. How are XML links formed? Why is there an additional way to create links, rather than the familiar method used with HTML?

10.14. What is an arc, in relationship to XLink?

10.15. What is XML Base?

10.16. What is XPointer?

10.17. What is XML Query?

 # Answers To Review Questions

10.1. XML is a subset of Standard Generalized Markup Language (SGML). SGML is actually a means of creating markup languages, called applications, and XML is a concise subset of these capabilities. Therefore, XML is a method for creating markup languages.

10.2. Authors can create markup languages with XML by defining elements and attributes with a DTD or an XML schema. An XML document may consist of one or more entities (roughly equivalent to files) that together make up the document.

10.3. Anyone can create an XML language for any purpose. For example, a company can create an XML language whose elements and attributes fit the way the company conducts ecommerce transactions internally. In this case, that XML language might be a standard for all ecommerce conducted within the company.

However, any individual or company can also create generic XML languages for ecommerce transactions across several companies or an entire industry. In fact, several competing versions of XML may be made available for ecommerce in an industry, and whether or not one becomes a standard depends upon how many companies decide to adopt one XML language to the exclusion of others.

Part of the power of XML is that, by the nature of its structure, authors can choose to use existing XML languages that have some elements and attributes they need, while at the same time adding new elements and attributes for specific purposes not covered by other XML languages.

10.4.   Basic XML documents contain text and markup identifying elements, attributes, and content or values, as well as references to DTDs or schemas (for validation) and namespaces (to identify elements and attributes when their names are the same but they refer to different XML languages).

When an XML document is read by an XML processor, the processor may validate the document, and then transform it into a format suitable for a particular platform. Therefore, the same XML document may end up looking quite different depending upon the platform for which it is transformed. In practice it is possible to write a single XML document that can be displayed on any number of platforms.

10.5.   Well-formedness means an XML document contains only one root element, and none of its elements overlap.

10.6.   Validating an XML document may occur when the document is processed by an XML processor. When an XML document is validated the elements and attributes in the document are checked against the DTD or schema to ensure they properly conform. Nonconforming documents should cause errors to be generated.

10.7.   XML Schema gives a database-like structure to XML documents, because not only do they define elements and attributes, they also define data types for elements and attributes, and provide constraints on the values or content elements and attributes can assume.

10.8.   XML namespaces are closed sets of names that may be applied to XML elements and attributes. If one XML language contains the element name "temperature" for instance, and another XML language uses this same name as well, some mechanism for differentiating between the two elements when both are used in an XML document is necessary (one might represent temperature in Fahrenheit while the other represents temperature in Centigrade). XML namespaces provide the solution, by allowing a unique prefix for elements that is referenced to the XML language the element comes from.

10.9.   XML elements and attributes are written lowercase, as XML is case sensitive. Like HTML elements, XML elements may or may not have attributes, and they may or may not be empty (contain content between the starting and ending tags). XML elements are written with angle brackets delimiting them, and ending XML tags use the slash to indicate that they are the ending tag (<myelement> </myelement>). Empty XML elements use the slash inside the tag to indicate they are both a starting and ending tag (<myelement />).

10.10.   XML documents usually consist of elements and subelements, called parent and child elements. The root element of an XML document is the parent of all other elements in the document, and forms the root of the tree-like structure of an XML document as represented in memory. Each element in the tree is called a *node*.

10.11.   The DOM can be used to address and modify nodes (elements) within an XML document. It provides the ability to read the values (current state) of element properties and methods for modifying those properties, as well as the content in elements. The Simple API for XML (SAX) provides the ability to read element properties and content but not change them.

10.12.   XML documents are transformed using eXtensible Stylesheet Language (XSL). XSL contains style sheet instructions that affect XML elements during the transformation process. First, XSL processors retrieve from an XML document a set of elements called the result tree (the original elements in the XML document is called the source tree). The XSL processor includes in the result tree formatting objects, and these formatting objects provide the data necessary for the final rendering to take place in the targeted platform, such as a browser. The end result may be, for example, an XHTML document with style sheet instructions for the browser, or an entirely different set of elements with formatting instructions appropriate for a cell phone, if that is the intended platform.

10.13. HTML links provide a one-way linking method, in which the user may click on the link and retrieve the resource specified in the *href* attribute, and may travel to a particular location within the resource. The simple XML link performs the same function, but the designers of XML have also built in the capability to provide much more elaborate link types, as well as elements whose purpose is to provide information about links.

XML links are formed when, within an XML element, a reference to the Xlink namespace is provided, and certain specific attributes are used. These attributes are: *type, href, role, arcrole, title, show, actuate, label, from,* and *to.*

10.14. An arc is the information required to negotiate from one side of a link to the other, namely, the URLs of both sides of the link and the direction of the link (from and to).

10.15. XML Base is a method of inserting into XML documents the base URL of an element or document in a manner similar to the HTML BASE element.

10.16. XPointer is a method of including in XML documents references to resources internal to the document without using links. Using XPointer, locations in the document can be found based on element type, attribute values, character content, and so forth.

10.17. XML Query is a query language for XML documents. It allows for retrieving from XML documents elements and their content, based on criteria supplied as part of the query, and sorting, filtering, deleting, updating, and otherwise performing typical query functions to the document, and constructing new documents from the result.

HTML Start Tag Reference

The following table lists HTML tags, showing the start tags, the function they perform, and how they relate to the major browsers and the World Wide Web Consortium's specifications for HTML.

Start Tag	Function	Netscape Navigator	Internet Explorer	WWW Consortium
< !– >	Starts a comment	3.0	3.0	3.2
< !doctype >	Starts the document type			3.2
< a >	Starts an anchor	3.0	3.0	3.2
< abbr >	Starts an abbreviation			4.0
< acronym >	Starts an acronym		4.0	4.0
< address >	Starts an address element	4.0	4.0	4.0
< applet >	Deprecated. Use < object >			
< area >	Starts an area inside an image map	3.0	3.0	3.2
< b >	Starts bold text	3.0	3.0	3.2
< base >	Starts a default reference to external resources	3.0	3.0	3.2
< basefont >	Deprecated. Use < style >			
< bdo >	Starts the direction of text display		5.0	4.0
< big >	Starts big text	3.0	3.0	3.2
< blockquote >	Starts a long quotation	3.0	3.0	3.2
< body >	Starts the body element	3.0	3.0	3.2
< br >	Inserts a single line break	3.0	3.0	3.2
< button >	Starts a push button		4.0	4.0
< caption >	Starts a table caption	3.0	3.0	3.2

Start Tag	Function	Netscape Navigator	Internet Explorer	WWW Consortium
< center >	Deprecated. Use < style >			
< cite >	Starts a citation	3.0	3.0	3.2
< code >	Starts computer code text	3.0	3.0	3.2
< col >	Starts attributes for table columns		3.0	4.0
< colgroup >	Starts groups of table columns		3.0	4.0
< dd >	Starts a definition description	3.0	3.0	3.2
< del >	Starts deleted text		4.0	4.0
< dfn >	Starts a definition term		3.0	3.2
< div >	Starts a section in a document	3.0	3.0	3.2
< dl >	Starts a definition list	3.0	3.0	3.2
< dt >	Starts a definition term	3.0	3.0	3.2
< em >	Starts emphasized text	3.0	3.0	3.2
< fieldset >	Starts a fieldset		4.0	4.0
< font >	Deprecated. Use < style >			
< form >	Starts a form	3.0	3.0	3.2
< frame >	Starts a subwindow (a frame)	3.0	3.0	4.0
< frameset >	Starts a set of frames	3.0	3.0	4.0
< h1 > to < h6 >	Starts header 1 to header 6	3.0	3.0	3.2
< head >	Starts information about the document	3.0	3.0	3.2
< hr >	Inserts a horizontal rule	3.0	3.0	3.2
< html >	Starts an html document	3.0	3.0	3.2
< i >	Starts italic text	3.0	3.0	3.2
< iframe >	Starts an inline subwindow (frame)		3.0	4.0
< img >	Starts an image	3.0	3.0	3.2
< input >	Starts an input field	3.0	3.0	3.2
< ins >	Starts inserted text		4.0	4.0
< kbd >	Starts keyboard text	3.0	3.0	3.2
< label >	Starts a label		4.0	4.0
< legend >	Starts a title in a fieldset		4.0	4.0
< li >	Starts a list item	3.0	3.0	3.2
< link >	Starts a resource reference	4.0	3.0	3.2
< map >	Starts an image map	3.0	3.0	3.2
< menu >	Deprecated. Use < ul >			
< meta >	Inserts meta information	3.0	3.0	3.2
< noframes >	Starts a noframe section	3.0	3.0	4.0
< noscript >	Starts a noscript section	3.0	3.0	4.0
< object >	Starts an embedded object		3.0	4.0
< ol >	Starts an ordered list	3.0	3.0	3.2
< optgroup >	Starts an option group			4.0
< option >	Starts an item in a list box	3.0	3.0	3.2
< p >	Starts a paragraph	3.0	3.0	3.2
< param >	Starts a parameter for an object	3.0	3.0	3.2

Start Tag	Function	Netscape Navigator	Internet Explorer	WWW Consortium
< plaintext >	Deprecated. Use < pre >			
< pre >	Starts preformatted text	3.0	3.0	3.0
< q >	Starts a short quotation		4.0	4.0
< samp >	Starts sample computer code	3.0	3.0	3.2
< script >	Starts a script	3.0	3.0	3.2
< select >	Starts a selectable list	3.0	3.0	3.2
< small >	Starts small text	3.0	3.0	3.2
< span >	Starts a section in a document		3.0	4.0
< strike >	Deprecated. Use < del >			
< strong >	Starts strong text	3.0	3.0	3.2
< style >	Starts a style definition	4.0	3.0	3.2
< sub >	Starts subscripted text	3.0	3.0	3.2
< sup >	Starts superscripted text	3.0	3.0	3.2
< table >	Starts a table	3.0	3.0	3.2
< tbody >	Starts a table body		4.0	4.0
< td >	Starts a table cell	3.0	3.0	3.0
< textarea >	Starts a text area	3.0	3.0	3.2
< tfoot >	Starts a fixed table footer		4.0	4.0
< th >	Starts a table header	3.0	3.0	3.2
< thead >	Starts a fixed table header		4.0	4.0
< title >	Starts the document title	3.0	3.0	3.2
< tr >	Starts a table row	3.0	3.0	3.2
< tt >	Starts teletype text	3.0	3.0	3.2
< u >	Deprecated. Use < style >			
< ul >	Starts an unordered list (bullets)	3.0	3.0	3.2
< var >	Starts a variable	3.0	3.0	3.2

INDEX

HTML Tags

< A >, 53, 54, 67, 68, 227
< APPLET >, 59, 64, 65, 66, 71, 227
< AREA >, 99, 100, 101, 104, 107, 158, 227

< BASE >, 58, 66, 70, 71, 128, 227
  XML, 223, 224, 226
< BASEFONT >, 48, 49, 65, 66, 69, 227
< BODY >, 7, 25, 26, 27, 29, 30, 40, 42, 44,
  46, 193, 227
  background and color attribute, 31, 44, 45,
  47, 66, 69, 178
< BR >, 38, 52, 90, 96, 97, 106, 227
  in XHTML, 196
< BUTTON >, 148, 227

< CAPTION >, 111, 112, 113, 114, 227
< COL >, 134, 228
< COLGROUP >, 134, 228

< DD >, 52, 228
< DIV >, 33, 228
< DL >, 52, 228
< !DOCTYPE >, 23, 26, 27, 43
  XHTML, 191, 193, 194, 202, 203, 204, 209
  XML, 215, 227
< DT >, 52, 228

< FONT >, 48, 49, 228
< FORM >, 8, 138, 139, 140, 228
< FRAME >, 122, 123, 124, 125, 126, 228
  targeting, 128
< FRAMESET >, 123, 124, 126, 228

< HEAD >, 27, 29, 228
< HR >, 40, 228
< HTML >, 27, 228

< IFRAME >, 130, 228
< IMG >, 86, 228
  alignment, 95
< INPUT >, 142, 228

< LABEL >, 153, 228
< LAYER >, 177, 180, 182
< LEGEND >, 228
< LI >, 43, 51, 52, 60, 68, 170, 228
< LINK >, 173, 228

< MAP >, 96, 228
< MENU >, 228
< META >, 28, 29, 41–44, 46, 51, 62, 169,
  183, 187

< NOBR >, 45

230